THE BOXING CLEVER
TWELVE RECIPE BOOKS IN ONE

BY JACQUI JONES & JOAN WILMOT

J&J PUBLISHING

Published by J & J Publishing

First published in Scotland in 2002 by
J & J Publishing
Ty Crwn, East Grange, Kinloss, Forres, Moray IV36 2UD

Reprinted 2004
Reprinted 2005
Reprinted 2007

Modified and electronic versions available 2021

Typeset & Design by Jacqui Jones and Tulin Oznur Tamturk

ISBN 978-1-7398469-0-9

FOR
ROBIN, BEN, JOE, SAM, ZAC, PETE, SEB, CHRIS &
ELLIE

J&J PUBLISHING
01343 850123

This book was first published in 2002.

Weekly Vegetable box schemes were becoming very popular at the time and we subscribed to our local scheme in the north-east of Scotland, called EarthShare. As subscribers, we received a weekly box of locally grown organic vegetables.

EarthShare is no longer operating, but this book is still valid today.

Since the first publication of this book the world has changed; most recently with the onset of the Covid-19 pandemic and lockdowns in 2020 /2021. As a result more people are growing their own vegetables and shopping locally.

This is a positive to emerge from the pandemic, and hopefully the habits will endure.

To make this book more accessible, it is now available on Print on Demand and ebook from www.amazon.co.uk.

Do you:

- **Grow your own produce?**
- **Have an allotment?**
- **Subscribe to a vegetable box scheme?**
- **Subscribe to a CSA scheme?**
- **Buy from a farmer's market or farm shop?**
- **Want to change to a plant-based diet or become a vegan?**
- **Want to join a community garden?**
- **Want to introduce more vegetables into your diet?**

If so, this book is for you!

CONTENTS

ACKNOWLEDGEMENTS

A book like this is rarely the product of one or two people. Throughout the three-year gestation period of the Boxing Clever Cookbook there have been many enthusiastic supporters who have given freely of their time and experience.

Special thanks must go to growers Mathis Rosenbusch and Christopher Raymont for the time they gave answering our many questions about growing. Thanks too, to the rest of the team at our local vegetable box scheme, EarthShare, for providing us with such a fabulous basis for our book.

Many of our friends and EarthShare subscribers have donated recipes and their names are woven into the text. We thank them for their contributions. We would like to thank Peter Jones and Robin Shohet, our respective husbands, for their tremendous support and help with re-writes.

Thanks to our children Sam, Zac, Seb, Ellie and Chris for their interest in the book and sampling the many meals. We include in this the successes as well as the failures, such as the bulgar cabbage parcels, which looked too much like boiled gonads to be palatable!!

Enjoy! Jacqui & Joan

Jacqui Jones
I live in our self-built eco house in Scotland. We grow vegetables and flowers for the house and keep a few hens.
I love creating meals from what our garden produces and I am particularly passionate about parsnips!

Joan Wilmot
I have four sons and work as a trainer and psychotherapist with my husband, Robin. Besides cooking, my other interests include sailing, horseriding and being a member of Findhorn Playback Theatre.

6

Dedicated to the memory of

Mathis Rosenbusch
1963 – 2018

Fay Blackburn
1943 – 2020

Nick Rodway
1946 - 2021

FOREWORD by Helen Browning

"The health of soil, plant, animal and (hu)man is one and indivisible".

- Lady Eve Balfour, founder of the Soil Association

2020 was an extraordinary year. The Covid-19 crisis brought great challenges for many of us but also provided an opportunity for us to take stock, and really notice how the world has changed. And us with it.

Over time we've become more and more disconnected from where our food comes from.

But as families and friends across the country were given the instruction to 'stay at home', we developed a new-found appreciation for the people around us - including those that are often overlooked but so crucial to our lives, health and happiness; nurses, schoolteachers, delivery drivers and farmers.

More people wanted to revitalise lost connections with their communities in new and more meaningful ways. As part of this, curiosity about local food production has grown.

Community Supported Agriculture (CSA) connects people, as directly as possible, to their food source. This book grew out of the CSA EarthShare, and its authors know only too well the importance of this link. Millions of people live in an urban existence with little sense of a connection with where their food comes from or how it is made. It's vital this connection is understood so we can all make food choices that align to our values; it's only together that we can transform the way we eat, farm and care for our natural world and build a better future.

By getting to know your local farmer, buying produce at a farm shop, having a vegetable box or being part of a CSA, you are keeping that connection alive. This is not altruism but an act of mutual reward - the benefits are immense.

Economically, buying direct can mean getting more for your money and more for the farmer. Environmentally, the nearer we are to the place where organic food is grown or reared, the more food miles are reduced and so is environmental pollution. Food that is produced locally that has not been stored or chilled tends to also be fresher and more nutritious. Culturally, local organic food has its own 'story', bringing a shared meaning at mealtimes and a deeper connection to the land.

We hope that, through food, we can all experience deeper connections with each other and with nature. The local organic movement began with people making small changes - just as we have - and together we're moving this understanding from strength to strength.

Helen Browning OBE
Chief Executive
of the Soil Association

WHAT IS A CSA SCHEME?

When consumers join a CSA scheme, they sign up for a year and pay a subscription in advance or in instalments. This means subscribers purchase a share of the seasonal harvest, either in one lump sum before the seeds are sown in early spring, or in several instalments throughout the growing season. Farmers receive a more stable and secure income and closer connection with their community and subscribers feel more connected to the land where their food is grown.

Subscribers make a commitment to support the farm throughout the season, and take on the costs and risks, the highs and lows of growing food, along with the farmer.

Subscribers can often be involved in working on the land for a discount on membership cost. They 'put their farmers face on their food' and receive a vegetable box weekly consisting of locally grown, organic, seasonal vegetables. The most common produce from CSA farmers is vegetables but they can include eggs, poultry, bread, fruit, pork lamb, beef, cheese and dairy produce.

WHAT IS A VEGETABLE BOX SCHEME?

Vegetable box schemes are a way of getting local and seasonal farm produce delivered to your home or a local pick-up point – usually weekly or sometimes fortnightly. As well as vegetables, boxes can also contain fruit, herbs, eggs, dairy produce, meat, honey or anything else you stipulate that you'd like from your local scheme. All depends on availability. It may come in a bag, as well as a box.

Most box scheme operators buy their produce from local farms or wholesalers, but a few do grow some of their own. Schemes vary considerably. Some buy in from other countries, so it is best if you speak directly to them and find out more before signing up.

Many box scheme operators offer small, medium and family size boxes and customers agree to pay a set price for a standard box of produce. Other schemes allow the customer to build their own box. The contents will vary each week depending on the seasonal vegetables available. They are usually guaranteed to include potatoes, carrots and onions.

9

EARTHSHARE

EarthShare was established in 1994 and was a not-for-profit CSA (Community Supported Agriculture) Scheme based in Forres, Moray in north-east Scotland. The plan was to break even each year by cutting out the middleman in the vegetable supply chain, minimising wastage and using subscriber help with the labour-intensive tasks such as weeding. It was one of the largest CSA schemes in the UK.

It would be impossible to say who or what was the most important factor in EarthShare. Without a combination of people, ideas and serendipity it would never have happened. For the purposes of this book we have picked two key players who were pivotal to the scheme.

Mathis Rosenbusch arrived here in north-east Scotland in 1993 along with his grey Ferguson tractor. A German biodynamic – and dynamic – farmer, he had farmed in Germany for 10 years before arriving. Despite not being born into an agricultural life, farming was his passion.

"It was something that made me happy and I just wanted to go for it," he said. "I am so passionate about farming I think I would be a farmer even if I wasn't paid for it."

Mathis' expertise was growing staple crops like brassicas, potatoes, root vegetables and more extensive field and tractor-based growing systems. He was also a master at finding, repairing and adapting old machinery, saving the project thousands of pounds in this way.

Our second key player was Christopher Raymont, who farmed organically in Berkshire from 1977 until he moved to Findhorn in Scotland on the Moray Coast in 1990 with his family to join the Findhorn Foundation, and work in its market garden, Cullerne.

The Findhorn Foundation is a world-famous eco-spiritual community. Established in 1963 by Peter and Eileen Caddy with their friend Dorothy Maclean, the community has evolved into a forum for the New Age. It is at the cutting edge of eco-friendly technology and lifestyle development.

Christopher and Mathis – who were drawn to the Foundation for different reasons – met and teamed up to form EarthShare in 1994. They realised that the separate entities of EarthShare and Cullerne Garden could operate much more efficiently for box scheme subscribers by joining forces. The partnership worked well. Cullerne Garden provided tunnel crops mainly from May to September and the field crops provided subscribers with the bulk of their vegetables between October and May.

Fruit for the boxes, including blackcurrants, raspberries, rhubarb and strawberries were grown on land owned by John Salt, a carpenter and part-time beekeeper at the nearby village of Rafford. He also grew amazing garlic.

Although not part of EarthShare, Wester Lawrenceton farm played an important role. Farmed by Pam and Nick Rodway, their land adjoined the EarthShare fields. The farm's 65 acres had at that time organic laying hens, dairy cows, sheep and a herd of milking goats. They also produced award-winning cheeses. The farm established a 'CowShare' scheme, where local people invested in the dairy herd. In return they got regular dairy produce as 'interest' on their loan.

10

INTRODUCTION TO THE
BOXING CLEVER COOKBOOK

It is difficult to pinpoint the exact 'eureka!' moment when the idea for writing the book started to develop. For Joan it grew from several years of struggling with increasing piles of boxes, all half-full, with vegetables at varying stages of decay.

Jacqui had subscribed to her local vegetable box scheme in her native Wales, but time constraints led to her giving it up. Like Joan, she had piled up boxes and often resorted to throwing unused, rotten vegetables into the compost bin.

They met at a training for Playback Theatre and after talking about box schemes, they realised that they had similar issues and the book was born. See page 181.

Throughout the book, reference is made to EarthShare, the CSA (Community supported Agriculture) scheme which we subscribed to. The name "Boxing Clever Cookbook" was the final decision. It was chosen because the vegetables arrive in a box, and to *"box clever"* is a British phrase describing how to use one's head and to make the best of what one has got.

We had fun putting the recipes together, and wanted this fun element to be part of the book. It became clear to us that the people who were subscribing to a box, ourselves included, fell into particular character types when it came to attitudes to *'the box'*. From that the *'sprout rating'* evolved. We described box-scheme users as *'Sprouters'* according to their often evangelical use of the box, and realised the sprout rating could be applied to anyone and anything. Have a go at rating yourself. You'll get the hang of it!

11

SPROUT RATING - A DO-IT-YOURSELF GUIDE

In the introduction, we talked about our unique 'sprout ratings' and here is your chance to rate yourselves and others. Using this exclusive un-scientifically tested formula you will be able to categorise those around you, even develop your own personal code for judging performance in all areas – even the bedroom. Experts (mainly us) have predicted that 'sprout ratings' will soon replace star signs as the opening chat-up gambit, so get in there first with this free guide.

ONE SPROUT RATING

Characteristics
- Starts the box scheme because they think it is a good idea
- By nature would prefer to buy organic vegetables from the supermarket on a need basis
- Has a broad-based approach to food and is willing to include a box scheme as part of their food shopping
- Often will give up the box after a period of time and will revert back to supermarket shopping

Forgivable faults
- Quickly loses interest in the box if vegetables are dirty or mis-shapen
- Good at ideas but poor to follow through. Needs instant gratification - wonders why the lettuce doesn't come with a salad dressing
- When it comes to food – easily persuaded to eat out or get a takeaway when faced with cooking a meal from the box

TWO SPROUT RATING

Characteristics
- Often chooses to lead a busy life but keen to take on the extra challenge of managing a vegetable box
- Can be a sinner or a saint in relation to the box, depending on their mood
- Often has boxes stacked up like London buses, over-whelmed by the very abundance of vegetables in the box
- Wants to be more creative with the box but finds it easier to compost than to cook

Forgivable faults
- Won't give up the box and risk feeling a failure
- With audience present, will punish themselves by eating 4-week old vegetables
- Gives vegetables generously to friends and family to lessen guilt trip to compost heap
- Over-committed to everything but the box

THREE SPROUT RATING

Characteristics
- Starts off with good intentions, and believes in the box scheme
- Occasionally gets behind with the boxes and fights to use them up weekly
- Will bail themselves out with creative use of freezer, becoming local expert on vegetable cryogenics
- Takes on too much

Forgivable faults
- Wracked with guilt when vegetable cryogenics fail and forced to empty year old frozen vegetables into wheelie bin
- Can exude self-confidence which, as we all know, often belies self-doubt
- An ideal candidate for a self-help group
- Two sprouter or five sprouter wannabes, depending on mood

FOUR SPROUT RATING

Characteristics
- Thoroughly researches all the issues involved between growing the food to serving it up on the table
- Even then, mulls everything over before making a choice
- Committed to eating locally grown organic food
- Keeps in touch with farming issues in the 'outside world'
- Often has an extensive network of personal contacts and a lively interest in anything that is happening with food
- Can be creative with food, recipes, and will manage the box well

Forgivable faults
- Works hard to promote the scheme – the Billy Graham of box schemes
- Earnest and Queen-like, their duty lies within the box
- **Never** leaves anything to chance
- Makes simplicity complicated

FIVE SPROUT RATING

Characteristics
- The box is one of the highlights of their week
- Could probably use twice as many vegetables as they receive
- Uses up all vegetables by midweek and hungry for more
- Shows genuine shock when told that some struggle with the contents of their box
- Managing the box is second nature, can turn any vegetable in the box into a meal.

Forgivable faults
- Crusader
- Lowers morale in lesser box subscribers
- Sometimes inflexible on that special dinner date
- Requires mouth-to-mouth resuscitation if shown prices on a restaurant menu, preferring to buy a new garden fork instead

MONTHLY VEGETABLE BOX CONTENTS

What to expect in your box - variety names are examples and vary from year to year

❄ JANUARY

FIELD CROPS - BRASSICAS	FIELD CROPS - ROOT VEGETABLES	FIELD CROPS - ONION FAMILY	FRUITS
Brussels sprouts (*Igor*) Cabbage, green (*Primo*) Cabbage, white (*Castello*) Curly kale (*Dwarf Green Curled*) Red cabbage (*Marner Lager Rot*) Swede (*Lizzy*) Winter kohlrabi (*Superschmelz*)	Beetroot (*Crimson King*) Carrots (*Bolero & Tip Top*) Parsnips (*Tender & True*) Potatoes (*Remarka*)	Leeks (*Musselburgh*) Onions (*Centurion & Sturon*)	

❄ FEBRUARY

FIELD CROPS - BRASSICAS	FIELD CROPS - ROOT VEGETABLES	FIELD CROPS - ONION FAMILY	FRUITS
Brussels sprouts and tops (*Igor*) Cabbage, green (*Primo*) Curly kale (*Dwarf Green Curled*) Green cauliflower (*Romanesco, Minaret*) Greens Purple sprouting broccoli (*Late*) Red cabbage (*Marner Lager Rot*) Swede (*Lizzy*) **CULLERNE TUNNEL CROPS** Oriental greens (*Ta Tsai, Mizuna*) Green salad (*Lambs lettuce*)	Beetroot (*Crimson King*) Carrots (*Bolero & Tip Top*) Parsnips (*Tender & True*) Potatoes (*Remarka*)	Leeks (*Musselburgh*) Onions (*Centurion & Sturon*)	

🌱 MARCH

FIELD CROPS - BRASSICAS	FIELD CROPS - ROOT VEGETABLES	FIELD CROPS - ONION FAMILY	FRUITS
Brussels sprouts (*Igor*) Cabbage, green (*Primo*) Curly kale (*Dwarf Green Curled*) Purple sprouting broccoli (*Late*) Red cabbage (*Marner Lager Rot*) Swede (*Lizzy*) **CULLERNE TUNNEL CROPS** Chicory (*Brussels Witloof*) Oriental greens (*Ta Tsai, Mizuna*) Pak Choi (*Joy Choi*) Spinach (*Primo*)	Carrots (*Bolero & Tip Top*) Parsnips (*Tender & True*) Potatoes (*Remarka*)	Leeks (*Musselburgh*)	**RAFFORD** Rhubarb

13

MONTHLY VEGETABLE BOX CONTENTS

What to expect in your box - variety names are examples and vary from year to year

🌱 APRIL

FIELD CROPS - BRASSICAS	FIELD CROPS - ROOT VEGETABLES	FIELD CROPS - ONION FAMILY	FRUITS
Beetroot leaf (*Crimson King*) Brussels sprouts (*Igor*) Cabbage, green (*Primo*) Purple sprouting broccoli (*Late*) Swede (*Lizzy*) **CULLERNE TUNNEL CROPS** Chicory (*Brussels Witloof*) Coriander Lettuce (*Wendel*) Parsley (*Curly & Italian Flat*) Radish (*French, Breakfast,* *Cherry Belle*) Rocket	Beetroot (*Crimson King*) Carrots (*Bolero & Tip Top*) Parsnips (*Tender & True*) Potatoes (*Remarka*)		**RAFFORD** Rhubarb

🌱 MAY

FIELD CROPS - BRASSICAS	FIELD CROPS - ROOT VEGETABLES	FIELD CROPS - ONION FAMILY	FRUITS
Purple sprouting broccoli (*Late*) **CULLERNE TUNNEL CROPS** Parsley (*Curly & Italian flat*) Radish (*French, Breakfast,* *Cherry Belle*) Spinach (*Medania*)	Carrots (*Bolero & Tip Top*) Potatoes (*Remarka*) **CULLERNE TUNNEL CROPS** New carrots (*Amsterdam Forcing,* *Earls Nantes, Indoor*)		**RAFFORD** Rhubarb

☀ JUNE

FIELD CROPS - BRASSICAS	FIELD CROPS - ROOT VEGETABLES	FIELD CROPS - ONION FAMILY	FRUITS
Basil plants Lettuce Oakleaf lettuce Parsley (*Curly & Italian Flat*) Parsley plants Spinach (*Medania*) Swiss Chard	Potatoes (*Remarka*) **CULLERNE TUNNEL CROPS** New carrots (*Amsterdam Forcing,* *Earls Nantes, Indoor*)		**RAFFORD** Rhubarb

MONTHLY VEGETABLE BOX CONTENTS

What to expect in your box - variety names are examples and vary from year to year

☼ JULY

FIELD CROPS - BRASSICAS	FIELD CROPS - ROOT VEGETABLES	FIELD CROPS - ONION FAMILY	FRUITS
CULLERNE TUNNEL CROPS Broad beans (*Aquadulce*) Coriander Cucumber (*Hana, Flamingo*) Lettuce (*6 or 7 varieties*) Peas/Mange tout (*Podding &* *Sugar Snap*) Parsley (*Curly & Italian Flat*)	Potatoes (*Remarka*) – first half of month New potatoes (*Aminka*) – second half of month **CULLERNE** New carrots – outdoor (*Nantes & Tip Top*)		**RAFFORD** Blackcurrants Raspberries Strawberries

☼ AUGUST

FIELD CROPS - BRASSICAS	FIELD CROPS - ROOT VEGETABLES	FIELD CROPS - ONION FAMILY	FRUITS
Calabrese (*Samson*) Cauliflower (*All Year Round*) **CULLERNE TUNNEL CROPS** Broad beans (*Aquadulce*) Courgettes (*All Green Bush*) Cucumber French beans (*Climbing & Dwarf*) Lettuce (*Cos, Crisphead, Little Gem,* *Oakleaf*) Parsley (*Curly & Italian Flat*) Peas (*Podding & Sugar Snap*) Tomatoes (*Matina, Sungold,* *Clementine*)	Beetroot (*Crimson King*) New potatoes (*Aminka*) **CULLERNE** Carrots (*Bolero & Tip Top*)	Onions (*Centurion & Sturon*) **RAFFORD** Garlic (*Christo*)	**RAFFORD** Blackcurrants Raspberries

☙ SEPTEMBER

FIELD CROPS - BRASSICAS	FIELD CROPS - ROOT VEGETABLES	FIELD CROPS - ONION FAMILY	FRUITS
Cabbage (*Primo*) Calabrese (*Samson*) Cauliflower (*All Year Round*) **CULLERNE TUNNEL CROPS** Cucumber French beans (*Climbing & Dwarf*) Lettuce (*6 or 7 varieties*) Small leaf greens Tomatoes (*Matina, Sungold,* *Clementine*)	Beetroot (*Crimson King*) New potatoes (*Aminka*) Carrots (*Bolero & Tip Top*) **CULLERNE** Courgette (*All Green Bush*) Daikon	Onions (*Centurion & Sturon*) **RAFFORD** Garlic (*Christo*)	

MONTHLY VEGETABLE BOX CONTENTS

What to expect in your box - variety names are examples and vary from year to year

❖ OCTOBER

FIELD CROPS - BRASSICAS	FIELD CROPS - ROOT VEGETABLES	FIELD CROPS - ONION FAMILY	FRUITS
Cabbage (*Primo*) Cauliflower (*All Year Round*) Red cabbage (*Marner Lager Rot*) **RAFFORD** Pumpkin **CULLERNE TUNNEL CROPS** Cucumber Spinach (*Perpetual*) Tomatoes (*Matina, Sungold, Clementine*)	Beetroot (*Crimson King*) Carrots (*Bolero & Tip Top*) Parsnips (*Tender & True*) Potatoes (*Remarka*) **CULLERNE** Courgette (*All Green Bush*)	Leeks (*Musselburgh*) Onions (*Centurion & Sturon*)	

❖ NOVEMBER

FIELD CROPS - BRASSICAS	FIELD CROPS - ROOT VEGETABLES	FIELD CROPS - ONION FAMILY	FRUITS
Cabbage, green (*Primo*) Curly kale (*Dwarf Green Curled*) Red Cabbage (*Marner Lager Rot*) Swede (*Lizzy*) Winter kohlrabi (*Superschmelz*) **RAFFORD** Pumpkin **CULLERNE TUNNEL CROPS** Green tomatoes Lettuce Oriental Greens (*Ta Tsai, Mizuna*) Spinach (*Giant Winter Prickly*)	Beetroot (*Crimson King*) Carrots (*Bolero & Tip Top*) Parsnips (*Tender & True*) Potatoes (*Remarka*)	Leeks (*Musselburgh*) Onions (*Centurion & Sturon*)	

❄ DECEMBER

FIELD CROPS - BRASSICAS	FIELD CROPS - ROOT VEGETABLES	FIELD CROPS - ONION FAMILY	FRUITS
Brussels sprouts (*Igor*) Cabbage, green (*Primo*) Curly kale (*Dwarf Green Curled*) Red Cabbage (*Marner Lager Rot*) Swede (*Lizzy*) Winter kohlrabi (*Superschmelz*)	Beetroot (*Crimson King*) Carrots (*Bolero & Tip Top*) Parsnips (*Tender & True*) Potatoes (*Remarka*)	Onions (*Centurion & Sturon*)	

16

STORAGE OF VEGETABLES

Once your box is in your hands, the following table may help you to store the vegetables so that they will keep fresher for longer. The leafy greens are the most vulnerable, needing either to be eaten or put in the fridge on the same day. Root vegetables will store well for a long time if stored in a cool, dark and dry place. If you like to keep vegetables in the fridge, investing in a larder fridge gives more space for storage.

VEGETABLE	HOW TO STORE
Beetroot	Upon storage the greens will quickly draw the moisture from the root, greatly reducing flavour and shrivelling the beetroot. Leave a 2.5cm (1") stem and the taproot intact to retain moisture and nutrients. After separating, beetroot will store well for about a week in perforated plastic bags in the fridge. Try to use the beetroots while they are still firm and fresh.
Broad Beans	Put into a perforated plastic bag in their skins and they will keep for up to 7 days in the fridge.
Brussels Sprouts	Remove any damaged outer leaves and store fresh unwashed sprouts in plastic bags in the fridge. The fresher the sprouts the better the flavour. Use within 2 days.
Cabbage	Put unwashed into plastic bags and refrigerate. If you plan to eat the cabbage raw, eat within a few days. Cabbage that you plan to cook can be stored for about 2 weeks
Cauliflower/Calabrese	Place in a perforated plastic bag in the fridge for up to 5 days. Pre-cut florets do not keep well, so store whole.
Carrots	Store carrots with the green tops trimmed. The tops rob the carrots of moisture and nutritional value. Carrots will keep for several weeks in the salad drawer of the fridge in perforated plastic bags. If you plan to use the green tops in soups or stews, store them separately, as they will only keep for a few days. Of all the root vegetables, carrots have a longer shelf life if kept in the fridge.
Chard, Swiss Chard, Leaf Beet, Spinach or Any Leafy Greens	These greens are extremely perishable. Put them straight into the fridge in newspaper and they will keep for up to three days. The leaves go limp, but as long as they are green they can be thoroughly refreshed by placing them in a bowl of cold water half an hour before use. Alternatively, put the unwashed leaves in plastic bags in the salad drawer for 2-3 days. The stalks can be kept for longer if separated from the leaves.
Chicory	Chicory is delicate and ideally should be eaten right away. It can be stored for a few days covered in a cool place or in the salad drawer of the fridge.
Chinese Greens, Pak Choi	Same as chard above.
Courgettes	Refrigerate unwashed in plastic bags for up to 7 days.
Cucumber	Put in loose or perforated plastic bags for up to 3 days in the fridge.
Curly Kale	Put in a perforated plastic bag, unwashed in the fridge. It will keep fresh for up to a week.
Kohlrabi	Kohlrabi stores well in the fridge for weeks in a sealed plastic bag. They can also be stored in a cool, dark place.

VEGETABLE	HOW TO STORE
Garlic	If garlic is stored around 12°C (55°F), fungi and other pathogens and pests are much less active than they are with the temperature in the 24–26°C (75-80°F) range. Keeping it cool, but not cool enough to sprout is the key to storing garlic well. Basically, any dark, cool place is fine as long as the humidity is not excessive. Garlic stored in oil at room temperature poses a danger of botulism. Garlic in oil can be kept in the refrigerator for a maximum of three weeks.
Leeks	Loosely wrap in plastic, unwashed, and refrigerate for up to 5 days.
Lettuce	Lettuce leaves should be free of wilt, rot and rust. Put fresh, unwashed leaves in plastic bags and refrigerate for up to 3 days.
Mushrooms	Mushrooms need to breathe because they deteriorate quickly when stored in plastic bags. Store in a brown paper bag in the fridge, or loose on a plate lined with kitchen paper.
Onions	Lay onions in a single layer of newspaper in a warm, well-ventilated place to cure for a few days. Leave undisturbed until the outer skin becomes papery and crispy dry. Rub off stringy roots. Hang in strings or in mesh bags away from moisture. If stored in a cool place they will last for months.
Parsley	Thoroughly wash fresh parsley and shake off excess moisture, wrap in paper towels, place in a plastic bag and refrigerate for up to one week; OR put stems in a glass of water, cover with a secured plastic bag and refrigerate and change the water every few days; OR put parsley in plastic bags and freeze.
Peas	Store unwashed peas in perforated plastic bags in the fridge for a few days. The sugar in them quickly begins to turn to starch even when under refrigeration; so the sooner they are eaten the better.
Potatoes	Potatoes must be stored properly – thick brown paper bags are best – and kept in the dark at all times. A cool place with good ventilation is important. Do not refrigerate potatoes. If potatoes start to sprout they can be eaten if the potato is still firm. Remove the sprouts and discard.
Pumpkin	Pumpkins should not be stored in the fridge or in a damp place. Moisture causes rapid deterioration. Whole unblemished pumpkin can be stored for up the 3–6 months in a cool, dry place.
Purple Sprouting Broccoli	Put into plastic bags, unwashed in the fridge for up to 3 days.
Radishes	Cut off tops because the leaves cause moisture and nutrient loss during storage. Topped radishes, placed in plastic bags and refrigerated, will keep for 5-7 days. Radish tops, stored separately in plastic bags in the fridge, will last for 2-3 days.
Rhubarb	Freshly harvested, unwashed stalks can be kept refrigerated in plastic bags, for up to three weeks.
Swede	Swede stores well in the fridge for weeks in a sealed plastic bag. They can also be stored in a cool, dark place.
Tomatoes	Keep in the salad drawer of the fridge.

THE STORE CUPBOARD

Apart from the vegetables in your box, the following ingredients have been used in the recipes. If you can build up a store cupboard to include these items, you will be able to attempt any recipe without extra shopping. We have also included the different types of cheese, dairy produce and fresh food used.

ALCOHOL

Beer
Cider
Gin
Orange liqueur
Red Wine
Sherry
Whisky
White wine

BAKING

Apple Juice
Baking powder
Bicarbonate of soda
Bread flour
Brown sugar
Caster sugar
Cocoa powder
Cornflour
Creamed coconut
Crystallized ginger
Dark chocolate
Demerara sugar
Desiccated coconut
Dried active yeast
Evaporated milk
Fresh yeast
Granulated sugar
Honey
Icing sugar

Lemon juice
Lime juice
Maple syrup
Marmalade
Molasses
Muscovado sugar
Orange juice
Pineapple juice
Plain flour
Self-raising flour
Semolina
Vanilla essence
Wholewheat flour

CHEESE

Brie
Camembert
Cheddar
Cottage
Cream
Edam
Feta
Gorgonzola
Gruyère
Mozzarella
Parmesan
Red Leicester
Ricotta
Roquefort
Stilton

COOKING OILS

Margarine
Olive Oil
Sesame Oil
Sunflower Oil
Vegetable Oil
Walnut Oil

DAIRY

Butter
Crème fraîche
Double cream
Eggs
Milk
Single cream
Sour cream
Whipping cream
Yoghurt, plain

DRIED FRUIT

Apricots
Currants
Dates
Prunes
Raisins

ESSENTIALS

Balsamic vinegar
Bouillon
Cider vinegar

Citric acid
Dijon mustard
English mustard
Horseradish
Malt vinegar
Mayonnaise
Miso
Red wine vinegar
Soy sauce/Tamari
Sundried tomatoes
Tofu
Tomato paste/purée
Vegetable suet
White wine vinegar
Wholegrain mustard
Worcestershire sauce

FRESH FOODS

Apples
Celery
Elderberries
Elderflowers
Ground elder
Lemons
Limes
Mushrooms
Olives, green & black
Oranges
Red/green chillies

FROZEN

Filo pastry
Puff pastry
Shortcrust pastry

GRAINS

Bulgar wheat
Oat bran
Oatmeal
Pearl barley

HERBS AND SPICES

Allspice
Basil
Bay leaves
Black peppercorns
Caraway seeds
Cardamom
Cayenne pepper
Celery salt
Celery seed
Chili powder
Cinnamon
Cloves
Coriander seed
Coriander, ground
Cumin
Curry powder
Dill weed

Fennel seeds
Garam masala
Garlic, fresh
Ginger powder
Ginger, fresh root
Juniper berries
Lavender flowers
Lemongrass
Marjoram
Mint
Mixed herbs
Mustard seeds
Nutmeg
Oregano
Paprika
Parsley
Poppy seeds
Rosemary
Sage
Salt
Sesame seeds
Sunflower seeds
Tamarind paste
Tarragon
Thyme
Turmeric

NUTS

Almonds
Cashew
Dry roasted peanuts

Ground almonds
Hazelnuts
Peanut butter
Peanuts
Pecan
Pine
Walnuts

PASTA

Cannelloni
Macaroni
Pasta shapes
Spaghetti
Tagliatelle

PULSES

Brown Lentils
Chickpeas
Red lentils

RICE

Arborio
Basmati
Brown
Jasmine
Long-grain

TINS & CARTONS

Butter beans
Cannellini beans
Chickpeas
Coconut Milk
Tomatoes
Passata
Water chestnuts

INTRODUCTION TO RECIPES

The recipes in this book may help you cope with any abundance of vegetables.

Most of the recipes are quickly and easily prepared and add flavours that are interesting. We have included recipes for familiar and unfamiliar vegetables. Many of the recipes have been tested on our own families and friends, along with hours of cooking, talking, drinking and laughing that have taken place to fine-tune the recipes since our decision to write the book.

We've listed the ingredients in each recipe in the order that you'll need them whilst cooking. On top of that, we've given you a brand-new recipe book each month to keep you inspired all year round as one of our aims was to look at the box of vegetables with a fresh eye. We are really good to you!

For those looking to become vegans, or have a more plant-based diet, many of the recipes in this book can be followed by using simple dairy substitutes for some ingredients. Manufacturers have huge ranges of products for vegans and our table shows some examples that can be used for our recipes.

Every month's recipes have a farming news preamble that will introduce you to the jobs that most vegetable farmers are dealing with - including when to plant out and when to harvest.

Lots of us have lost touch with the hard work that produces our most basic food, so this part of the book may help re-connect with what's going on in our farming communities.

Dairy	Vegan Substitute
Milk	Non-dairy milks which include soy, oat, rice, hazelnut, cashew, almond and hemp
Cream/Yoghurt	Coconut milk, Oatly Plain Oatgurt
Butter or spreads	Dairy-free such as Stork, Trex or Flora
Eggs	**Aquafaba** which is water from a can of chickpeas or garbanzo beans for meringues, mousses, sponges or brownies *1 tablespoon = 1 egg yolk* *2 tablespoons = 1 egg white* *3 tablespoons = 1 whole egg* Treat your aquafaba as you would an egg
Cream cheese and cheese	Violife Creamy Original or Violite Epic Mature Cheddar flavour
Parmesan	Nutritional Yeast Flakes - great for sprinkling on dishes

FARMING NEWS FOR JANUARY

*T*he main activity is harvesting. Potato grading or dressing is done weekly. This is where the potatoes are put across a grader and the small, green and rotten ones are taken out.

 ## HARVESTING

As EarthShare fields are close to the sea, they do not suffer from hard frosts. As a result, Mathis is able to leave the following vegetables in the ground and harvest them weekly or as needed: Brussels sprouts, carrots, red and green cabbage, chicory, curly kale, kohlrabi, leeks, parsnips and swede.

Mathis has a rhythm of harvesting twice a week. On Tuesdays he crops for the Findhorn Foundation kitchens and on Thursdays he crops for EarthShare subscribers. The freshly-picked vegetables are driven from the fields to the box-packing sheds at Cullerne on Thursday evenings.

Two to three people compile an average of 120 boxes – they start packing the boxes on Friday mornings.

Robust field crops are packed first. During the morning, more fragile produce – just picked from the tunnels at Cullerne – arrives at the packing shed, and this is placed on top.

To complete the boxes, weekly *'box notes'* are included. They include news, views and recipes, and the quarterly newsletter, *'The Onion String'*, to which subscribers are encouraged to contribute. These are produced by EarthShare Director and Administrator, Pam Bochel.

The completed boxes are then driven to three separate pick-up points at Elgin, Forres and the Findhorn Foundation for subscribers to collect.

 ## MAINTENANCE AND MACHINERY

In addition to the general maintenance tasks, Mathis often undertakes a project or two to occupy himself during this time of year. One year he converted the grey 'Fergie' tractor from its paraffin/petrol mixture to run on LPG – probably the first such eco-friendly tractor in the UK. At Cullerne, Christopher looks after the tools. He sharpens them and oils the wooden handles. The Rotavator and power tools receive their winter maintenance.

 ## PESTS AND DISEASES

At this time of year the crops still in the ground are relatively disease free. The only disease evident is parsnip canker, or rust, as gardeners call it, where they can crack a little and go brown but that has not been too much of a problem to date. Cabbages and other brassicas can suffer from the cabbage root fly, which eats the roots away and kills the plant.

Scotland is the perfect place for growing swede because it is windy and cool so there is less chance of it being affected by root fly.

 ## PLANTING

The early potatoes are put into boxes for chitting – this is to allow the tubers to sprout. However, they are put in the light so as not to become leggy.

WEATHER

The weather can be very cold and windy in Scotland at this time of year, but thankfully working days are short. The sun doesn't peek over the horizon until nearly 8am, and it starts to get dark at about 3pm.

Mathis and Milan on the Ferguson Tractor

21

Manfred and Barbara Hafner Box Packing

JANUARY
RECIPES

BEETROOT AND CARROT CURRY
(Serves 4)

- 1 tsp coriander seed
- ½ tsp ground cinnamon
- ¼ tsp black pepper
- Pinch of chilli powder
- 2 tbsp olive oil
- 450 g (1 lb/2 cups) beetroot, peeled and diced
- 450 g (1 lb/2 cups) carrots, peeled and diced
- 300 ml (10 fl oz/½ pint) water
- Salt to taste

1 Roughly grind all the spices together in a spice grinder or with a pestle and mortar.
2 Heat olive oil in pan. Add the spices and stir for about 30 seconds.
3 Add beetroot and carrot and stir for further 2 minutes.
4 Add water and salt to taste, cover and cook on low heat for about 15 minutes, stirring occasionally, or until vegetables are cooked.
5 Serve with rice.

BEETROOT, ORANGE KISSED
(Serves 4)

- 450 g (1 lb/2 cups) beetroot, scrubbed but not topped and tailed
- 1 tbsp butter or margarine
- ½ tsp cornflour
- 150 ml (¼ pint/5 fl oz) orange juice
- 2 tbsp brown sugar
- ¼ tsp ground ginger
- Salt and black pepper
- 2 tbsp raisins
- Strips of orange peel

1 Place beetroot in a pan with cold, salted water. Bring to the boil. Cover the pan and return to the boil. Reduce heat and simmer until cooked, about one hour.
2 Drain, allow to cool, peel and slice.
3 Melt the butter or margarine in a pan, add cornflour with orange juice, brown sugar, ginger, salt and pepper. Stir continuously until thick.
4 Add beetroot and raisins to the sauce and heat through.
5 Garnish with strips of orange peel.

Sprout snippet: You can use any root vegetable for chips or crisps. Slice with a potato peeler or cheese slice and deep fry or lay the slices on a baking tray, brush with oil and sprinkle with herbs of your choice.

BEETROOT PESTO

- 200 g (7 oz) beetroot, scrubbed but not topped and tailed
- 2 tbsp olive oil
- 150 g (5 oz) toasted pine nuts
- 5 crushed cloves of garlic
- 2 tbsp fresh basil, chopped
- Zest and juice of one lemon
- 225 ml (8 fl oz/1 cup) olive oil
- 150 g (5 oz) grated Parmesan cheese
- Salt and black pepper

1 Preheat oven 180ºC (350ºF/Gas 4).
2 Place beetroot on a baking tray, brush with olive oil and roast for about one hour or until cooked. Cool, skin and quarter.
3 Toast pine nuts in a hot dry frying pan

stirring until golden, about 5 minutes.

4 Place all ingredients in a blender and zap until smooth. You may need to add a little more olive oil.

5 Serve as a dressing, in sandwiches, as a dip with vegetable sticks, crackers or with pasta.

Sprout Snippet: Beetroot contains more natural sugar than starch, so it is particularly delicious when roasted. Roasting concentrates the sugar rather than leaching it out into the cooking liquid.

BRUSSELS SPROUTS WITH CARAWAY SEEDS
(Serves 4)

- *450 g (1 lb/2 cups) Brussels sprouts, trimmed with outer leaves removed*
- *50 g (2 oz) butter or margarine*

- *150 ml (¼ pint/5 fl oz) water*
- *2 garlic cloves, peeled and crushed*
- *½ tsp caraway seeds*
- *Salt and black pepper*

1 Thinly slice sprouts lengthwise.

2 Heat butter or margarine and water in a pan and add sprouts when water boils.

3 Cover, reduce heat and simmer for about 5 minutes, or until the sprouts are just cooked.

4 Add garlic and the caraway seeds and cook until water has almost evaporated.

5 Season and transfer to a serving dish.

BRUSSELS SPROUTS AND CHESTNUTS WITH MAPLE GLAZE
(Serves 4)

- *175 g (6 oz/¾ cup) tinned chestnuts*
- *450 g (1 lb/2 cups) Brussels sprouts, trimmed with outer leaves removed*
- *5 tbsp maple syrup*
- *25 g (1 oz) butter or margarine*
- *Salt and black pepper*

1 Drain chestnuts.

2 Cut an X in the base of each sprout. Put into boiling salted water. Return to boil, reduce heat and simmer until tender, about 5-10 minutes. Drain and leave to cool.

3 Quarter each sprout.

4 Put maple syrup into a pan and warm. Add sprouts, butter and chestnuts.

5 The syrup and butter will thicken and glaze the sprouts. Season and serve.

BRUSSELS SPROUTS WITH LEMON
(Serves 4)

- *450 g (1 lb/2 cups) Brussels sprouts, trimmed with outer leaves removed*
- *4 tbsp spring onions, chopped*
- *25 g (1 oz) butter or margarine*
- *1½ tsp grated lemon zest*
- *Salt and black pepper*

1 Place sprouts in a pan of boiling salted water. Cook until sprouts are still slightly crisp, about 5 minutes.

2 Drain and put back into pan.

3 Combine rest of the

24

ingredients together in a bowl and add the sprouts. Stir.

4 Transfer to serving dish.

BRUSSELS SPROUTS WITH WINE AND HONEY-GLAZED

(Serves 4)

You can use broccoli instead of Brussels sprouts

- *450 g (1 lb/2 cups) Brussels sprouts, trimmed with outer leaves removed*
- *150 (¼ pint/5 fl oz) water*
- *4 tbsp dry red wine*
- *3 tbsp honey*
- *1 tbsp soy sauce*
- *¼ tsp black pepper*
- *1 tsp cornflour*

1 Cut an X into the base of each Brussels sprout about ¼" deep.

2 Put them into a pan of boiling salted water and boil for about 5 minutes. Do not drain.

3 In a bowl combine wine, honey, soy sauce and pepper and add to Brussels sprouts. Stir well.

4 Bring back to the boil, reduce heat, and simmer for a further 5 minutes.

5 Mix cornflour with a little water, stir into the pan quickly and cook until sauce is thickened.

6 Transfer to serving dish.

CABBAGE AND CELERY BAKE

(Serves 4)

- *450 g (1 lb/2 cups) cabbage, coarsely chopped*
- *175 g (6 oz) celery, sliced*
- *Salt to taste*
- *1 tsp fennel seeds*

Sauce

- *25 g (1 oz) butter or margarine*
- *50 g (2 oz/½ cup) plain flour*
- *425 ml (¾ pint/2 cups) milk*
- *150 ml (¼ pint/5 fl oz) beer*
- *225 g (8 oz/1 cup) Cheddar cheese, grated*
- *Salt and black pepper*

1 Preheat oven 180ºC (350ºF/Gas 4).

2 Place the cabbage, celery, salt and fennel seeds in a pan of boiling water. Bring back to boil, reduce heat and simmer for about 5 minutes and drain well.

3 Transfer to buttered oven dish.

4 Melt the butter or margarine in a pan, add flour and cook,

stirring continuously for 1 minute. Slowly add milk, stirring continuously until sauce is smooth and thick.

5 Add the beer and stir until foam disappears. Cook until heated through.

6 Add cheese and stir until melted. Season to taste.

7 Pour sauce over vegetables, top with breadcrumbs and bake for 30 minutes.

Sprout snippet: The nasty odour problem of cabbage is a result of overcooking. Cabbage contains rich sources of sulphur containing compounds that break down during cooking. The longer the cabbage is cooked, the smellier the compounds become. The solution: brief cooking time in stainless steel pans.

CABBAGE WITH SPICES, GINGER AND COCONUT MILK
(Serves 4)

- 2 tbsp olive oil
- ½ tsp black mustard seeds
- 1 onion, chopped
- 2 garlic cloves, crushed
- 1 green chilli, seeded and finely chopped
- 1 tsp turmeric
- 2.5 cm (1") piece fresh root ginger, peeled and finely chopped
- 2 tsp ground coriander
- 1 tsp ground cumin
- 1 bay leaf
- ¼ tsp ground cinnamon
- Salt and black pepper
- 450 g (1 lb) cabbage, cut into medium sized strips
- 2 tbsp cider vinegar
- 1 x 400 ml (14 fl oz) tin coconut milk

1 Heat oil in a pan, fry the mustard seeds until they crackle.
2 Add the onion, garlic, chilli, turmeric, ginger, coriander, cumin, bay leaf, cinnamon. Season to taste.
3 Fry for another 2-3 minutes.
4 Add cabbage and vinegar.
5 Stir in coconut milk and simmer gently, stirring occasionally until the cabbage is cooked.
6 Serve with rice.

Sprout snippet: To relieve an upset stomach and stimulate digestion, drink 1 tbsp of olive oil before eating.

CARROT, LEEK AND OLIVE STEW
(Serves 4)

- 1 tbsp olive oil
- 3 medium leeks, sliced
- 2 cloves garlic, crushed
- 3 medium carrots peeled and diced
- 1 medium potato, finely diced
- 2 tbsp tomato paste or purée
- ¼ tsp dried thyme
- ¼ tsp dried oregano
- Salt and black pepper
- 500 ml (16 fl oz/2 cups) water or vegetable stock
- 90 g (3 oz/½ cup) ripe olives, pitted and chopped

1 Heat oil in pan and sauté leek and garlic until soft.
2 Add the carrots, potatoes and seasonings.
3 Add water or stock, cover and bring to boil.
4 Reduce heat and simmer for about 15-20 minutes.
5 During last 5 minutes of cooking, stir in olives.
- Serve with rice, roast potatoes or breads.

CURLY KALE PESTO

- 225 g (8 oz/1 cup) curly kale, chopped
- 1½ tsp dried basil
- 2-4 garlic cloves
- 2 tbsp Parmesan
- 50 g (2 oz/¼ cup) sunflower seeds
- 175 ml (6 fl oz/¾ cup) olive oil
- Salt and black pepper

1 Blend curly kale, basil, sunflower seeds, garlic and Parmesan in a food processor.

2 Gradually add olive oil. Season to taste. A little more olive oil may be needed.
3 Keeps well in jars in the refrigerator for up to 3 days.

Sprout snippet: We found that keeping food in jars in the fridge rather than in a dish with cling-film keeps food fresher and is more appealing.

CURLY KALE AND POTATO RISOTTO
(Serves 6)
- *2 tbsp olive oil*
- *25 g (1 oz) butter or margarine*
- *1 medium onion, chopped*
- *2 medium potatoes, peeled or with skin, cut into 1.25 cm (½") chunks*
- *350 g (12 oz/1½ cups) curly kale, chopped finely*
- *350 g (12 oz/1½ cups) Arborio rice*

- *150 ml (¼ pint/5 fl oz) white wine*
- *950 ml (32 fl oz/1½ pints/4 cups) hot vegetable stock*
- *2 tbsp Parmesan cheese, grated*
- *Salt and black pepper*

1 In a large pan, heat the oil and butter or margarine. Add the onion, potatoes and curly kale.
2 Sauté until kale wilts, about 5-10 minutes.
3 Add rice and stir briefly, until rice turns opaque, about one minute.
4 Add wine and stir until evaporated.
5 Add boiling stock. Simmer until rice is cooked, about 18 minutes.
6 Add the Parmesan and season to taste.

Sprout snippet: Arborio rice is a pearly-looking, round, fat, Italian, white rice and forms the foundation of risotto. It has a higher than normal amount of soluble starch that is released during cooking. The starch makes the risotto creamy. It takes about 18 minutes to cook. It is done when it is al dente: tender on the outside and firm in the centre.

CURLY KALE WITH TOASTED SESAME SEEDS
(Serves 4)
- *1¼ tsp sesame oil*
- *2 garlic cloves, crushed*
- *450 g (1 lb/2 cups) curly kale, cut into fine strips*
- *2 tbsp vegetable stock*
- *2 tsp soy sauce*
- *Salt and black pepper*
- *1¼ tsp sesame seeds, toasted*

1 In a pan, heat oil. Add garlic and sauté for 10 seconds.
2 Add curly kale and stock. Cover and cook for about 5 minutes or until the kale has wilted. You may need to add more liquid.
3 Add soy sauce.
4 Put into a serving dish and keep warm.
5 Toast the sesame seeds in a hot, dry frying pan until slightly browned and fragrant. Shake pan frequently. Watch that they do not burn.
6 Top the kale with sesame seeds and extra freshly ground black pepper.

27

Burns' Night is a key event in the Scottish year, and it is celebrated in Scotland, or wherever people of Scottish descent live in the world.

A Burns' supper is traditionally held on 25th January, the date when Scotland's most famous poet, Robert Burns, was born.

He wrote his 'Address to the Haggis' during his first visit to Edinburgh in 1786. The poem, which is highly patriotic and atmospheric, is very suitable for reciting in a loud voice. The centrepiece is the haggis, borne on a silver platter by the cook, preceded by a kilted bagpiper. Others follow, bearing the dishes of swede (neeps) and potato (tatties).

The 'Address' is declaimed and the haggis is then stabbed ceremonially with the black knife (sgean dhu), kept in the Scot's stocking and large amounts of whisky are consumed.

We could not write this book without including a haggis recipe! This is a completely different and unusual way to serve haggis.

HAGGIS BURGERS WITH WHISKY SAUCE
(Serves 4)
Burgers
- *450 g (1 lb) haggis*
- *1 egg, beaten*

Coating
- *50 g (2 oz) flour*
- *1 egg, beaten*
- *125 g (4 oz) breadcrumbs*
- *2 tbsp olive oil for frying*

Sauce
- *Knob of butter or margarine*
- *3 tbsp whisky*
- *4 tbsp double cream*
- *50 ml (¼ cup/2 fl oz) vegetable stock*
- *1 tsp Dijon mustard*
- *Salt and black pepper*

1 Take haggis out of its skin and put into a bowl.
2 Add beaten egg and mix together.
3 Form into burgers, coating each one with flour.
4 Dip each burger into egg then coat in breadcrumbs.
5 Heat olive oil in a pan and fry burgers until golden brown, turning once.
6 For the **sauce**, heat pan and melt butter. Add 3 tbsp whisky and light with lighter to burn off alcohol.
7 Add cream, stock and mustard once the flame is out.
8 Allow to thicken and season to taste. Pour sauce over burgers.
9 Serve with mashed *neeps* (swede) and *tatties* (potatoes).

KOHLRABI WITH BROWN SUGAR AND GINGER
(Serves 6)
- *700 g (1½ lb/3 cups) kohlrabi, peeled and sliced 0.6 cm (¼") thick*
- *25 g (1 oz) butter or margarine*
- *2 tbsp brown sugar*
- *½ tsp ground ginger*
- *Salt and black pepper*

1 Put kohlrabi into a pan with salted water. Bring to the boil, reduce heat, simmer until tender, about 10 minutes. Drain.
2 Melt butter or margarine in a pan. Add brown sugar, ginger, salt and pepper and stir.
3 Pour over the kohlrabi, mix well and serve.

28

KOHLRABI, SWEDE AND POTATO SOUP
(Serves 6)

- 1 tbsp olive oil
- 1 onion, chopped
- 2 garlic cloves
- 450 g (1 lb/2 cups) kohlrabi, peeled and diced
- 450 g (1 lb/2 cups) swede, peeled and diced
- 450 g (1 lb/2 cups) potato, peeled and diced
- 950 ml (32 fl oz/1¾ pints/4 cups) stock
- Salt and black pepper
- ¼ tsp ground nutmeg

To serve:
- 150 ml (5 fl oz/¼ pint) sour cream

1 Heat oil in pan, add onion and garlic and sauté for about 4 minutes or until onion is transparent.
2 Add kohlrabi, swede, potato and stock and stir well.
3 Bring to the boil, cover, reduce heat and simmer for about 30 minutes or until the vegetables are tender.
4 In a food processor, blend until smooth.
5 Return to pan and add salt, pepper and nutmeg.
6 Ladle into bowls and top with sour cream.

LEEK, CARAMELISED PEAR, AND BRIE TART
(Serves 4)
Shortcrust Pastry
- 175g (6 oz/1½ cups) plain flour
- ¼ tsp salt
- Pinch sugar
- 90 (3 oz) butter or margarine
- 4-5 tbsp cold water

Filling
- 3 pears, peeled, cored and diced
- 4 tbsp olive oil
- 3 large leeks, sliced and washed
- 90 g (3oz/½ cup) pine nuts
- Salt and black pepper
- Pinch of nutmeg
- 225 g (8 oz/1 cup) Brie cheese

1 Preheat oven 200ºC (400ºF/Gas 6).
2 To make pastry, combine flour, salt and sugar in a bowl.
3 Cut the butter or margarine into cubes and rub into flour until it looks like fine breadcrumbs.
4 Add water to form a dough. Knead on a floured board.
5 Wrap up in plastic and allow to rest in fridge for at least 30 minutes.
6 On lightly floured board, roll out dough in a circle and place in a 24 cm (9½")
round pie dish.
7 Prick pastry with fork and blind bake for 5–10 minutes until it has just a hint of colour.
8 Heat 2 tbsp oil in a pan, sauté pears until golden brown, stirring frequently. Remove from the pan and set aside.
9 Heat remaining oil in the pan and sauté leeks until they are translucent.
10 Lightly toast the pine nuts in a hot dry frying pan.
11 Combine pears, leeks, pine nuts, salt, pepper and nutmeg in a bowl.
12 Spoon mixture into pastry case and dot the top with all of the Brie.
13 Bake for about 10 minutes, or until cheese has melted.

29

LEEK, POTATO, PRUNE AND APPLE PIE WITH STOUT
(Serves 4)

- *50 g (2 oz) dried prunes*
- *150 ml (¼ pint/5 fl oz) stout such as Black Bishop or Guinness*
- *275 g (10 oz) frozen puff pastry*
- *1 tbsp olive oil*
- *1 medium onion, thinly sliced*
- *225 g (8 oz/1 cup) potatoes, thinly sliced*
- *1 leek, sliced and washed*
- *1 medium cooking apple, cored, peeled and sliced*
- *6 sage leaves, chopped*
- *3 cloves*
- *¼ tsp cinnamon*
- *Salt and black pepper*
- *2 tbsp double cream or yoghurt*
- *Beaten egg to glaze*

1. Preheat oven 200ºC (400ºF/Gas 6).
2. Marinate the prunes in stout for 2 hours.
3. De-frost pastry and roll out to line medium pie dish with large flaps overlapping.
4. Put olive oil in a pan, sauté onions and potatoes until softened.
5. Add leek and sauté for 2 minutes.
6. Remove from heat and stir in apple, sage leaves, cloves, cinnamon, salt and pepper.
7. Stir in 2 tablespoons of double cream or yoghurt.
8. Drain prunes (retain marinade), chop and add to mixture.
9. Pour into pie dish.
10. Pull over pastry flaps, leaving hole in the centre.
11. Brush with beaten egg and bake for 30 minutes or until golden.
12. Use prune marinade to make extra gravy.
13. Melt 25 g (1 oz) butter or margarine in a pan, add 25 g (1 oz) plain flour, and cook gently for 2-3 minutes, stirring constantly with a wooden spoon.
14. Gradually add the prune marinade and up to ½ pint of stock until desired thickness is achieved.
15. Season to taste.
16. Serve with green vegetables.

PARSNIP AND CARROT PURÉE
(Serves 4)

- *450 g (1 lb/2 cups) parsnips, peeled and sliced*
- *450 g (1 lb/2 cups) carrots, peeled and sliced*
- *225 ml (8 fl oz/1 cup) milk or single cream*
- *50 g (2 oz) butter or margarine*
- *½ tsp vanilla essence*
- *Salt and black pepper*

1. Put parsnips into salted water. Bring to the boil, reduce heat and simmer until tender. Drain.
2. Put carrots into salted water. Bring to the boil, reduce heat and simmer until tender. Drain.
3. Place cooked parsnips in a food processor. Add half the milk or cream, half of the butter or margarine, blend until smooth.
4. Season to taste. Set aside - keep warm.
5. Rinse blender, add

carrots, rest of the milk and butter or margarine, vanilla essence and blend until smooth.

6 Season to taste.

7 Spoon parsnip into half of a small serving bowl. Spoon carrot in the other half. Pull a small rubber spatula through the mixture to create a marbled pattern.

PARSNIP AND POTATO CASSEROLE
(Serves 4)

- 225 g (8 oz/1 cup) parsnips, peeled and chopped
- 225 g (8 oz/1 cup) potatoes, peeled and chopped
- 90 g (3 oz) cream cheese
- 1 tbsp grated Parmesan cheese
- 2 tbsp milk
- 25 g (1 oz) butter or margarine
- 2 tbsp parsley, chopped
- Salt and black pepper

1 Preheat oven 190ºC (375ºF/Gas 5).

2 Place parsnips and potatoes in a pan with salted water. Bring to the boil, reduce heat and simmer until tender, about 10 minutes.

3 Drain and return vegetables to pan.

4 Mash well, stir in rest of ingredients and season.

5 Pour mixture into a greased baking dish and bake for about 20 minutes until mixture is bubbly.

PARSNIP CAKE WITH WALNUT AND CINNAMON FROSTING

- 125 g (4 oz/½ cup) butter or margarine
- 150 ml (¼ pint/5 fl oz) olive oil
- 225 g (8 oz/1 cup) granulated sugar
- 225 g (8 oz/1 cup) brown sugar
- 4 eggs
- 225 g (8 oz/2 cups) plain flour
- 1 tsp baking powder
- 1 tsp bicarbonate of soda
- 1 tsp ground cinnamon
- 1 pinch salt
- 700 g (1½ b/3 cups) parsnips, peeled and grated
- 150 g (5 oz/1 cup) walnuts, chopped
- 1 tsp vanilla essence

For the frosting
- 175 g (6 oz) cream cheese
- 125 g (4 oz/½ cup) butter or margarine
- 150 g (5 oz/1 cup) walnuts, chopped
- 1 tsp ground cinnamon
- 350 g (12 oz) icing sugar

1 Preheat oven 180ºC (350ºF/Gas 4).

2 Grease 2 x 24 cm (9½") cake tins.

3 Combine butter or margarine, oil, granulated sugar, brown sugar and cream mixture until smooth.

4 Add eggs, one at a time.

5 Sieve flour, baking powder, bicarbonate of soda, cinnamon and salt into a bowl and mix.

6 Fold in flour mixture to butter /sugar mixture.

7 Add the parsnips, walnuts and vanilla. Mix well.

8 Pour mixture into prepared cake tins

and spread evenly.

9 Bake for 30 minutes, or until a knife inserted into the centre of the cake comes out clean.

10 Remove from the oven and cool.

11 For the frosting, combine the cream cheese, butter or margarine, and mix well.

12 Add walnut pieces and cinnamon and mix well.

13 Add the icing sugar a little at a time and mix until the frosting is spreadable.

14 Spread half the frosting between the cake pieces and the other half on top of the cake.

POTATO CAKES WITH GOAT'S CHEESE
(Makes 4 cakes)

- *50 g (1 lb) potatoes, coarsely grated*
- *1 tsp dried thyme*
- *2 garlic cloves, crushed*
- *1 onion, finely chopped*
- *Salt and black pepper*
- *2 tbsp olive oil*
- *50 g (2 oz) butter or margarine*
- *125 g(4 oz) goat's cheese*

1 After grating the potatoes, using your hands, squeeze out as much of the thick starchy liquid as possible.

2 Add the thyme, garlic, onion and seasoning.

3 Heat olive oil and butter or margarine in a pan.

4 Divide mixture into

four spoonfuls and place in a frying pan, spacing them well apart. Press firmly down with a spatula.

5 Cook for 3-4 minutes on each side or until golden. Drain on kitchen paper.

6 Preheat the grill.

7 Put a slice of cheese on top of each potato cake and grill for 2-3 minutes until lightly golden.

8 Serve with a light salad.

RED CABBAGE WITH APRICOTS AND BALSAMIC VINEGAR
(Serves 6-8)

- *1 tbsp olive oil*
- *1 onion, thinly sliced*
- *½ tsp allspice*
- *¼ tsp ground nutmeg*
- *700 g ½ lb/ cups) red cabbage, thinly sliced*

- *125 g (4 oz/½ cup dried apricots, sliced*
- *4 tbsp balsamic vinegar*
- *Salt and black pepper*

1 Heat olive oil in pan, add onion, allspice and nutmeg and stir for 1 minute.

2 Add cabbage and apricots. Sauté until well coated, about 2 minutes.

3 Add vinegar and cook until cabbage is crisp-tender, about 5 minutes.

4 Season to taste.

RED CABBAGE WITH CHESTNUT SAUCE
(Serves 6)

- *1 tbsp olive oil*
- *2 onions, chopped*
- *2 cloves garlic, crushed*
- *½ tsp ground coriander*
- *1 large red cabbage, sliced*

32

- 450 g (1 lb/2 cups) chestnuts, peeled and chopped
- 225 ml (8 fl oz/1 cup) vegetable stock
- 2 tbsp red wine vinegar
- Salt and black pepper
- 2 ripe pears, peeled and sliced

1   In a large pan, heat oil and cook onions, garlic and coriander until onions are soft.
2   Add cabbage and cook for 3–5 minutes.
3   Add chestnuts, stock, vinegar, salt and pepper.
4   Cover and cook on low heat for about 15 minutes.
5   Add pears and cook for about another 10 minutes.
6   Serve with crispy roast potatoes.

RED CABBAGE, SWEET AND SOUR
(Serves 4)

- 1 tbsp olive oil
- 700 g (1½ lb/3 cups) red cabbage, chopped finely
- 225 g (8 oz/1 cup) carrots, grated
- 1 onion, chopped
- 2 cloves garlic, crushed
- ½ tsp ground ginger
- ¼ tsp cayenne pepper

For the blender

- 125 g (4 oz/½ cup) prunes, pitted
- 150 ml (¼ pint/5 fl oz) apple juice
- 4 tbsp vinegar
- 2 tbsp soy sauce
- 2 tbsp cornflour

1   In a large pan, heat oil, add cabbage, carrots, onion, garlic, ginger and cayenne pepper. Cook until vegetables are soft, about 10 minutes.

2   Put the rest of the ingredients into a blender and purée until smooth.
3   Add to the cooked vegetables and mix together. Continue cooking until liquid is thickened.

Now for our first swede recipes. In America swede is called rutabaga and is said to be one of the world's least understood vegetables and may also be the most maligned. Noses turn up at the very word. Yet under the rough skin of this unappealing tuber, a treasure lies hidden: flesh rich and flavourful, the colour of gold.

SWEDE IN CIDER
(Serves 4)

- 1 tbsp olive oil
- 1 onion, chopped
- 450 g (1 lb/2 cups) swede, peeled and diced
- 1 tsp dried tarragon
- ½ tsp dried thyme
- 2 tbsp dried currants
- ½ tsp ground cinnamon
- 450 ml (16 fl oz/2 cups) dry cider
- Salt and black pepper
- 150 ml (5 fl oz/¼ pint) cream

1   Heat oil in a pan and sauté the onion until soft, about 5 minutes.
2   Add swede and sauté until browned.
3   Add tarragon, thyme, currants, cinnamon, cider and season to taste.
4   Bring to the boil, reduce heat and simmer for about 15 minutes or until swede is cooked and liquid has reduced.
5   Stir in the cream and serve with rice.

SWEDE AND LEEK SOUP

(Serves 4-6)

- 2 tbsp olive oil
- 700 g (1½ lb/3 cups) swede, peeled and diced
- 225 g (8 oz/1 cup) potatoes, peeled and diced
- 450 g (1 lb/2 cups) leeks, sliced and washed well
- 1 garlic clove, crushed
- ½ tsp mixed herbs
- 1.5 L (2½ pints/6 cups) vegetable stock
- Salt and black pepper
- 150 ml (¼ pint/5 fl oz) milk

1 Heat the oil in a large pan and sauté swede, potatoes, leeks and garlic for about 5 minutes.
2 Add the mixed herbs, vegetable stock and season to taste.
3 Bring to the boil, reduce heat and simmer for about 30 minutes or until vegetables are soft.
4 Soup can be left like this, or blended if you like a smooth texture.
5 Stir in the milk, reheat and serve.

In Scotland, swede (called 'neeps') is traditionally served mashed with lots of butter and pepper.

SWEDE PURÉE WITH CHEESE AND PEARS

(Serves 6-8)

- 450 g (1 lb/2 cups) swede, peeled and sliced
- 450 g (1 lb/2 cups) pears, peeled and cored
- 1 tbsp olive oil
- 1 onion, chopped
- 50 g (2 oz) Cheddar cheese, cubed
- Salt and black pepper
- ½ tsp nutmeg, grated

1 Put swede into salted water. Bring to the boil, reduce heat and simmer until tender, about 10-15 minutes.
2 Drain and set aside.
3 Steam pears over boiling water for about 5-10 minutes, or until pears are tender.
4 Heat oil in a pan and sauté onion until tender, about 5 minutes.
5 Transfer onion to food processor. Add swede, pears and cheese. Process until smooth.
6 Season to taste.
7 Transfer to a serving bowl and sprinkle with nutmeg. Can be served hot or chilled.

SWEDE PURÉE WITH CREME FRAICHE, GINGER AND NUTMEG

(Serves 4)

- 700g (1½ lb/3 cups) swede, peeled and diced
- 25 g (1 oz) butter or margarine
- ½ tsp ground ginger
- ¼ tsp ground nutmeg
- Salt and black pepper
- 2 tbsp crème fraîche

To garnish

- Extra crème fraîche
- 2 tbsp parsley, chopped
- Black pepper

1 Put swede in salted water and bring to the boil. Reduce heat and simmer for about 15 minutes or until tender.

2 Drain. Purée in a food processor until smooth.
3 Transfer purée into a pan. Stir in butter or margarine, ginger and nutmeg. Season to taste. Gently heat through.
4 Stir in crème fraîche and place mixture into a serving dish.
5 Garnish with a swirl of crème fraîche, parsley and freshly ground black pepper.

SWEDE PURÉE WITH GROUND ELDER
(Serves 4)
The Romans introduced ground elder into Britain as a source of vitamin C.

- 2 handfuls of ground elder, washed and sliced into 2 cm (¾") lengths
- 450 g (1 lb) swede, peeled and diced
- 2-3 tbsp single or double cream
- 50 g (2 oz) butter or margarine
- Salt and black pepper

1 Put sliced elder into boiling salted water. Bring back to the boil, reduce heat and simmer for about 10 minutes or until tender. Drain.
2 Put swede into salted water, bring to the boil, reduce heat and simmer until tender, about 20 minutes. Drain.
3 Mash swede with cream and butter or margarine. Season.
4 Add ground elder, stir and serve.

Sprout snippet: : Ground elder or Jack jump-about is every gardener's nightmare so we were amazed to discover that it is edible. You can eat it on its own like spinach by heating a knob of butter in a pan, adding some water and cooking the ground elder leaves for about 10 minutes. Drain, and add salt, pepper, nutmeg, lemon juice. Serve. Can be added to stews.

Ground elder or Jack jump-about

SWEDE PUREE WITH WHISKY AND CREAM
(Serves 4-6)

- 900 g (2 lb) swede, peeled and cubed
- 45 g (½ oz) butter or margarine
- 3 tbsp whisky
- 2 tbsp single cream
- Salt and black pepper

1 Put swede in a pan with salted water, bring to the boil, reduce heat and simmer until tender, about 15 minutes. Drain.
2 Transfer swede to a food processor.
3 Add butter or margarine, whisky, cream and season.
4 Process until smooth.

Sprout Snippet: *Do you know what the difference is between a swede and a turnip? In some areas you ask for a swede and receive a large orange-fleshed vegetable. In other areas you need to ask for a turnip to receive a large orange-fleshed vegetable.*

On top of this, a swede is called a rutabaga or yellow turnip in the United States. In Scotland, they call swede neeps.

One definition of a turnip, as we understand, is that it is a smaller cousin of the swede or rutabaga. It has white flesh with a purple trimming and green top. It has a sharper taste and is most frequently available during the summer before the new crop of swede or rutabaga. Some people call it a 'white turnip'.

Confused? So are we!

Be reassured the recipes work with all three, whatever you call it!

Rutabaga, Swede or Neeps

FARMING NEWS FOR FEBRUARY

*P*otato grading or dressing is done weekly.

HARVESTING

Broccoli, Brussels sprouts, green and red cabbage, cauliflower, chicory, curly kale, leeks, parsnip and swede continue to be cropped.

In addition, the harvesting of oriental greens from polytunnels at Cullerne commences. Most of the oriental greens come from Northern China and Japan, which have much colder winters than Scotland. These varieties of salad greens always do well in the conditions created within the polytunnels, better than over-wintered lettuce, which is subject to mildew.

PLANTING

Christopher sows the first carrots, lettuce, radish and spinach in modules in the polytunnels at Cullerne, ready for April.

The carrots are ready to crop in late May to dovetail with the end of the last season's carrots.

WEATHER

The weather is best described as lousy: windy and too cold to work on machines outside.

It beats the canker, root fly and anything else to become the pest this month.

Pak Choi

Christopher Raymont with trailer of EarthShare vegetables

FEBRUARY RECIPES

FEBRUARY RECIPES

BEETROOT PIE
(Serves 4)
- 450 g (1 lb/2 cups) beetroot, cooked and peeled
- 125 g (4 oz/½ cup) onion, peeled
- 1 egg
- 50 g (2 oz/¼ cup) flour
- 1 tbsp mustard
- 8 tbsp cream
- Salt and back pepper

1 Preheat oven 180°C (350°F/Gas 4).
2 Blend beetroot and onion in a food processor until smooth.
3 Add remaining ingredients and blend thoroughly.
4 Place mixture into an oiled baking dish. Set the dish in a shallow baking or roasting tin, with about 2.5 cm (1") of cold water and bake for about 20-30 minutes.
5 Serve with millet, potatoes or potato cakes with goat's cheese on page 32.

BEETROOT AND WALNUT HOUMOUS
(Serves 4)
- 2 beetroot, scrubbed but not topped and tailed
- 1 onion, chopped
- 400 g tin chickpeas
- 5 cloves garlic
- 45 g (1½ oz/2 tbsp) tahini
- 90 g (3 oz/½ cup) toasted walnuts
- 1 tsp ground cumin
- 2-4 tbsp olive oil
- Salt and black pepper
- 2 tbsp water
- 2 tsp lemon juice

1 Place beetroot in a pan with cold, salted water. Bring to the boil, reduce heat and simmer until cooked, about one hour. Drain, remove skin, and quarter.
2 Put beetroot, onion, drained chickpeas and rest of the ingredients into a food processor and blend thoroughly. Season to taste.
3 Serve as a starter or light lunch on pitta bread.

BRUSSELS SPROUTS WITH OLIVE AND RED PEPPER SAUCE
(Serves 4)
- 225 g (8 oz/1 cup) Brussels sprouts, trimmed with outer leaves removed
- 2 tbsp olive oil
- 1 garlic clove, crushed
- 15 black olives, chopped
- 1 red pepper, chopped
- Salt and black pepper

To serve:
- Spaghetti, for 4

1 Put Brussels sprouts into boiling salted water. Bring back to the boil, cover, reduce heat, simmer until tender, then quarter.
2 In a large pan, heat oil and sauté garlic for about 2 minutes.
3 Add Brussel sprouts, olives, red pepper and season to taste.
4 Sauté until pepper is just cooked.
5 Cook spaghetti for 4, add to Brussels sprouts and stir.
6 Serve immediately.

BRUSSELS SPROUTS, ORANGE AND HONEY GLAZED

(Serves 4)

- 450 g (1 lb/2 cups) Brussels sprouts, trimmed with outer leaves removed
- ½ fresh orange, peeled and cut into wedges
- 25 g (1 oz) butter or margarine
- 1 tbsp honey
- ¼ tsp ground cloves

1 Put Brussels sprouts into boiling salted water, bring back to the boil, reduce heat and simmer until tender, about 10 minutes. Drain.
2 Add rest of the ingredients to the pan and stir well.
3 Transfer to serving dish.

Sprout snippet: Many people who do not like Brussels sprouts are often haunted by childhood memories of smelly, green, mushy globs that had to be eaten before pudding. Fresh Brussels sprouts, properly cooked, are delicate in flavour. Try some of these recipes and give them another chance.

CABBAGE WITH COCONUT

(Serves 4)

- 3 tbsp olive oil
- ¼ tsp mustard seeds
- ¼ tsp chilli powder
- 450 g (1 lb/2 cups) cabbage, shredded
- ¼ tsp turmeric
- 2½ tsp mustard powder
- 2 tbsp water
- 50 g (2 oz) desiccated coconut
- Salt and black pepper

1 Heat oil in pan and fry mustard seeds until they pop.
2 Add chilli powder, cabbage, turmeric and cook gently for about 5 minutes, stirring occasionally. Cover and simmer until the cabbage is tender.
3 Mix mustard powder with water to make a paste and add to pan.
4 Add coconut, salt and pepper. Cook, stirring occasionally until most of the liquid is absorbed.
5 Serve with boiled rice or bread.

CABBAGE, SPICED

(Serves 4)

- 2 tbsp olive oil
- 2 medium onions, sliced in rings
- ½ tsp cumin seeds
- 450 g (1 lb/2 cups) cabbage or spring greens, shredded
- ¼ tsp chilli powder
- 1 tsp garam masala
- Salt and black pepper
- Lemon wedges to serve

1 Heat oil in large pan. Add onions and fry until golden brown, about 10 minutes, stirring from time to time.
2 Add cumin seeds and cook over a medium heat for one minute.
3 Add cabbage and cook until leaves are shiny and tender.
4 Add chilli, garam masala and season. Cook for 3 minutes, stirring constantly.
5 Serve with lemon wedges.

Sprout snippet: To relieve constipation, drink a mixture of one teaspoon each of olive oil and lemon juice before breakfast.

CARROT BAKE WITH HORSERADISH AND CHEESE
(Serves 4)
- 450 g (1 lb/2 cups) carrots, washed or peeled and cut into 1.25 cm (½") slices
- 2 tbsp onion, chopped
- 4 tbsp mayonnaise
- 4 tbsp water
- 1 tbsp creamed horseradish
- Salt and black pepper

Topping
- 125 g (4 oz) fresh breadcrumbs
- 1 tbsp olive oil
- 125 g (4 oz) Cheddar cheese, grated

1 Preheat oven 190ºC (375ºF/Gas 5).
2 Bring carrots to boil in salted water. Reduce heat and simmer until just tender. Drain and place in a baking dish, set aside.
3 In a bowl combine the onion, water, mayonnaise and horseradish. Season and mix well.
4 Pour over carrots.
5 Mix together the topping ingredients and sprinkle on top of the carrots.
6 Bake for about 25 minutes or until golden.

CARROTS, BUTTERED WITH TARRAGON
(Serves 4)
- 4 large carrots, cut into batons
- 50 g (2 oz/½ stick) butter or margarine
- 2 tbsp fresh tarragon, or 1 tsp dried
- Salt and black pepper

1 Preheat oven 190ºC (375ºF/Gas 5).
2 Place half the carrots in greased ovenproof dish.
3 Dot with half the butter and sprinkle with half the tarragon.
4 Place second half of carrots on top of first, dot with the rest of the butter and tarragon.
5 Season.
6 Cover and bake for about 30 minutes or until carrots are tender.

CARROT AND COCONUT SOUP
(Serves 4)
- 125 g (4 oz/½ cup) red lentils
- 225 g (8 oz/1 cup) carrots, grated
- ½ medium onion, chopped
- 2 cloves garlic, chopped
- 1 tbsp tomato purée
- 600 ml (1 pint/20 fl oz) vegetable stock or water
- 1 tbsp creamed coconut
- Salt and black pepper

1 Cook lentils, carrots, onion, garlic and tomato purée in the water or stock for 20 minutes, or until lentils are soft.
2 Add coconut and simmer for about 3 minutes.
3 Liquidise until smooth.
4 Season to taste and reheat gently adding more liquid if necessary.

CAULIFLOWER AND BRUSSELS SPROUTS TOPS, WITH SPICES AND LIME JUICE
(Serves 4-6)
- 2 tbsp olive oil
- 1 onion, thinly sliced
- 2 garlic cloves, chopped
- 1 cauliflower (white

or green), broken into florets
- 1 carrot, peeled and chopped
- 3 medium potatoes, peeled and cubed
- ½ tsp turmeric
- 1 tsp ground cumin
- 1 tsp mustard seeds
- Salt and black pepper
- 450 g (1 lb/2 cups) Brussels sprouts tops, chopped
- Juice and zest of one lime

1. Heat oil in a large pan and sauté the onion and garlic until browned, about 8-10 minutes.
2. Add the cauliflower, carrot and potato. Mix well.
3. Add the turmeric, cumin, mustard seeds, and season.
4. Add sprout tops with 150 ml (¼ pint/5 fl oz) water.

5. Cover and cook until the sprout tops have wilted, about 3-5 minutes.
6. Add the lime zest and juice.
7. Serve with rice.

CURLY KALE AND CHICKPEA BALTI
(Serves 4)
- 1 tbsp olive oil
- 1 medium onion, chopped
- 2 garlic cloves, crushed
- 1 tsp cumin seeds
- 1 tbsp ground coriander
- 1 tsp turmeric
- 225 g (8 oz/1 cup) curly kale, cut into fine strips
- 1 x 400 g tin tomatoes
- 1 x 400 g tin chickpeas, drained and rinsed
- Salt and black pepper

1. Heat oil in a pan and add onion and garlic. Sauté for about 3 minutes.
2. Add cumin seeds, coriander, and turmeric and sauté for another 2-3 minutes.
3. Add the curly kale, tomatoes and chickpeas. Bring to the boil, reduce heat and simmer for 5-10 minutes, or until the kale is cooked.
4. Season to taste.
5. Serve with rice or chapattis.

CURLY KALE WITH GARLIC AND CINNAMON
(Serves 4)
- 1 tbsp olive oil
- 1 onion, chopped
- 2 cloves garlic
- ½ tsp ground cinnamon
- 450 g (1 lb/2 cups) curly kale, chopped

- 225 ml (8 fl oz/1 cup) vegetable stock
- 1 tsp red wine vinegar
- Salt and black pepper

1. Heat oil in pan and sauté onion for 5 minutes. Add garlic and cook for further 2 minutes.
2. Stir in the cinnamon.
3. Add kale and mix.
4. Add vegetable stock and wine vinegar. Bring to boil, reduce heat, cover and simmer for about 15 minutes or until kale is tender.
5. Season to taste.

CURLY KALE WITH RED PEPPERS
(Serves 4)
- 2 tbsp olive oil
- 1 medium onion, chopped
- 2 garlic cloves, crushed

42

- 1 large red pepper, seeded and chopped
- 450 g (1 lb/2 cups) curly kale, finely chopped
- Salt and black pepper

1 Heat oil in a pan, sauté onion, garlic and red pepper for about 5 minutes or until onions become transparent.
2 Add curly kale and mix well so that it gets coated with the oil mixture. Add up to 4 tablespoons of water if kale appears a little dry.
3 Sauté for about 10 minutes until kale is cooked.
4 Season to taste.

LEEKS AND GREENS WITH PASTA
(Serves 4-6)

Any greens can be used for this recipe such as sprout tops, Chinese cabbage, beetroot tops, chard, purple sprouting broccoli.

- 3 tbsp olive oil
- 450 g (1 lb/2 cups) leeks, sliced and washed well
- 2 garlic cloves, crushed
- 900 g (2 lb/4 cups) mixed greens, chopped
- Salt and black pepper
- 450 g (1 lb) pasta

To garnish:
- 1 tbsp Parmesan cheese, grated

1 In a large pan, heat 2 tbsp oil, add the leeks and sauté until very soft.
2 Add garlic and sauté for about a minute.
3 Add chopped greens, continue cooking for about another 5-8 minutes until greens are tender. Season.
4 Meanwhile, cook pasta, following instructions on packet. Drain and toss with greens and leeks.
5 Add another tbsp of olive oil and sprinkle with Parmesan.

LEEK AND LEMON SOUP
(Serves 4)

- 2 tbsp olive oil
- 4 medium leeks, washed well and finely sliced
- 1 medium onion, chopped
- 6 celery sticks, chopped
- 2 bay leaves
- 1 litre (1¾ pints) vegetable stock
- Salt and black pepper
- Juice and grated zest of 1 lemon

1 In a large pan, heat olive oil and add leeks, onion, and celery. Stir until completely coated with oil. Add bay leaves. Sauté until vegetables are soft.
2 Add stock, bring to the boil, reduce heat and simmer for about 40 minutes. Adjust seasoning.
3 Stir in juice and lemon zest just before serving.

LEEK AND LENTIL RISOTTO
(Serves 4)

- 1 tbsp olive
- 4 leeks, washed and chopped
- 4 cloves garlic, sliced or crushed
- 1 red pepper, finely chopped
- 600 ml (1 pint/2½ cups) vegetable stock or water

- *225 g (8 oz/1 cup) Arborio rice*
- *225 g (8 oz/1 cup) red lentils*
- *Salt and black pepper*
- *½ tsp dried basil*

To garnish
- *1 tbsp chopped parsley*
- *75 g (3oz) finely grated carrots*

1 Heat oil in a pan, sauté leeks, garlic and red pepper until soft.
2 Add stock or water and stir in rice, lentils, basil and season to taste.
3 Bring to boil, then reduce heat and simmer, covered, for about 10 minutes or until rice and lentils are cooked.
4 Garnish with parsley and carrot.

LEEKS WITH PEARS AND MASHED POTATO
(Serves 4)
- *8 medium potatoes (peeled or not, as you prefer) cut into cubes*
- *3 ripe pears, peeled, cored and cut into cubes*
- *1 tbsp olive oil*
- *225 g (8 oz/1 cup) leeks, washed well and sliced*
- *Knob of butter or margarine*
- *Salt and black pepper*

1 Put potatoes and pears into salted water, bring to the boil, reduce heat and simmer for 5–10 minutes, until tender.
2 Heat oil a in pan and sauté leeks until lightly browned and quite soft. Set aside.

3 When potatoes and pears are cooked, mash with a knob of butter or margarine, and season to taste.
4 Stir in sautéed leeks and serve.

LEEK AND THREE-CHEESE PÂTÉ WITH VERMOUTH
(Makes about 3 x 225 g ½ lb jars)
- *2 tbsp olive oil*
- *3–5 cloves garlic, crushed*
- *2 large leeks, washed and cut into long thin strips*
- *1 tsp soy sauce*
- *2 tbsp dry vermouth*
- *340 g (12 oz) Brie cheese, sliced*
- *225 g (8 oz) blue cheese, sliced*
- *225 g (8 oz) cream cheese*
- *½ tbsp black pepper*

1 Heat oil in pan. Add garlic and leeks. Sauté until golden brown.
2 Stir in soy sauce and dry vermouth. Sauté until liquid is absorbed. Cool.
3 Place the three cheeses in a food processor. Add leek mixture and pepper. Pulse until combined.
4 Transfer to serving dish.
5 Serve with flat breads and crusty olive bread.

LEEK AND TOMATO SOUP WITH BASIL CREAM
(Serves 4)
- *1 tbsp olive oil*
- *2 medium leeks, washed and chopped*
- *2 x 400 g tins tomatoes*
- *1 tbsp butter or margarine*

44

- *1 tbsp brown sugar*
- *Salt and black pepper*
- *4 tbsp single or double cream*
- *1 tbsp fresh basil, chopped*

1 Heat oil in pan and sauté leeks until tender.
2 Add tomatoes, bring to the boil, reduce heat and simmer for 10 minutes.
3 Place vegetables in blender and purée until smooth. Return to pan.
4 Stir in butter or margarine, add sugar and season.
5 Mix cream and basil together in a pan and stir well. Add salt to taste, and heat through.

To Serve

6 Ladle soup into bowls and garnish with basil cream.

LEEK AND WALNUT SOUP
(Serves 4)

- *4 medium leeks, washed and coarsely chopped*
- *10 fl oz (½ pint/1¼ cups) vegetable stock*
- *5 fl oz (¼pint/½ cup) white wine*
- *¼ tsp salt*
- *1 tbsp sugar*
- *125 g (4 oz/½ cup) chopped walnuts*
- *1 tsp vinegar*

1 Place leeks, stock and wine in large pan with lid. Bring to boil, reduce heat and simmer for about 12 minutes, or until just cooked.
2 Add salt, sugar, nuts and vinegar. Simmer uncovered for about 7 minutes.
3 Ladle into individual serving bowls.

PARSNIP AND EROTIC BANANA EXPERIENCE
Perfect for St. Valentine's Day.

(Serves 4)

- *4 medium sized parsnips, peeled and left whole*
- *4 cabbage leaves, blanched*
- *1 tbsp olive oil*
- *2 spring onions, chopped*
- *1 red pepper, chopped*
- *4 tbsp lemon juice*
- *4 tbsp maple syrup*
- *2 bananas, mashed*

1 Put whole parsnips into salted water. Bring to the boil, reduce heat and simmer until tender, about 15-20 minutes. Drain and keep warm.
2 Blanch 4 cabbage leaves by putting them into boiling water, quickly return to the boil, and simmer for about 2 minutes.
3 Immediately after blanching, drain and plunge the cabbage leaves into cold water to cool and to prevent further cooking. Put on serving dish.
4 Heat oil in a pan and sauté the spring onions, red pepper, lemon juice and maple syrup until sauce gives a glossy coating.
5 Add bananas and heat through gently.
6 Cut parsnips in half lengthwise, almost to the base and spread apart and lay on blanched cabbage leaves.
7 Spoon the banana mixture into the cut parsnip and serve.

45

PARSNIPS WITH HONEY AND ORANGE

(Serves 4-6)

- *700 g (1½ lb/3 cups) parsnips, peeled and diagonally sliced*
- *25 g (1 oz) butter or margarine*
- *1 tbsp honey*
- *4 tbsp orange juice*
- *Grated zest of one orange*
- *Salt and black pepper*

1. In a pan, cook parsnips in salted water until just tender, about 10 minutes.
2. Drain and remove from pan. In same pan heat butter or margarine, honey, juice and orange zest together.
3. Toss with parsnips and season to taste.

POTATOES WITH FETA CHEESE AND OLIVES

(Serves 6-8)

- *75 ml (3 fl oz) olive oil*
- *900 g (2 lb) potatoes, peeled*
- *1 tbsp fresh rosemary or 1 tsp dried rosemary*
- *275 g (10 oz) Feta cheese, crumbled*
- *125 g (4 oz) black and green olives, pitted*
- *300 ml (½ pint/10 fl oz) vegetable stock*
- *Salt and black pepper*

1. Preheat oven 180ºC (350ºF/Gas 4).
2. Grease an ovenproof dish with some of the olive oil.
3. Place potatoes in a pan of salted water, bring to the boil, reduce heat and simmer for about 15-20 minutes, or until just tender.
4. Drain and cool slightly.
5. Cut the potatoes into thin slices.
6. Layer potatoes in an ovenproof dish with olives, rosemary and Feta.
7. Drizzle with olive oil and pour over the stock.
8. Season to taste.
9. Cover with foil and bake for about 35 minutes.
10. Serve.

PURPLE SPROUTING BROCCOLI WITH POTATOES AND DILL

(Serves 4)

- *700 g (1½ lb/3 cups) potatoes, peeled and cut into chunks*
- *1 medium onion, chopped*
- *½ tsp dried dill weed or 4 fresh dill sprigs*
- *225 g (½ lb/1 cup) purple sprouting broccoli*
- *3 tbsp lemon juice*
- *1 tbsp olive oil*
- *Salt and black pepper*

1. Bring potatoes, onion and dill to boil in salted water, reduce heat and simmer until tender, about 10-15 minutes. Drain and remove dill sprigs if using fresh dill.
2. Put broccoli into boiling salted water, return to boil, reduce heat and simmer until tender, about 5-10 minutes. Drain.
3. Place potatoes, onion and broccoli a large bowl. Add lemon juice, olive oil and pepper. Mix well.
4. Serve warm or chill to serve as a salad.

PURPLE SPROUTING BROCCOLI QUICHE IN POTATO CRUST

(Serves 6)

- 4 medium potatoes, peeled and cut into 0.6 cm (¼") slices
- 350 g (12 oz/1½ cups) purple sprouting broccoli, including stalks, roughly chopped
- 225 g (8 oz/1 cup) Cheddar cheese, grated
- 225 g (8 oz/1 cup) cottage cheese
- 2 eggs, beaten
- 1 medium onion, chopped
- 1½ tsp Dijon mustard
- Salt and black pepper

Topping
- 50 g (2 oz/¼ cup) Cheddar cheese, grated

1 Preheat oven 190ºC (375ºF/Gas 5).
2 Put potatoes into salted water, bring to the boil, reduce heat and simmer for about 5-10 minutes or until potatoes are cooked but holding their shape. Drain.
3 Grease a 24 cm (9½") pie dish. Arrange the sliced, boiled potatoes in a single layer over the bottom and sides of the dish to form a crust. Brush sides with oil.
4 Excluding the topping, combine broccoli and rest of ingredients together in a large bowl and mix well.
5 Pour the broccoli mixture into the crust. Top with grated cheese.
6 Bake for about 30 minutes, or until the top is golden brown and a sharp knife inserted into the centre of the quiche comes out clean.
7 Let the quiche sit for 5 minutes before slicing and serving.

PURPLE SPROUTING BROCCOLI WITH SESAME SAUCE

(Serves 6)

- 900 g (2 lb/4 cups) purple sprouting broccoli, chopped into bite-sized pieces
- 50 g (2 oz/¼ cup) sesame seeds, toasted
- 4 tbsp soy sauce
- ½ tsp honey
- 2 tsp sesame oil

1 Put broccoli into boiling, salted water, return to boil, reduce heat and simmer until just tender, about 5 minutes. Cool.
2 Put sesame seeds in a dry frying pan and toast until golden brown and fragrant, stirring occasionally.
3 Mix toasted sesame seeds with remaining ingredients in a large bowl. Add broccoli and marinade for at least 1 hour.
4 Serve on a bed of lettuce leaves.

RED CABBAGE CREAMY SOUP

(Serves 4-6)

- 2 tbsp olive oil
- 1 leek, finely sliced and washed
- 1 medium onion, finely sliced
- 900 g (2 lb/4 cups) red cabbage, sliced
- 350 g (12 oz/1½ cups) potatoes, thinly sliced
- 1 L (1¾ pints) vegetable stock
- 150 ml (¼ pint/5 fl oz) milk or cream

- *Salt and black pepper*

1 Heat oil in a pan and sauté leek and onion until soft, but not browned.
2 Add red cabbage, potatoes and stock.
3 Cover, bring to the boil, reduce heat and simmer for about 30 minutes or until vegetables are tender.
4 Purée in a food processor.
5 Pour soup back into pan and stir in milk or cream.
6 Season to taste.

SWEDE AND CARROTS WITH CHEESY CELERY SAUCE
(Serves 4-6)

- *450 g (1 lb/2 cups) swede, peeled and diced*
- *350 g (12 oz/1½ cups) carrots, peeled and sliced*
- *¼ tsp ground ginger*
- *150 ml (¼ pint/5 fl oz) water*
- *½ tsp salt*
- *1 medium onion, peeled and chopped*
- *125 g (4 oz/½ cup) celery, diced*
- *1 tbsp olive oil*
- *3 tbsp flour*
- *300 ml (½ pint/1¼ cups) milk*
- *120 g (4 oz) Cheddar cheese, grated*
- *Salt and black pepper*

1 In a pan, combine the swede, carrots, ginger and water.
2 Season.
3 Cover and cook over medium heat for 10–15 minutes or until vegetables are tender. Drain and reserve liquid.
4 In a pan, sauté onion and celery in oil until tender.
5 Stir in flour and seasoning.
6 Gradually add milk, reserved vegetable liquid and stir until thickened.
7 Add cheese and stir until melted.
8 Add vegetables and serve.

SWEDE, BAKED WITH GRUYÈRE CHEESE AND CREAM
(Serves 4)

- *2 tbsp plain four*
- *Salt and black pepper*
- *450 g (1 lb/2 cups) swede, peeled, quartered sliced*
- *1 clove garlic, crushed*
- *75 g (3 oz) Gruyère cheese, grated*
- *15 g (½ oz) butter or margarine*
- *575 ml (20 fl oz/1 pint/ 2½ cups) single cream*

1 Preheat oven 190ºC (375ºF/Gas 5).
2 Mix flour, salt and pepper into a mixing bowl. Add the swede slices and toss well to coat the slices in flour.
3 Grease an ovenproof dish with oil and rub the crushed garlic over the inside of the dish.
4 Layer the swede slices in the dish with the grated Gruyère cheese, ending with a layer of cheese.

5 Dot 15 g (½ oz) butter over the surface of the swede and pour over the cream.

6 Bake for about one hour until golden brown and the swede is tender.

SWEDE ROASTED WITH MAPLE SYRUP

(Serves 4)

- *450 g (1 lb/2 cups) swede, peeled and diced*
- *2 tbsp olive oil*
- *15 g (½ oz) butter or margarine*
- *Salt and black pepper*
- *2 tbsp maple syrup*

1 Preheat oven 190ºC (375ºF/Gas 5).

2 Place swede on a baking tray. Drizzle over olive oil and dot with butter or margarine. Season to taste.

3 Roast in oven for about 10 minutes, stirring occasionally.

4 Pour over maple syrup and mix well, and roast for about another 10 minutes or until golden brown and tender, stirring occasionally.

SWEDE ROASTED SOUP WITH CREAM

(Serves 4)

- *450 g (1 lb/2 cups) swede, peeled and diced*
- *3 tbsp olive oil*
- *Salt and black pepper*
- *1 medium onion, chopped*
- *2 carrots, sliced*
- *2 cloves garlic, crushed*
- *½ tsp dried thyme*
- *1 L (1¾ pints/36 fl oz) vegetable stock*
- *150 ml (5 fl oz/¼ pint) single cream*

1 Preheat oven 190ºC (375ºF/Gas 5).

2 Place swede on a baking tray. Drizzle over 2 tablespoons of the olive oil and add seasoning.

3 Roast for about 20 minutes or until golden brown and tender, stirring occasionally.

4 Heat remaining oil in a pan, stir in onion, carrots, garlic and thyme and cook for 4-5 minutes until softened but not browned.

5 Add roasted swede with the stock. Bring gently to the boil, reduce heat, cover and simmer for about 15 minutes, stirring occasionally.

6 Purée the soup in a food processor until smooth.

7 Transfer soup to a pan. Stir in most of the cream, keeping some for garnish and gently heat through.

To serve:

8 Ladle into individual bowls, garnish with a swirl of cream.

FARMING NEWS FOR MARCH

*I*n the words of Mathis: "Muck spreading and cultivating, tilling and ploughing. The sap is rising and the farmer is getting excited and restless".

One of the EarthShare celebrations takes place near to the time of the Spring Equinox, 21/22 March. Called the Spring Blessing, it is held in the fields where many of the crops are grown.

Water collected from the Findhorn River, some EarthShare seed potatoes, broad bean seeds and onion sets are placed together on the ground and subscribers form a large circle around them. They link hands and sing, led by Sheila Pettit. They ask for blessings for their land and its crops in the coming year, including field land, Cullerne gardens and Rafford.

Some subscribers plant the first of the seed potatoes, others put in broad beans and onion sets. While the planting takes place, a group of subscribers walk around the boundaries of the EarthShare fields to view and bless the land.

HARVESTING

Brussels sprouts, carrots, chicory, curly kale, green and red cabbage, purple sprouting broccoli, parsnips, swede, leeks, and potatoes.

Rhubarb from Rafford, spinach and exotic salad greens such as Mizuna and Pak Choi from the polytunnels at Cullerne.

MAINTENANCE AND MACHINERY

This is often the month the EarthShare Land Rover gets its spring maintenance and anti-rusting painting of the chassis. This is particularly important because of the corrosive salt on the roads and in the atmosphere from being so close to the sea.

PLANTING

The first onion sets are planted, as are parsnips and the early potatoes in the open fields. The broad beans are also planted using EarthShare's own saved seed. First outdoor sowings at Cullerne of rocket, radish and peas.

WEATHER

Often wetter than we want. Mathis is frequently seen at field gates waiting eagerly for dry days to start the fieldwork.

Red and Green Cabbages

MARCH
RECIPES

MARCH RECIPES

BRUSSELS SPROUTS WITH BALSAMIC VINEGAR
(Serves 6)

- *700 g (1½ lb/3 cups) Brussels sprouts, washed and trimmed*
- *2 tbsp olive oil*
- *2 cloves garlic, crushed*
- *1 onion, peeled and chopped*
- *4 tbsp balsamic vinegar*
- *25 g (1 oz) butter or margarine*
- *Salt and black pepper*

1 Bring salted water to the boil, add Brussels sprouts, return to the boil. Reduce heat and simmer until just tender, about 10 minutes. Drain.
2 In a large frying pan, heat the oil, add the garlic and onion. Sauté for a few minutes until onion is tender.
3 Add the Brussels sprouts and heat through.
4 Add vinegar, butter or margarine and season to taste. Mix well.
5 Serve immediately.

BRUSSELS SPROUTS IN BEER
(Serves 4)

- *450 g (1 lb/2 cups) Brussels sprouts, washed and trimmed*
- *275 ml (½ pint/1¼ cups) beer, to cover sprouts*
- *25 g (1 oz) butter or margarine*
- *Salt and black pepper*

1 Place sprouts in a pan and pour over enough beer to cover them.
2 Bring to the boil, reduce heat, and simmer for about 10 minutes, or until crisp-tender. Add more beer if needed.
3 Drain, add butter or margarine. Season.
4 Serve immediately.

BRUSSELS SPROUTS IN MUSTARD SAUCE
(Serves 4)

- *150 ml (¼ pint/5 fl oz) vegetable stock to cook sprouts*
- *450 g (1 lb/2 cups) Brussels sprouts, washed and trimmed*
- *1 tbsp olive oil*
- *1 medium onion, peeled and chopped*
- *1 tsp Dijon mustard*
- *Salt and black pepper*
- *1 tbsp cornflour*
- *150 ml (¼ pint/5 fl oz) milk*

1 Bring stock to the boil, add Brussels sprouts, cover and return to the boil. Reduce heat and simmer until just tender, about 10 minutes.
2 Reserve the stock, so drain the sprouts over a bowl.
3 Put drained sprouts into a serving dish and keep warm.
4 Heat oil in a pan and sauté the onion until transparent.
5 Remove from heat, add reserved stock. Stir in mustard and seasoning. Return to the heat.
6 Mix the cornflour with milk, add to the stock and cook, stirring continuously until the sauce is thickened and smooth. Add more water if needed.

52

7   Pour the mustard sauce over the Brussels sprouts and stir to coat.
8   Serve immediately.

CABBAGE FRIED RICE
(Serves 4-6)
- *450 g (1 lb/2 cups) Basmati rice*
- *2 tbsp olive oil*
- *650 ml (24 fl oz/3 cups) vegetable stock or water*
- *450 g (1 lb/2 cups) cabbage, cut into fine strips*
- *225 g (8 oz/1 cup) carrots, cut into sticks*
- *1 onion, chopped*
- *1-2 garlic cloves, crushed*
- *2.5 cm (1") piece fresh root ginger, peeled and finely chopped*
- *1 tbsp fresh parsley, chopped*
- *Salt and black pepper*

1   Wash the rice.
2   Heat oil in a pan and fry the rice until the water the rice has been washed in has evaporated.
3   Add the water or stock. Bring to the boil, reduce heat and simmer until rice is cooked, about 8-10 minutes. Do not overcook.
4   Drain and keep warm.
5   Put cabbage and carrots into boiling water, and cook until the carrots are crisp-tender, about 5-10 minutes. Drain and keep warm.
6   In another pan, add remaining oil and fry onion, garlic and ginger until onions are soft.
7   Add vegetables and parsley to the onion and garlic mixture.
8   Add rice, mix well.

CABBAGE FRUIT SALAD
(Serves 4)
- *1 apple, cored, unpeeled and diced.*
- *1 tbsp fresh lemon juice*
- *450 g (1 lb/2 cups) cabbage, finely sliced or grated*
- *125 g (4 oz/½ cup) raisins*
- *4 tbsp pineapple juice*
- *2 tsp fresh lemon juice*
- *1 tbsp sugar*
- *125 ml (4 fl oz/½ cup) sour cream*

1   Coat apple in 1 tbsp of lemon juice to prevent darkening.
2   In a bowl put cabbage, apples, raisins, pineapple juice, lemon juice, sugar and sour cream and mix well.
3   Refrigerate.

CARROTS WITH APRICOTS AND GINGER
(Serves 6-8)
- *700 g (1½ lb/3 cups) carrots, peeled and sliced*
- *2 tbsp olive oil*
- *1 onion, finely chopped*
- *1-2 garlic cloves, crushed*
- *2.5 cm (1") piece of fresh root ginger, peeled and chopped*
- *125 g (4 oz) dried apricots, chopped*
- *2 tbsp brown sugar*
- *1 tbsp balsamic vinegar*
- *Salt and black pepper*

1   Put carrots in salted water, bring to the boil, reduce heat and simmer for 10 minutes or until soft.
2   Drain and keep warm.
3   Heat oil in a pan, add onion, garlic,

ginger, apricots, brown sugar, vinegar, and season. Cook for about 4 minutes, stirring frequently.

4 Pour glaze over carrots, heat through and serve.

CARROTS WITH COUSCOUS AND THYME
(Serves 3-4)

- *2 tbsp olive oil*
- *225 g (8 oz/1 cup) carrots, coarsely grated*
- *2 tsp lemon juice*
- *¼ tsp sugar*
- *300 ml (10 fl oz/½ pint/1¼ cups) water*
- *½ tsp fresh thyme or ¼ tsp dried thyme*
- *Salt and black pepper*
- *225 g (8 oz/1 cup) couscous*

1 Heat oil in a pan and cook carrots, for about 3 minutes,

stirring frequently.

2 Add lemon juice, sugar, one tbsp of water, thyme, and season to taste. Simmer covered for about 2 minutes.

3 Add remaining water, bring to the boil and stir in the couscous.

4 Remove pan from heat, cover and let the couscous stand for about 5 minutes. You may need to adjust the water.

5 Fluff the couscous with a fork and serve.

CARROT AND CHOCOLATE CAKE
This cake is made without eggs. It doesn't rise much, but is very moist, dark and full of chocolate flavour.

- *350 g (12 oz/1½ cups) carrots, peeled and grated*
- *150 g (5 oz/¾ cup) granulated sugar*
- *125 ml (4 fl oz/½ cup) vegetable oil*
- *225 ml (8 fl oz/1 cup) boiling water*
- *175 g (6 oz/1½ cups) wholewheat flour*
- *1½ tsp baking powder*
- *125 g (4 oz/½ cup) cocoa powder, unsweetened*
- *1 tsp cinnamon*
- *Pinch of salt*

1 Preheat oven 180ºC (350ºF/Gas 4).

2 Mix together the carrots, sugar and oil in a large bowl.

Pour water over the mixture.

3 In another bowl mix together flour, baking powder, cocoa, cinnamon and salt. Add to the carrot mixture and stir well.

4 Pour into a lightly greased and floured 20 cm (8") square pan and bake for about 35 minutes, or until a knife inserted into the centre of the cake comes out clean.

5 Remove from tin and cool on a wire rack.

CHICORY, BRAISED
(Serves 4)

- *2 tbsp olive oil*
- *900 g (2 lb/4 cups) chicory, washed and separated into spears*
- *1 onion, chopped*

- *Juice of ½ lemon*
- *Salt and black pepper*

1 Heat oil in frying pan and fry chicory on all sides until golden.
2 Add chopped onion lemon juice and season.
3 Cover the pan and simmer for about 25 minutes, turning the chicory occasionally. Add water if needed.

If chicory is bitter, 1 teaspoon of sugar can be added to remove bitter taste. Serve with cheese, Béchamel or tomato sauce.

CHICORY AND CAMEMBERT FLAN
(Serves 4)

- *450 g (1 lb/2 cups) shortcrust pastry*
- *1 small onion, finely chopped*
- *2 heads chicory, finely sliced*
- *125 g (4 oz) Camembert, roughly chopped*
- *2 eggs*
- *150 ml (¼ pint/ fl oz) milk or single cream*
- *1 tbsp parsley*
- *Salt and black pepper*

1 Preheat oven 190ºC (375ºF/Gas 5).
2 Roll out the pastry and line a 20 cm (8") fluted flan case. Chill for 30 minutes.
3 Prick the pastry base and blind bake for 15 minutes.
4 Remove from oven and sprinkle onions, Camembert and chicory over the pastry base.
5 Beat eggs and milk or cream together, add parsley, season and pour into pastry case.
6 Place on a baking

tray and return to the oven for 30–35 minutes, until filling is set and golden.
7 Can be served hot or cold.

CHICORY AND CARROT SALAD
(Serves 4)

- *2 tsp white wine vinegar*
- *1 tsp Dijon mustard*
- *¼ tsp sugar*
- *1 tsp water*
- *Salt and black pepper*
- *3 tbsp olive oil*
- *900 g (2 lb/4 cups) chicory, rinsed and torn into pieces*
- *125 g (4 oz/½ cup) carrot, coarsely grated*

1 In a bowl mix the vinegar, mustard, sugar and water together and season to taste.
2 Add the oil in a stream, whisking,

until the dressing has emulsified.
3 Add to the chicory and carrot and mix.

CHICORY AND POTATOES
(Serves 6)

- *2 tbsp olive oil*
- *3 cloves garlic, crushed*
- *900 g (2 lb/4 cups) potatoes, peeled and sliced*
- *1 celery stick, cut into thin slices*
- *450 g (1 lb/2 cups) chicory, washed, and cut into 5 cm (2") pieces*
- *Salt and black pepper*
- *50 g (2 oz/¼ cup) chopped mint*
- *150 ml (¼ pint/5 fl oz) water*
- *2 tbsp lemon juice*

1 Heat oil in a large pan. Add garlic, potatoes, celery,

chicory, salt, pepper and mint. Stir well to coat ingredients with oil.

2 Cover and cook, stirring frequently, for 5–10 minutes, until chicory has wilted.

3 Add water, stirring well. Cover and cook for about 15 minutes, stirring frequently, or until potatoes are tender. Add more water if needed.

4 Just before serving, stir in lemon juice.

CHICORY WITH RICE AND PARMESAN
(Serves 4)
- 125 g (4 oz/½ cup) rice
- 4 tbsp olive oil
- 225 g (8 oz/1 cup) onion, chopped
- 3 cloves garlic, crushed

- 900 g (2 lb/4 cups) chicory, washed, dried and chopped
- 125 g (4 oz/½ cup) sorrel leaves or 1 tsp lemon juice
- 2 tbsp Parmesan
- Salt and black pepper
- 125 g (4 oz/½ cup) fresh breadcrumbs

1 Preheat oven 190ºC (375ºF/Gas 5).

2 Bring salted water to the boil, add the rice, return to boil, simmer until cooked, about 10 minutes. Drain, and keep warm.

3 In a large pan, heat the oil and cook onions until soft, about 5 minutes.

4 Add garlic, stir for about 30 seconds.

5 Add the chicory, and stir to coat with the oil. Cook chicory until wilted and add

sorrel (if used) or lemon juice, and cook until tender, about 5 minutes.

6 When the chicory is tender, add the rice with one tablespoon of Parmesan. Mix well and season.

7 Put in a greased, deep, baking dish.

8 Mix remaining Parmesan with breadcrumbs and sprinkle on the top. Drizzle with olive oil and bake for 30–40 minutes.

9 Can be served hot or cold.

CURLY KALE FRIED IN BEER BATTER
For the beer batter
- 125 g (4 oz) plain flour
- 225 ml (8 fl oz) beer
- Salt and black pepper
Oil for deep-frying
- Curly kale leaves,

torn into pieces to be dipped in batter
- Salt for sprinkling the leaves
- Lemon wedges to serve

1 Sift flour into a bowl and make a hole in the centre.

2 Gradually add the beer to the flour and beat until smooth.

3 Season.

4 Let batter stand, covered, for one hour, before using.

5 Heat oil in a pan, dip one piece of kale into the batter, coating it thoroughly.

6 Fry in the oil for about 30 seconds on each side, or until golden.

7 Transfer kale once fried onto kitchen paper towels to drain, and sprinkle lightly with salt.

8   Repeat until all leaves are cooked.

9   Serve with lemon wedges.

CURLY KALE WITH CURRIED LENTILS
(Serves 4)

- *135 g (4 oz/½ cup) brown lentils*
- *2 tbsp olive oil*
- *1 tsp curry powder*
- *1 medium onion, chopped*
- *4 cloves*
- *1 tbsp raisins*
- *125 g (4 oz/½ cup) carrot, peeled and diced*
- *125 g (4 oz/½ cup) potato, peeled and diced*
- *Salt and black pepper*
- *350 ml (12 fl oz/1½ cups) water*
- *225 g (8 oz/1 cup) curly kale, chopped*

For the topping:
- *2 tbsp plain yoghurt*

1   Rinse and soak lentils in water for about 15 minutes. Drain.

2   In a pan heat oil and sauté curry powder, onion and cloves for about 2 minutes.

3   Add raisins, carrot, potato and soaked lentils. Season to taste.

4   Add water, bring to boil, reduce heat and simmer until lentils are tender, about 15 minutes.

5   Place kale on top of lentils, and cook until reduced by half, about 5-10 minutes. When done, lentils should be tender but not mushy.

6   Remove from heat. Gently stir to mix kale with lentils.

7   Put in dish and top with yoghurt.

CURLY KALE WITH MASHED POTATOES
(Serves 4)

- *225 g (8 oz) curly kale, chopped finely*
- *700 g (1½ lb/3 cups) potatoes, peeled and quartered*
- *1 garlic clove, peeled*
- *50 g (2 oz/½ stick) butter or margarine*
- *150 ml (¼ pint/5 fl oz) milk or single cream*
- *Salt and black pepper*

1   Bring ¼ cup salted water to the boil. Add kale, bring back to the boil, reduce heat and simmer until just tender, about 5-10 minutes stirring occasionally. Drain and keep warm.

2   Place potatoes and garlic together in a pan, cover with water, bring to the boil, reduce heat and simmer until cooked, about 15 minutes. Drain well and return to the pan.

3   Add the butter or margarine to the potatoes, and mash with a potato masher. Gradually add the milk or cream and season to taste.

4   Add cooked kale to the potato mixture, stir well and serve.

LEEK, MUSHROOM AND CASHEW NUT CANNELLONI

(Serves 4)

Filling

- 2 tbsp olive oil
- 225 g (8 oz/1 cup) mushrooms, chopped
- 450 g (1 lb/2 cups) leeks, chopped and washed
- 50 g (2 oz/¼ cup) cashew nuts, toasted
- Freshly grated nutmeg
- ¼ tsp dried thyme
- Salt and black pepper
- 1 x 500 g packet Cannelloni tubes

Sauce

- 1 tbsp olive oil
- 1 onion, chopped
- 1 garlic clove, crushed
- 3 tsp plain flour
- 175 ml (6 fl oz/¾ cup) crème fraîche
- Salt and black pepper
- Freshly grated nutmeg

Topping

- 25 g (1 oz/½ cup) Parmesan or Cheddar cheese, grated
- 25 g (1 oz/½ cup) fresh breadcrumbs

1 Preheat oven 180ºC (350ºF/Gas 4).

2 Heat olive oil in a pan and sauté the mushrooms and leeks for about 5 minutes or until soft.

3 Toast the cashew nuts by frying them in a hot, dry, frying pan until golden.

4 Add the toasted cashew nuts to the mushrooms and leeks, add nutmeg, thyme and season to taste.

5 Fill 8–12 cannelloni tubes with the leek mixture and arrange in a greased, oven-proof dish.

6 To make the sauce, heat oil in a pan, add the onion and garlic and cook until soft, about 5 minutes.

7 Stir in the flour, add the crème fraîche to form a sauce. Add nutmeg and season to taste.

8 Pour sauce over cannelloni, and sprinkle with cheese and breadcrumbs.

9 Bake in the oven for about 25 minutes or until golden and bubbling.

LEEK OMELETTE

(Serves 4)

- 1 tbsp olive oil
- 900 g (2 lb/4 cups) leeks, chopped and washed
- 4 eggs
- 2 tbsp milk
- Salt and black pepper

1 Heat oil in a pan, add leeks and sauté until softened, about 3-4 minutes.

2 Break eggs into a bowl, add milk and season. Beat until blended, but not foamy.

3 Pour eggs on top of leeks, so that the egg mixture coats the leeks.

4 Cook until bottom of omelette is golden, about 1-2 minutes.

5 Carefully turn the omelette over. Cook until just set, about one minute. Cut into 4 and serve.

OLIVE CAKE (CAKE AUX OLIVES)

This cake can be served as a starter or as a main course with salad.

- 150 g (5 oz) self-raising flour
- 3 eggs
- Salt and black pepper
- 120 ml (4 fl oz/½ cup) olive oil

- *120 ml (4 fl oz/½ cup) full cream milk, warmed*
- *75 g (3 oz) olives (black, green or a mixture), chopped*
- *125 g (4 oz) Gruyère cheese, cut into tiny squares*
- *200 g (7 oz) ham or streaky bacon, cut in squares (optional)*

1 Preheat oven 180ºC (350ºF/Gas 4).
2 Mix together flour, eggs, salt, pepper, oil and milk.
3 Add olives, cheese, and ham or bacon (if used).
4 Put into a greased loaf tin and bake for 35-45 minutes or until cooked.

PAK CHOI WITH GINGER AND SOY SAUCE
(Serves 2-3)

- *2 tbsp olive oil*
- *1-2 garlic cloves, crushed*
- *1 x 2.5 cm (1") piece root ginger, peeled and finely chopped*
- *450 g (1 lb/2 cups) pak choi, chopped*
- *1 tbsp soy sauce*
- *Black pepper*

1 Heat oil in a pan and sauté garlic and root ginger for about 1-2 minutes.
2 Add pak choi and cook for about 3-5 minutes or until cooked.
3 Add the soy sauce, pepper, stir well, and serve.

PARSNIP AND CARAWAY CAKE
- *225 g (8 oz) self-raising flour*
- *1 tsp bicarbonate of soda*
- *225 g (8 oz) parsnip, grated*
- *½ tsp caraway seed*
- *180 g (6 oz) soft margarine*
- *125 g (4 oz) caster sugar*
- *2 eggs, beaten*
- *Zest and juice of one lemon*

Lemon water icing
- *125 g (4 oz) icing sugar*
- *1 tbsp warm water*
- *1 tbsp lemon juice*

1 Preheat oven 180ºC (350ºF/Gas 4).
2 Sieve together flour and bicarbonate of soda.
3 Stir in the parsnip and caraway seed.
4 Cream together the margarine and sugar and stir in the eggs gently. Fold in the flour mixture, lemon zest and juice to make a dropping consistency.
5 Place mixture into a greased and floured 20 cm (9") round cake tin and bake for 25–30 minutes.
6 Cool on a wire rack.
7 To make the lemon water icing, sift icing sugar into a bowl.
8 Add water and lemon juice until the mixture is thick enough to coat the back of a wooden spoon. Drizzle over cake.

PARSNIP, CARROT AND POTATO CAKE WITH APPLE
- *180 g (6 oz) soft margarine*
- *180 g (6 oz) caster sugar*
- *3 eggs, beaten*
- *225 g (8 oz) self-raising flour*
- *½ tsp ground nutmeg*
- *125 g (4 oz/½ cup)*

59

grated carrot
- 125 g (4 oz/½ cup) parsnip, grated
- 125 g (4 oz/½ cup) potato, grated
- 125 g (4 oz/½ cup) eating apple, grated
- Zest and juice of 1 orange

Orange water icing
- 125 g (4 oz/½ cup) icing sugar
- 1 tbsp warm water
- 1 tbsp fresh orange juice

1 Preheat oven 180ºC (350ºF/Gas 4).
2 Cream together the margarine and sugar, and stir in the eggs gently.
3 Sieve together the flour and nutmeg, add carrot, parsnip, potato and apple. Mix well.
4 Fold flour mixture into the creamed mixture and stir in the orange zest and juice.
5 Turn into a greased and floured 24 cm (9½") round cake tin and bake for 45–50 minutes or until a skewer comes out clean.
6 Turn on to a wire rack to cool.
7 To make the orange water icing, sift icing sugar into a bowl.
8 Add water and orange juice until the mixture is thick enough to coat the back of a wooden spoon. Drizzle top of cake with orange water icing.

PARSNIP AND CARROTS WITH HONEY AND ALMONDS
(Serves 4)
- 75 g (3 oz) almonds, slivered
- 50 g (2 oz) butter or margarine
- 450 g (1 lb/2 cups) parsnips, peeled and cut into long, thin strips
- 450 g (1 lb/2 cups) carrots, peeled and cut into long strips
- 2 tbsp lemon juice
- 2 tbsp honey
- 1 tsp wholegrain mustard
- Salt and black pepper

1 Preheat oven 180ºC (350ºF/Gas 4).
2 Toast almonds in a hot, dry frying pan for about 3 minutes, stirring frequently. Keep checking them so that they do not burn.
3 Melt margarine or butter in a pan, add parsnips and carrots and cook gently until tender, about 5-10 minutes.
4 Add toasted almonds, lemon juice, honey, mustard and heat through. Season and serve.

PARSNIP, LEEK AND GINGER SOUP
(Serves 4-6)
- 1 tbsp olive oil
- 450 g (1 lb/2 cups) leeks, sliced into rings and washed
- 2 tbsp fresh ginger root, grated
- 700 g (1½ lb/3 cups) parsnips, peeled and roughly chopped
- 150 ml (¼ pint/5 fl oz) dry white wine
- 1.5 L (2¾ pints/5½ cups) vegetable stock

To garnish
- 2 tbsp cream
- ½ tsp paprika

1. Heat oil in a large pan and add leeks and ginger. Cook for about 2-3 minutes, until the leeks begin to soften.
2. Add parsnips and cook for about 10 minutes.
3. Pour in wine and stock and bring to the boil. Reduce heat and simmer for about 20 minutes or until the parsnips are tender.
4. Purée in a blender until smooth. Check seasoning.
5. Reheat and serve with a swirl of cream and paprika.

POTATOES WITH BLUE CHEESE AND WALNUTS
(Serves 4)
- *450 g (1 lb) potatoes, cut into wedges*
- *1 onion, sliced*
- *125 g (4 oz) blue cheese, mashed*
- *150 ml (¼ pint/5 fl oz) single cream*
- *Salt and black pepper*
- *50 g (2 oz) walnut pieces*

1. Put potatoes into salted water, bring to the boil, reduce heat and simmer until tender, about 15 minutes.
2. Add onion to the pan for the last 5 minutes or so of cooking.
3. Drain, put into a shallow serving dish and keep warm.
4. In a small pan, melt cheese and cream gently. Do not allow to boil, but heat until it scalds.
5. Season to taste.
6. Pour sauce over the potatoes and onion. Top with walnuts.

PURPLE SPROUTING BROCCOLI WITH HORSERADISH AND WALNUTS
(Serves 4)
- *1 tbsp olive oil*
- *2 cloves garlic, crushed*
- *700 g (1½ lb/3 cups) purple sprouting broccoli, chopped*
- *4 tbsp water*
- *150 ml (¼ pint/5 fl oz) sour cream*
- *1 tsp creamed horseradish*
- *¼ tsp dried thyme*
- *½ tsp dried marjoram*
- *Salt and black pepper*
- *125 g (4 oz/½ cup) walnuts, toasted and chopped*

1. Heat oil in a pan and sauté the garlic for about 1 minute.
2. Add broccoli and water. Cover and cook until tender or until most of the liquid has gone.
3. Add sour cream, horseradish, thyme, marjoram and season to taste.
4. Add nuts, toss and serve.

PURPLE SPROUTING BROCCOLI, LENTILS, BULGAR WHEAT AND YOGHURT
(Serves 4)
- *1 tbsp olive oil*
- *1 medium onion, chopped*
- *125 g (4 oz/½ cup) bulgur wheat*
- *125 g (4 oz/½ cup) red lentils*
- *425 ml (¾ pint/15 fl oz) water*
- *225 g (8 oz/1 cup) purple sprouting broccoli, chopped*
- *Salt and black pepper*
- *225 ml (8 fl oz/1 cup) plain yoghurt*

1. Heat oil in a pan, sauté onion and bulgar wheat until onion is soft.
2. Stir lentils and water into onion and bulgar mixture and bring to the boil.
3. Sprinkle broccoli over mixture, cover, simmer for about 15 minutes or until water absorbed and broccoli is cooked.
4. Season to taste.
5. Top with yoghurt and serve.

PURPLE SPROUTING BROCCOLI AND MUSHROOM DIP
(Serves 4)
- *450 g (1 lb/2 cups) purple sprouting broccoli, chopped*
- *1 tbsp olive oil*
- *2 garlic cloves*
- *½ medium onion, chopped*
- *125 g (4 oz/½ cup) mushrooms, chopped*
- *175 g (6 oz/¾ cup) cottage cheese*
- *4 tbsp plain yoghurt*
- *Salt and black pepper*

1. Cook broccoli in boiling salted water until crisp-tender, about 3-5 minutes. Drain and rinse under cold water.
2. In a pan, heat oil. Add garlic, onion and mushrooms and cook until onion is tender. Transfer to blender.
3. Add broccoli, cottage cheese, yoghurt and seasoning to the blender and process until smooth
4. Transfer to a bowl and serve.

RED CABBAGE WITH PEARS AND BROWN SUGAR
(Serves 6)
- *50 g (2 oz) butter or margarine*
- *2 tsp olive oil*
- *1 onion, finely chopped*
- *1 clove of garlic, crushed*
- *3 tbsp brown sugar*
- *1 tbsp tomato purée*
- *2 tbsp red wine vinegar*
- *Salt and black pepper*
- *450 g (1 lb/2 cups) red cabbage, quartered, cored, and shredded*
- *2 ripe medium pears, peeled, cored and cut into thin strips*

To garnish:
- *Parsley, chopped*

1. Melt the butter or margarine in a pan and add oil.
2. Add the onion and garlic. Cook for one minute without browning.
3. Add sugar, tomato purée, red wine vinegar and season. Mix and cook for one minute.
4. Increase heat and add cabbage and pears, cook, stirring frequently until crisp-tender. Put into serving dish.
- Garnish with chopped parsley

RED CABBAGE SALAD WITH RAISINS AND GINGER
(Serves 4)
- *125 g (4 oz/½ cup) raisins, soaked*
- *450 g (1 lb/2 cups) red cabbage, grated*
- *1 tbsp root ginger, finely chopped*
- *Juice of 1 lemon*
- *1 tsp olive oil*
- *¾ tsp ground coriander*

- *¼ tsp cayenne pepper*
- *Salt and black pepper*

1. Soak raisins in water until softened.
2. Put red cabbage and drained, softened raisins in a bowl with ginger.
3. Mix lemon juice, olive oil, coriander and cayenne pepper together to make the dressing. Season.
4. Pour the dressing over the cabbage just before serving.

RHUBARB WITH LENTILS AND POTATOES
(Serves 4)

- *225 g (8 oz) red lentils*
- *2 medium potatoes, peeled and sliced*
- *1 tbsp olive oil*
- *2 garlic cloves, crushed*
- *2 tsp ground coriander*
- *2 tsp ground cumin*
- *1 tsp chilli powder*
- *1 tsp fresh ginger root, grated*
- *225 g (8 oz) rhubarb, sliced, and 150 ml (¼ pint) water*
- *50 g (2 oz) sugar*
- *50 g (2 oz) desiccated coconut*
- *Salt and black pepper*

1. In a pan, cover lentils with water. Bring to boil, reduce heat and simmer.
2. Once lentils are simmering, add potatoes, and simmer until tender, about 10-15 minutes.
3. Remove from heat, drain and set aside.
4. Heat oil in a pan, fry garlic, coriander, cumin, chilli, and ginger for about 1-2 minutes.
5. Add rhubarb and water, bring to the boil, reduce heat and simmer until cooked, about 10 minutes.
6. Add sugar, coconut, and season to taste.
7. Stir in potatoes and lentils and heat through gently.
8. Put into bowls and garnish with coconut
9. Serve with rice or crusty bread and chutney.

RHUBARB STICKY CAKE

- *180 g (6 oz) butter or soft margarine*
- *180 g (6 oz) caster sugar*
- *3 eggs, beaten*
- *180 g (6 oz) self-raising flour*
- *Pinch of salt*
- *About 2 tbsp milk*
- *450 g (1 lb/2 cups) rhubarb, sliced into 2.5 cm (1") pieces*
- *1 tbsp Demerara sugar*

Topping
- *50 g (2 oz) butter or soft margarine*
- *90 g (3 oz) plain flour*
- *25 g (1 oz) caster sugar*

1. Preheat oven 190ºC (375ºF/Gas 5).
2. Grease and line a 24 cm (9½") round cake tin.
3. Cream together the butter or margarine and sugar, stir in eggs, fold in flour and salt. Add milk to give a dropping consistency.
4. Turn the cake mix into the tin.
5. Toss sliced rhubarb with Demerara sugar.
6. Arrange rhubarb on top of the cake mix.

7 Make topping by rubbing butter or margarine into flour and stir in sugar.

8 Sprinkle topping mixture on top of the rhubarb and bake in the oven for 40–45 minutes or until skewer comes out clean.

9 Cool on a wire rack.

SPINACH WITH FETA AND CHICKPEAS
(Serves 4)

- 450 g (1 lb) chickpeas, cooked or 400 g tinned
- 150 ml (¼ pint/5 fl oz) water
- 1 tbsp olive oil
- 450 g (1 lb/2 cups) spinach, washed and chopped
- 1 tsp ground cumin
- 1 tbsp lemon juice
- 225 g (8 oz) Feta cheese, crumbled
- Salt and black pepper

1 Combine chickpeas, water, oil, spinach and cumin in a pan.

2 Bring to the boil, reduce heat, cover and simmer until spinach is just tender, about 5–10 minutes.

3 Stir in lemon juice, Feta, and season.

4 Serve immediately.

SPINACH WITH LENTILS AND COCONUT MILK
(Serves 4)

- 125 g (4 oz/½ cup) red lentils
- 450 g (1 lb/2 cups) fresh spinach, washed and chopped
- 2 tbsp olive oil
- 2 cloves garlic, crushed
- 1 onion, chopped
- 1 green pepper, deseeded and diced
- 1 tbsp mustard
- 2 tsp curry powder
- 2 tsp turmeric
- Pinch of cinnamon
- 225 ml (8 fl oz/1 cup) water
- 150 ml (¼ pint/5 fl oz) coconut milk
- Salt and black pepper

1 Wash the lentils and mix with spinach.

2 Heat oil in a pan, add garlic, onion, green pepper, mustard, curry powder, turmeric and cinnamon.

3 Sauté for about 5 minutes, stirring frequently or until onion is soft.

4 Add the lentils and spinach and stir.

5 Add water and coconut milk, bring to the boil, reduce heat and simmer for about 10-15 minutes, or until lentils are cooked. Season.

SPINACH WITH ORANGE AND WALNUTS
(Serves 4)

- 900 g (2 lb/4 cups) spinach, washed and chopped
- Zest and juice of one orange
- 50 g (2 oz/½ cup) walnuts
- Salt and black pepper

1 Place spinach, zest and orange juice in a frying pan over a high heat. Cook and stir until spinach has wilted and just cooked, about 3–5 minutes.

2 Add walnuts and stir well.

3 Season and serve immediately.

SPINACH WITH PINE NUTS AND RAISINS
(Serves 4)

- 2 tbsp olive oil
- 3 cloves of garlic, crushed
- 4 tbsp seedless raisins
- 4 tbsp pine nuts
- 900 g (2 lb/4 cups) fresh spinach, washed and roughly chopped
- 2 tbsp Parmesan, grated

1 Heat oil in a pan. Add garlic, raisins and pine nuts and cook for about 2 minutes.
2 Add spinach. Cook until spinach is just cooked, about 5 minutes.
3 Transfer to serving dish and sprinkle Parmesan over the top.
4 Serve immediately.

SPINACH WITH SESAME SEEDS
(Serves 4)

- 900 g (2 lb/4 cups) fresh spinach, washed and roughly chopped
- 50 g (2 oz/¼ cup) sesame seeds
- 2 tbsp light soy sauce
- Juice of ½ lemon
- Black pepper

1 Place spinach in a saucepan with only the water that clings to the leaves after washing. Do not season.
2 Cover, bring to the boil, reduce heat and cook just until leaves wilt, stirring once or twice, about 3-5 minutes.
3 Drain and keep warm.
4 Heat pan, add the sesame seeds and dry fry for about 2 minutes, or until golden brown, stirring frequently. Remove from heat.
5 Transfer spinach to serving dish. Mix soy sauce with lemon juice, season and pour over spinach.
6 Sprinkle toasted sesame seeds on top and serve.

SPINACH, SPICY FRIED
(Serves 4)

- 2 tbsp olive oil
- 2 medium onions, finely sliced
- 2 cloves garlic, crushed
- 1 tsp fresh root ginger, finely grated or ¼ tsp ground ginger
- 1 tsp cumin seeds or ground cumin
- ½ tsp ground coriander
- ½ tsp ground turmeric
- ½ tsp chilli powder
- 900 g (2 lb/4 cups) fresh spinach, well washed and roughly chopped
- Salt and black pepper

1 Heat oil in pan and fry the onion until golden.
2 Add garlic and ginger and fry for a further minute.
3 Add coriander, cumin, tumeric and chilli.
4 Add spinach, stir and cook uncovered until spinach has wilted and just cooked. Add a little water to prevent spinach sticking to the pan if needed.
5 Season to taste.
6 Serve with rice, chapattis or other Indian breads.

SPINACH AND PURPLE SPROUTING BROCCOLI CURRY
(Serves 4-6)

- *2 tbsp olive oil*
- *2 onions, chopped*
- *3 cloves garlic, crushed*
- *½ tsp chilli powder*
- *2 tbsp fresh ginger, chopped finely, or 1 tsp ground ginger*
- *2 tsp ground cumin*
- *2 tsp ground coriander*
- *4 fresh tomatoes (or 1 x 400 g (14 oz) tin*
- *450 g (1 lb/2 cups) purple sprouting broccoli, washed and trimmed*
- *450 g (1 lb/2 cups) fresh spinach*
- *Salt and black pepper*

1. Heat oil in a pan and sauté onions until just tender but not brown.
2. Add garlic, chilli, ginger, cumin and coriander. Mix to coat spices in oil.
3. Add tomatoes, and sprouting broccoli. Cover and cook for about 10 minutes until broccoli is just tender.
4. Add spinach and cook for another 5 minutes or until spinach is tender.
5. Season to taste.

SPINACH, STIR FRIED WITH GINGER AND ALMONDS
(Serves 4)

- *1 tbsp miso*
- *2 tbsp soy sauce*
- *1 tsp wine vinegar*
- *2 tbsp almonds, chopped*
- *1 tbsp sesame oil*
- *900 g (2 lb/4 cups) spinach, washed and chopped*
- *½ tsp ground ginger*

1. Mix miso, soy sauce and wine vinegar together. Set aside.
2. Heat wok or frying pan over high heat. Add almonds and stir-fry until edges turn golden. Transfer to plate.
3. Heat sesame oil in wok or frying pan, add spinach and ginger, and stir-fry until just tender, about 3 minutes.
4. Add miso, soy sauce and wine vinegar mixture to spinach.
5. Add almonds. Stir and serve.

SWEDE BRUSCHETTA
(Serves 4)

- *4 tbsp olive oil*
- *2 garlic cloves, crushed*
- *1 onion, chopped*
- *225 g (8 oz) swede, peeled and cut into small cubes*
- *1 tsp rosemary leaves, chopped*
- *1 tbsp balsamic vinegar*
- *8 thick slices of bread (sourdough or ciabatta)*
- *2 garlic cloves lightly crushed for rubbing over toast*
- *Salt and black pepper*

1. Heat 2 tablespoons of oil in a pan. Add garlic, onion and swede. Sauté, until the swede has softened and golden brown.
2. Transfer to a bowl. Add rosemary and balsamic vinegar. Keep warm.
3. Toast the bread until golden on both sides but still soft in the centre.
4. Rub the cloves of garlic over the surface of the toast.

5 Pile the swede mixture on top of the toast, drizzle on the rest of the olive oil and season.

6 Serve.

SWEDE AND LEEK FRITTERS WITH LEMON, OREGANO AND TOMATO SAUCE

(Makes about 12)

For the sauce

- *1 x 400 g (14 oz) tin of Italian plum tomatoes, mashed*
- *150 ml (¼ pint/5 fl oz) vegetable stock*
- *Juice of 1 lemon*
- *1 tsp dried oregano*
- *Salt and black pepper*

For the fritters

- *700 g (1½ lb/3 cups) swede, peeled and grated*
- *4 tbsp oil for frying*
- *1 medium leek, washed and chopped*
- *3 eggs, beaten*
- *4 tbsp plain flour*
- *Salt and black pepper*
- *Oil for frying*

1 For the sauce, put tomatoes, stock, lemon juice, oregano and seasoning in a pan. Bring to the boil, reduce heat, and simmer for about 15 minutes, stirring occasionally.

2 To make fritters, place swede, leek, eggs, flour, salt and pepper in a bowl and mix well. This will make a batter.

3 Heat 4 tbsp oil in a pan. Spoon in one tablespoon of the batter at a time into the pan ensuring that the pan is not too crowded.

4 Cook until lightly browned on one side, turn and brown on the other side.

5 Drain on kitchen paper towels.

6 Repeat until all the fritters are cooked.

7 To serve, top the fritters with sauce.

SWEDE WITH SPINACH AND CORIANDER

(Serves 4-6)

- *1 tbsp olive oil*
- *1 medium onion, chopped*
- *1 tsp coriander seed, crushed*
- *½ tsp turmeric*
- *¼ tsp cayenne pepper*
- *Salt and black pepper*
- *4 tbsp plain yoghurt*
- *450 g (1 lb/2 cups) spinach, washed and chopped*
- *450g (1 lb/2 cups) swede, peeled and diced*
- *1 garlic clove, crushed*
- *150 ml (¼ pint/5 fl oz) water*

1 Heat oil in a pan and sauté onion until golden.

2 Add coriander, turmeric, cayenne pepper, salt, pepper and yoghurt. Cook for about 5 minutes, stirring frequently.

3 Add half the spinach along with swede and garlic.

4 Cook, covered for about 3 minutes.

5 Stir in rest of spinach and water.

6 Cook, covered, for about 15-20 minutes or until swede is tender.

7 Serve.

FARMING NEWS FOR APRIL

*P*otato grading or dressing is carried out weekly.

🗓 HARVESTING

Brussels sprouts, carrots, parsnips, spring cabbage, spring cauliflower, swedes, purple sprouting broccoli. Rhubarb from Rafford, herbs such as coriander and parsley from Cullerne, as well as chicory, lettuce, radish and rocket salad.

🌱 PLANTING

This is the month for planting potatoes, the two varieties being Remarka for the main crop and Aminka for the earlies. Mathis chose Remarka because they grow into big potatoes. One of the differences between subscribers in Germany and in Scotland was that Scottish subscribers wanted bigger potatoes.

It is also the month for planting onion sets. Further south in the UK onions grow easily from seed, but that is not possible up here because of the shorter growing season. The season is just about long enough for onion sets that were sown as seeds in the middle of the previous year.

Originally from Mediterranean countries, onions have gradually crept further north into Scotland as varieties have been developed that will cope better with the colder climate. The same applies to garlic.

Chicory is sown during this month, and Christopher sows the first batch of lettuce destined for planting outside. These are sown in modules within the Cullerne propagation tunnel.

⚙ MAINTENANCE AND MACHINERY

The onion planting machine, which is used to plant onion sets, is another example of Mathis' ingenuity.

He modified a precision drill to plant the onion sets onto ridges. He saved the frame and the roller from the drill and fitted a seat on the back of the tractor. Someone sits on the seat and feeds the onion sets into a tube so that they get planted on top of the ridge and the furrows get closed again. EarthShare is able to plant one acre of land, about 100,000 onion sets, in six hours.

🐛 PESTS AND DISEASES

Wood pigeons are a big pest this month, as they seem to think the vegetables are being grown solely for them.

Using a bird-scarer with a wide repertoire of sounds keeps them at bay.

Julie Adams and Nicky Molnar potato grading

Rhubarb

APRIL
RECIPES

APRIL RECIPES

BEETROOT CASSEROLE WITH ORANGE AND HONEY
(Serves 4)

- 4 tbsp olive oil
- 225 g (8 oz) onions, chopped
- 450 g (1 lb) beetroot, peeled and diced
- 1 tbsp tomato purée
- 1 tbsp honey
- Salt and black pepper
- ½ tbsp cornflour
- 300 ml (½ pint/10 fl oz) orange juice

1 Preheat oven 180ºC (350ºF/Gas 4)
2 Heat oil in a pan, add onions and sauté until soft.
3 Add beetroot and cook for about another 5 minutes.
4 Add tomato purée and honey and transfer to baking dish. Season.
5 Mix cornflour with orange juice, pour over beetroot and bake for about 35 minutes or until beetroot is cooked.

BEETROOT AND CHOCOLATE LOAF

- 225 g (8 oz) self-raising flour
- 25 g (1 oz) cocoa powder
- Pinch of salt
- 1 tsp baking powder
- 125 g (4 oz) caster sugar
- 125 g (4 oz) beetroot, peeled and grated
- 75 g (3 oz) dark chocolate, melted
- 75 g (3 oz) butter, melted
- 2 eggs, beaten

1 Preheat oven 180ºC (350ºF/Gas 4).
2 Grease and line a 900 g (2 lb) loaf tin.
3 Sift together flour, cocoa powder, salt and baking powder.
4 Stir in sugar, beetroot, melted chocolate, butter, and eggs.
5 Turn into a greased tin and bake for 45–50 minutes until firm on top and until a skewer inserted comes out clean.
6 Cool on a wire rack.

BEETROOT LEAF, STIR FRIED WITH COCONUT AND RAISINS
(Serves 4)

- 2 tbsp olive oil
- 2 garlic cloves, chopped
- 450 g (1 lb) beetroot leaf, washed and chopped
- 2 tbsp desiccated coconut
- 2 tbsp raisins
- 4 tbsp orange juice
- Salt and black pepper

1 Heat oil in a pan and sauté the garlic for about 2 minutes.
2 Add beetroot leaf and cook until wilted.
3 Add coconut, raisins and orange juice. Season to taste.
4 Heat for about another 5 minutes and serve.

BEETROOT IN A TANGY MUSTARD SAUCE
(Serves 4-6)

- 700 g (1½ lb/3 cups) beetroot, scrubbed but not topped and tailed
- 1 tbsp olive oil
- 50 g (2oz/¼ cup) onions, chopped
- 1 tbsp flour
- 120 ml (4 fl oz) vegetable stock
- 3 tbsp Dijon mustard
- 4 tbsp cream or fromage frais
- Salt and black pepper

To garnish:
- *Chopped parsley*

1. Place beetroot in a pan with salted water. Bring to the boil, cover, return to the boil. Reduce heat and simmer for about an hour until beetroot is cooked.
2. Drain under cold water, peel and slice.
3. Heat oil in a pan, add onions and cook for about 4 minutes.
4. Turn heat down, stir in flour and cook for 2 minutes, stirring continuously.
5. Gradually add the stock, mustard and cream or fromage frais. Cook for a few minutes until thick.
6. Add the cooked beetroot and heat for a few minutes until warm. Season to taste.

7. Put into a serving dish, and garnish with parsley.

BRUSSELS SPROUTS IN PECAN SAUCE
(Serves 4)
- *450 g (1 lb/2 cups) Brussels sprouts, washed and trimmed*
- *45 g (1½ oz) butter or margarine*
- *50 g (2 oz/¼ cup) Pecan nuts, chopped*
- *Salt and black pepper*

1. Bring salted water to the boil, add Brussels sprouts, cover and return to the boil. Reduce heat and simmer until just tender, about 10 minutes. Drain, and keep warm.
2. Heat butter or margarine in a small pan and brown the Pecans, stirring frequently, about 2 minutes. Do not let them burn. Season to taste.
3. Pour the Pecans over the Brussels sprouts. Serve.

BRUSSELS SPROUTS WITH RICE
(Serves 6)
- *450 g (1 lb/2 cups) Brussels sprouts, washed and trimmed*
- *1 tin 400 g (14 oz) condensed cream of mushroom soup*
- *225 ml (8 fl oz/1 cup) milk*
- *300 ml (½ pint/1¼ cups/10 fl oz) water*
- *Knob of butter (optional)*
- *Salt and black pepper*
- *¾ tsp caraway seeds*
- *150 g (5 oz/¾ cup) Basmati rice*

1. Bring salted water to the boil, add Brussels sprouts, cover the pan and return to the boil. Reduce heat and simmer until just cooked. Drain and keep warm.
2. In a pan, gently heat undiluted soup, milk, water, butter, salt, pepper and caraway seeds stirring occasionally.
3. Add rice, reduce heat, then cover and simmer until rice is cooked.
4. Stir in Brussels sprouts and mix.
5. Transfer to serving dish.

BRUSSELS SPROUTS SATAY
(Serves 4)
- *450 g (1 lb/2 cups) Brussels sprouts*
- *1 tbsp smooth peanut butter*
- *3 tbsp tamari or soy sauce*
- *2 tbsp vegetable oil*

- *4 tbsp toasted pine nuts, chopped*

1. Put Brussels sprouts into boiling salted water. Return to boil, reduce heat and simmer for about 5-6 minutes until crisp tender. Drain well.
2. Mix peanut butter with 2 tbsp tamari or soy sauce to form a smooth paste.
3. Heat oil in a pan, quickly stir fry the sprouts for about 2 minutes.
4. Remove from heat and stir half the peanut paste into the pan.
5. Transfer to a serving dish.
6. Drizzle with remaining paste and tamari or soy sauce.
7. Sprinkle with pine nuts.
8. Serve warm or cold.

Sprout snippet: Tamari is wheat free and is a popular option instead of using soy sauce for those who have wheat allergies.

CABBAGE AND BARLEY SOUP WITH TAHINI
(Serves 4)

- *75 g (3 oz) pearl barley*
- *1 tbsp olive oil*
- *1 onion, thinly sliced*
- *1 garlic clove, crushed*
- *450 g (1 lb/2 cups) cabbage, cut into fine strips*
- *Vegetable stock – enough to make up 1 L (1¾ pints/36 fl oz) with barley water*
- *1 bay leaf*
- *1-2 tbsp tahini*
- *Salt and black pepper*

1. Cook the pearl barley according to the instructions on the packet.
2. Reserve the liquid.
3. Heat oil in a pan. Sauté onion and garlic until onion is soft.
4. Add cabbage and the cooked barley, with the cooking water and make it up to 1 L (1¾ pints/ 36 fl oz) with vegetable stock.
5. Bring to the boil, add bay leaf and simmer until the cabbage is just cooked, but still crunchy.
6. Remove from heat and stir in tahini.
7. Season and serve.

CABBAGE CHOWDER WITH CORIANDER AND WHISKY
(Serves 8)

- *900 g (2 lb/4 cups) cabbage, cut into fine strips or grated*
- *450 g (1 lb/2 cups) carrots, peeled and cut into strips*
- *700 g (1½ lb/3 cups) potatoes, peeled and diced*
- *450 ml (16 fl oz/2 cups) vegetable stock*
- *1 tbsp fresh coriander, chopped*
- *1-2 tbsp whisky*
- *450 ml (16 fl oz/2 cups) milk*
- *2 tbsp cream*
- *Salt and black pepper*

1. Put the cabbage, carrots, potatoes and stock in a pan.
2. Bring to the boil, reduce heat and simmer until vegetables are cooked.
3. Add coriander, whisky, milk and cream. Heat through.
4. Season to taste.

72

CABBAGE WITH HONEY AND WINE
(Serves 4)

- 1 tbsp olive oil
- 1 onion, finely chopped
- 4 tbsp cider vinegar
- 2 tsp honey
- 125 ml (4 fl oz) white wine
- 125 ml (4 fl oz) vegetable stock
- 450g (1lb/2 cups) cabbage cut into fine strips
- Salt and black pepper

1 Heat oil in a pan and sauté onion until soft.
2 Add cider vinegar, honey, white wine and vegetable stock. Bring to the boil.
3 Reduce heat, add the cabbage. Cover and simmer until crisp-tender.
4 Season to taste.
5 Serve with rice or an omelette.

CARROTS WITH NOODLES
(Serves 4-6)

- *1 tbsp olive oil*
- *1 onion, chopped*
- *225 g (8 oz) carrots, grated*
- *150 ml (¼ pint/5 fl oz) orange juice*
- *1 tbsp cider vinegar*
- *Salt and black pepper*
- *175 g (6 oz) egg noodles, cooked*

1 Heat oil in a pan, add the onion and carrots. Sauté for about 3 minutes.
2 Add the orange juice, vinegar and season to taste.
3 Bring to the boil and cook for about 2-3 minutes.
4 Cook egg noodles according to packet instructions.
5 Stir the cooked noodles into the carrot mixture and serve.

CARROT AND PEANUT BUTTER BISCUITS

- *125 g (4 oz) peanut butter*
- *50 g (2 oz) margarine*
- *90 g (3½ oz) brown sugar*
- *50 g (2 oz) sugar*
- *1 egg*
- *½ tsp vanilla essence*
- *125 g (4 oz/1 cup) plain flour*
- *1 tsp bicarbonate of soda*
- *½ tsp salt*
- *125 g (4 oz/1 cup) 100% bran cereal*
- *225 g (8 oz/1 cup) carrots, grated*
- *100 g (3½ oz) chopped peanuts or sunflower seeds*

1 Preheat oven 180ºC (350ºF/Gas 4).
2 Cream peanut butter, margarine, brown sugar, sugar, egg and vanilla essence until light and fluffy.
3 Mix together flour, bicarbonate of soda and salt and fold into creamed mixture.
4 Stir in cereal, carrots and peanuts or sunflower seeds.
5 Form into 2.5 cm (1") balls and place on a greased baking sheet, about 5 cm (2") apart. Flatten with a fork.
6 Bake for 10-12 minutes or until lightly browned.
7 Cool on a wire rack.

CHICORY AND BEETROOT SALAD WITH WALNUTS
(Serves 4-6)

- *450 g (1 lb/2 cups) beetroot, scrubbed, but not topped and tailed*
- *225 g (8 oz/1 cup) walnuts*
- *2 tsp Dijon mustard*
- *½ tsp dried tarragon*

73

- 2 cloves garlic, crushed
- Salt and black pepper
- 4 tbsp white wine vinegar
- 175 ml (6 fl oz/¾ cup) olive oil
- 450 g (1 lb/2 cups) chicory, trimmed washed and chopped roughly

1   Place the beetroot in salted water, bring to boil, reduce heat and simmer until tender, about 1 hour. Drain, peel and slice. Allow to cool.
2   Add the walnuts to a hot, dry pan. Cook, watching constantly, stirring frequently, until the walnuts start to brown and they smell toasted, about 5 minutes.
3   In a jar with a lid, combine mustard, tarragon, garlic, salt, pepper, vinegar and olive oil. Put on lid and shake until ingredients are blended well.
4   Arrange beetroot in a serving bowl.
5   Place chicory on top, pour dressing over chicory and sprinkle with walnuts.

CHICORY AND RED LEICESTER SALAD WITH HONEY
Dressing
- 150 ml (¼ pint/5 fl oz) natural yoghurt
- 2 tsp honey
- 2 tsp lemon juice
- 1 tsp French mustard
- Zest of one orange, grated

Salad
- 225 g (8 oz) red Leicester cheese, cubed
- 2 chicory heads, sliced
- 2 sweet apples, peeled, cored and chopped
- 2 oranges, peeled and segmented

To garnish:
- Chopped parsley

1   For dressing, mix yoghurt, honey, lemon juice, mustard and orange zest together.
2   Put cheese, chicory, apples and oranges in a bowl.
3   Add dressing and mix.
4   Top with chopped parsley and serve.

CHICORY WITH WARM APPLE AND CIDER THYME DRESSING
(Serves 4)
- 450 g (1 lb/2 cups) chicory, trimmed, washed and roughly chopped

Dressing
- 150 ml (¼ pint/5 fl oz) cider
- 1 apple, chopped
- 2 tbsp lemon juice
- 1 tbsp olive oil
- ½ tsp dried or fresh oregano
- ½ tsp dried or fresh thyme

1   Put chicory into serving bowl.
2   Combine dressing ingredients together in a small pan and boil for 3–5 minutes, until the juices are slightly thickened and apple is soft, but not broken down.
3   Allow the dressing to cool slightly, pour over the chicory and serve immediately.

PARSNIP AND APPLE BAKE WITH CORIANDER AND PARSLEY

(Serves 4)

- *450 g (1 lb/2 cups) parsnips, peeled and grated*
- *1 medium apple, grated and mixed with 2 tsp lemon juice*
- *1 onion, finely chopped*
- *1 tbsp fresh coriander, chopped*
- *1 tbsp fresh parsley, chopped*
- *2 eggs, beaten*
- *Salt and black pepper*

1 Preheat oven 180ºC (350ºF/Gas 4).
2 Mix parsnips, apple, onion, coriander and parsley together.
3 Add egg to bind the mixture. Season.
4 Put into a greased baking dish and bake until browned.

PARSNIP, CARROT AND SPROUTING BROCCOLI CURRY

(Serves 4)

- *2 tbsp olive oil*
- *1 onion, finely chopped*
- *1 tbsp ground cumin*
- *2 tsp ground coriander*
- *½ -1 tsp cinnamon*
- *1 tsp turmeric*
- *3 garlic cloves, crushed*
- *1 tbsp fresh root ginger, finely chopped*
- *1 fresh green chilli, seeded and chopped*
- *300 ml (10 fl oz/½ pint/1¼ cups) plain yoghurt*
- *300 ml (10 fl oz/½ pint/1¼ cups) water*
- *Salt and black pepper*
- *350 g (12 oz/1½ cups) parsnips, peeled and diced*
- *350 g (12 oz/1½ cups) carrots, peeled and cut into sticks*
- *225 g (8 oz) broccoli, chopped*

To garnish:
- *Fresh coriander, chopped*

1 In a large pan, heat the oil and sauté the onion until golden.
2 Stir in the cumin, coriander, cinnamon and turmeric. Cook for about 1 minute.
3 Add the garlic and ginger. Add the chilli and cook for about another minute, stirring continuously.
4 Stir in the yoghurt, a little at a time. Cook, stirring continuously, for about 2 minutes.
5 Stir in the water and season to taste.
6 Add parsnips, carrots and broccoli. Bring to the boil, reduce heat, cover and simmer until vegetables are tender.

To garnish
- Sprinkle with chopped coriander.

PARSNIPS WITH MAPLE SYRUP AND DIJON MUSTARD SAUCE

(Serves 4)

- *450 g (1 lb/2 cups) parsnips, peeled and cut into diagonal slices, 0.6 cm (¼") thick*
- *1 tbsp maple syrup*
- *1 tsp Dijon mustard*
- *50 g (2 oz) butter or margarine*
- *Salt and black pepper*

1 Place the parsnips in a pan with salted water. Bring to the boil, reduce heat and simmer until tender, about 15 minutes. Drain and keep warm.
2 Whilst parsnips are cooking, in a small pan combine maple syrup, mustard, butter or margarine, salt and pepper.

75

3   Heat gently and stir until the butter or margarine has melted.
4   Pour sauce over parsnips. Stir to coat them well.
5   Serve with potatoes with lemon tahini sauce on page 93.

POTATO CURRY, THAI STYLE

- *2 tbsp olive oil*
- *1 onion, chopped*
- *2.5 cm (1") piece root ginger, peeled and grated*
- *3 garlic cloves, crushed*
- *1-2 fresh green chillies, seeded and chopped*
- *900 g (2 lb) potatoes, peeled and diced*
- *1 x 440 ml (14 fl oz) can coconut milk*
- *Juice of 2 limes or lemons*
- *Salt and black pepper*

- *1 x 2.5 cm (1") piece fresh lemon grass (optional)*

1   Heat the oil in a pan, add the onion and fry until golden brown.
2   Add the ginger, garlic and chilli and fry for another 2 minutes, stirring constantly.
3   Add the potatoes, coconut milk, lime or lemon juice and lemon grass (if used). Season to taste.
4   Bring to the boil,reduce heat and simmer for about 35 minutes.
5   Remove lemon grass before serving with jasmine rice.

PURPLE SPROUTING BROCCOLI WITH MACARONI AND BLUE CHEESE SAUCE
(Serves 4-6)

- *450 g (16 oz/2 cups) macaroni*
- *450 g (1 lb/2 cups) purple sprouting broccoli, chopped*
- *25 g (1 oz) butter or margarine*
- *35 g (1 oz/¼ cup) flour*
- *½ tsp dried mustard*
- *Salt and black pepper*
- *175 ml (6 fl oz) milk*
- *150 ml (¼ pint/5 fl oz) yoghurt*
- *225 g (8 oz) Stilton cheese, crumbled*

1   Preheat oven 180ºC (350ºF/Gas 4).
2   Cook macaroni in boiling water until just cooked. Drain.
3   Cook broccoli in boiling salted water for 3 minutes or until tender. Drain.
4   In a pan, melt the butter or margarine, add flour, mustard, salt and pepper and cook for 2 minutes, stirring continuously with a wooden spoon.
5   Gradually add the milk using a whisk. Whisk briskly until smooth. Remove from the heat.
6   Stir in the yoghurt and Stilton.
7   Add sauce to the macaroni and mix.
8   Gently fold in the broccoli.
9   Grease an ovenproof dish and fill with the mixture.
10 Bake for about 20 minutes or until browned.
11 Top with bread-crumbs or cheese before baking.

PURPLE SPROUTING BROCCOLI WITH BAKED POTATOES
(Serves 5)

- 5 potatoes, baked
- 700 g (1½ lb/3 cups) purple sprouting broccoli
- 25 g (1 oz) butter or margarine
- 1 tbsp plain flour
- 225 ml (8 fl oz/1 cup) milk
- ¼ tsp powdered mustard
- 120 g (4 oz/½ cup) Cheddar cheese, grated
- Salt and black pepper

1 Put broccoli in a pan of boiling, salted water. Simmer until cooked.
2 In another pan, melt butter or margarine. Add flour and stir to make a smooth paste.
3 Stir in milk a little at a time and cook on a low heat, stirring continuously, until thickened.
4 Add the mustard.
5 Stir in cheese and cook until melted.
6 Fold in broccoli and season to taste.
7 Serve over hot baked potatoes.

PURPLE SPROUTING BROCCOLI AND CARROTS WITH LIME DRESSING
(Serves 4-6)

- 2 carrots, thinly sliced diagonally
- 450 g (1 lb/2 cups) purple sprouting broccoli, chopped

Dressing
- 1 tbsp sesame oil
- 1 tbsp soy sauce
- 2 tsp honey
- 3 tbsp fresh lime juice (about 1 lime)
- Salt and black pepper

1 Bring 5 cm (2") of water to boil in a pan. Add vegetables, cover and simmer until just cooked.
2 Drain, plunge into cold water and drain again.
3 Whisk the dressing ingredients together.
4 Combine vegetables and dressing. Serve.

PURPLE SPROUTING BROCCOLI AND CREAMY CARROT SLAW
(Serves 4)

- 3 tbsp mayonnaise
- 1½ tbsp lemon juice
- 1½ tsp onion, grated
- 1½ tsp Dijon mustard
- 350 g (12 oz/1½ cups) purple sprouting broccoli, chopped
- 225g (8 oz/1 cup) carrots, peeled & grated
- Salt and black pepper

1 Combine lemon juice, mayonnaise, onion and mustard in a medium bowl. Whisk to blend.
2 Add broccoli and carrots. Mix.
3 Season to taste and refrigerate before serving.

PURPLE SPROUTING BROCCOLI PESTO (RECIPE I)
(Makes about 3 x 450 g jars)

- 450 g (1 lb/2 cups) purple sprouting broccoli, with stalks, chopped
- 175 g (6 oz/1 cup) walnuts
- 175 g (6 oz) Parmesan cheese, cut into chunks
- 225 ml (8 fl oz/1 cup) olive oil
- 3 cloves garlic
- Salt and black pepper

1 Put all ingredients in a food processor. Season to taste.
2 Serve with pasta or use as a dip.

PURPLE SPROUTING BROCCOLI PESTO (RECIPE 2)

(Makes about 3 x 450 g jars)

- *450 g (1 lb/2 cups) purple sprouting broccoli, chopped*
- *175 ml (6 fl oz/¾ cup) olive oil*
- *175 g (6 oz) grated Parmesan cheese*
- *8 sun-dried tomatoes*
- *125 g (4 oz) unsalted cashew nuts*
- *3 cloves garlic*
- *Salt and black pepper*

1 Immerse broccoli into boiling salted water, bring back to the boil, reduce heat and simmer until just tender. Drain and cool.
2 In a food processor, purée broccoli, and rest of ingredients until smooth.
3 Serve over pasta.

PURPLE SPROUTING BROCCOLI WITH TAGLIATELLE, FETA CHEESE AND OLIVES

(Serves 4-6)

- *350 g (12 oz/1½ cups) tagliatelle*
- *450 g (1 lb/2 cups) purple sprouting broccoli*
- *4 tbsp olive oil*
- *3 tbsp pine nuts*
- *175 g (6 oz) Feta cheese, crumbled*
- *175 g (6 oz) black olives, pitted and halved*
- *125 g (4 oz/½ cup) Parmesan cheese, grated*
- *2 tbsp fresh basil, chopped*
- *Salt and black pepper*

1 Cook tagliatelle in boiling salted water until just cooked (al dente).
2 Add broccoli to tagliatelle, continue to boil until broccoli is just cooked.
3 Drain tagliatelle and broccoli and transfer to a large bowl.
4 Heat oil in pan and add the pine nuts and stir until golden brown, about 2 minutes. Remove from heat.
5 Pour pine nuts with oil over tagliatelle and broccoli and toss to coat.
6 Add Feta, olives, Parmesan and basil and stir well.
7 Season to taste.

RADISH AND POTATO SALAD

- *225 g (8 oz/1 cup), potatoes peeled and quartered*
- *225 g (8 oz/1 cup) radishes, washed and grated finely*
- *1 small onion, finely chopped*
- *Bunch of parsley, chopped*
- *4 tbsp sour cream*
- *1 tbsp Dijon mustard*
- *Salt and black pepper*

1 Put potatoes into salted water, bring to the boil, reduce heat and simmer until tender, about 10-15 minutes. Drain and cool.
2 Chop potatoes, add rest of the ingredients to the potatoes and mix.
3 Serve.

RHUBARB, GINGER AND ORANGE MOUSSE
(Serves 4)

- *450 g (1 lb) rhubarb, washed and cut into chunks*
- *125 g (4 oz) brown sugar*
- *1 tbsp orange juice*
- *½ tsp ground ginger*
- *300 ml (½ pint/10 fl oz) whipping cream*

1. Put rhubarb, sugar, orange juice and ginger in a pan, bring to the boil, reduce heat and simmer until tender, about 10-15 minutes.
2. Allow to cool.
3. Whip the cream until it is stiff and fold in the rhubarb mixture.
4. Chill before serving.

ROCKET STIR-FRY WITH RADISH AND PARSLEY
(Serves 2)

- *2 tbsp olive oil*
- *2 garlic cloves, chopped*
- *A good handful of rocket, washed and chopped*
- *6-8 radishes, washed and quartered*
- *1 tbsp parsley, chopped*
- *Salt and black pepper*

1. Heat oil in a pan and fry the garlic for about 2 minutes.
2. Add rocket, radishes and parsley and stir-fry for about 5 minutes.
3. Season to taste and serve.

SWEDE WITH CORIANDER, PARSLEY AND PARMESAN
(Serves 4)

- *1 tbsp olive oil*
- *1 onion, chopped*
- *450 g (1lb) swede, peeled and cut into small cubes*
- *1 tbsp fresh coriander*
- *1 tbsp fresh parsley*
- *2 tbsp Parmesan*
- *Salt and black pepper*

1. Heat oil in a pan and fry the onion for about 2-3 minutes, or until soft.
2. Add the swede and fry gently until golden brown, about 10-15 minutes.
3. Add coriander, parsley and Parmesan. Season to taste.
4. Serve.

FARMING NEWS FOR MAY

Sowing, ploughing and planting remain the major activities this month.

 **HARVESTING**

May is when the last of the sprouting broccoli and the carrots are harvested and the time when the new carrots are coming through in the polytunnels at Cullerne. Spinach from Cullerne is picked. This is a crop that would have been sown the previous summer and already yielded a harvest that season. Over the winter the spinach plants are kept covered with straw so that they will not be eaten by the deer, which are very much part of the food chain in Scotland. Often in both directions, so to speak. Just before it goes to seed in the spring it is possible to get one more crop off these leafy greens. Rhubarb grown at Cullerne is a wonderfully reliable harbinger of spring.

 MAINTENANCE AND MACHINERY

Mathis flame-weeds the beetroot, carrots and parsnips with a blow torch fitted with a gas bottle and mounted on the front of the tractor. He designed this and it burns off the weeds before the crops emerge.

At Cullerne, polytunnels need to be reskinned every 5-7 years in May after the early spring crops are harvested and before the summer crops are planted. If it is done in the winter, when the warm weather comes, the polythene expands and in high winds the loose polythene would whip, split and blow away.

 PESTS AND DISEASES

May and September are usually the months when the carrot fly flies and lays its eggs.

The carrot fly is probably the most challenging pest here. It deposits its eggs in the soil and then the maggots feed on the carrots.

 PLANTING

May is the month for planting beetroot and carrots. Mathis plants Phacelia, a blue flower that keeps away the carrot fly and attracts bees amongst the crops. It is pretty too.

This is also the month to sow all the brassicas, including purple sprouting broccoli and cauliflowers. Cauliflowers are particularly difficult to grow in our part of Scotland because they are sensitive to cold weather.

Pigeons and cabbage root fly enjoy them as much as we do, adding to the workload, but Mathis perseveres because the subscribers really like them.

This is also the period when the summer crops are planted in the polytunnels at Cullerne. Tomatoes, French beans, and cucumber go in. Christopher tries to do this without clearing away the old crops completely so that he can continue to reduce 'the hungry gap' until the outdoor beds are ready.

The hungry gap is that period before the new season's vegetables are ready, and the winter crops are tailing off.

 WEATHER

May is usually the driest, warmest and prettiest month of the year in Scotland.

May Vegetable Box

Spinach

MAY
RECIPES

MAY RECIPES

CARROTS WITH GINGER, COCONUT AND SPINACH
(Serves 4-6)

- 2 tbsp olive oil
- 1 onion, chopped
- 2 garlic cloves, crushed
- ½ tsp turmeric
- 700 g (1½ lb/3 cups) carrots, roughly grated or cut into thin strips
- 1.25 cm (½") fresh root ginger, peeled and grated
- ½ tsp ground coriander
- 125 g (4 oz) desiccated coconut
- 350 g (12 oz) fresh spinach, chopped
- Salt and black pepper

1 Heat oil in a pan, sauté the onion, garlic and turmeric until onions are soft.
2 Add carrots, ginger, coriander, coconut, spinach, salt and pepper.
3 Simmer for 10 minutes or until the carrots are cooked.
4 Serve.

CARROTS WITH WHITE WINE AND HERBS
(Serves 4)

- 450 g (1 lb/2 cups) carrots, peeled or scrubbed and cut into chunks
- 450 ml (16 fl oz/2 cups) water
- 350 ml (12 fl oz/1½ cups) dry, white wine
- 225 ml (8 fl oz/1 cup) white wine vinegar
- 3 sprigs parsley
- 1 sprig rosemary
- 3 mint leaves
- 3 basil leaves
- 1 bay leaf
- 1-2 garlic cloves, peeled
- 1 tbsp sugar
- 4 tbsp olive oil
- Salt and black pepper

1 Place carrots in a pan, cover with the water, wine and vinegar.
2 Add herbs, garlic, sugar, olive oil, salt and pepper.
3 Bring to the boil and simmer, uncovered, for 30 minutes.
4 Strain the liquid into a serving dish, add carrots, mix and serve.

PURPLE SPROUTING BROCCOLI WITH GARLIC AND MACARONI
(Serves 4)

- 450 g (1 lb/2 cups) macaroni
- 450 g (1 lb/2 cups) purple sprouting broccoli, chopped
- 2-4 tbsp olive oil
- 6 cloves garlic, chopped
- 120 g (4 oz/½ cup) Cheddar cheese, grated
- Salt and black pepper

1 Cook the macaroni following instructions on the packet. Drain, transfer to a serving dish and keep warm.
2 Put broccoli into boiling, salted water, return to the boil. Reduce heat and simmer until crisp-tender. Drain.
3 Heat oil in pan and add the garlic. Cook for about 2 minutes.
4 Add broccoli and cheese to the pan and season to taste Mix well and heat gently until cheese has melted.
5 Pour broccoli, cheese and oil mixture over macaroni and stir.
6 Sprinkle more cheese on top and serve.

PURPLE SPROUTING BROCCOLI, POTATO AND CHEESE SOUP
(Serves 4)

- 1 tbsp olive oil
- 225 g (8 oz/1 cup) onion, chopped
- 700 g (1½ lb/3 cups) potatoes, peeled and cut into 1.25 cm (½") cubes
- 20 fl oz (1 pint/2½ cups) boiling water
- ½ tbsp bouillon
- 450 g (1 lb/2 cups) purple sprouting broccoli, chopped
- 175 g (6 oz) Cheddar cheese, grated
- Salt and black pepper

1 Heat oil in pan. Add the onion and sauté for 5 minutes.
2 Add potatoes, water, bouillon and broccoli. Cover, bring to boil, reduce heat and cook until vegetables are tender.
3 Pour into a blender

and process until smooth.
4 Return to the pan and gradually add the cheese, stirring until heated through and the cheese has completely melted.
5 Season to taste.

PURPLE SPROUTING BROCCOLI AND ROASTED GARLIC CHEESE SPREAD

- 2 bulbs garlic, separated into individual cloves, unpeeled
- 2-3 tbsp olive oil
- 225 g (8 oz/1 cup) purple sprouting broccoli, chopped
- 225 g (8 oz) cream cheese
- 2 tsp chives
- Salt and black pepper

1 Preheat oven 190ºC (375ºF/Gas 5).
2 Coat garlic cloves liberally with olive

oil. Place on foil and roast for about 30 minutes in oven or until soft.
3 Cool, remove pulp from garlic. Discard skins. Set aside.
4 Immerse broccoli into boiling salted water, return to boil, reduce heat and simmer until just tender. Set aside and cool.
5 Combine broccoli, garlic, cream cheese and chives in a food processor. Process until smooth. Season to taste.
6 Put in serving dish and chill before serving.

PURPLE SPROUTING BROCCOLI SLAW
(Serves 8)

- 450 g (1 lb/2 cups) purple sprouting broccoli, chopped
- 225 g (8 oz/1 cup)

celery, chopped
- 1 onion, chopped
- 225 g (8 oz/1 cup) black olives, pitted and halved
- 3 hard-boiled eggs, chopped
- 225 g (8 oz) mayonnaise

1 Put broccoli into boiling, salted water, return to boil, reduce heat and simmer until just tender. Drain and cool.
2 Combine cooled broccoli, celery, onion, olives and eggs together.
3 Mix in mayonnaise. Refrigerate before serving.

PURPLE SPROUTING BROCCOLI WITH SPICY CHICKPEA SAUCE
(Serves 4)

- 450 g (1 lb/2 cups)

83

purple sprouting broccoli

- 1 x 400 g (14 oz) can chickpeas, drained
- 150 ml (¼ pint/5 fl oz) plain yoghurt
- 2 garlic cloves, peeled
- 2 tbsp water
- 2 tsp olive oil
- 2 tsp lemon juice
- ¼ tsp ground cumin
- ¼ tsp cayenne pepper
- Salt and black pepper

1 Put broccoli into boiling, salted water, return to boil, reduce heat and simmer until tender, Drain and keep warm.

2 In a food processor add drained chick-peas, yoghurt, garlic, water, olive oil, lemon juice, cumin, cayenne pepper and seasoning and blend until smooth.

3 Taste to check seasoning.
4 Heat sauce in a pan.
5 Put cooked broccoli into a serving dish, spoon the sauce over and stir.

PURPLE SPROUTING BROCCOLI WITH TOFU AND JASMINE RICE
(Serves 4)

- 225 g (8 oz/1 cup) Jasmine rice
- 2 tsp brown sugar
- 4 tsp tamari
- 2 tbsp olive oil
- 1 tsp dried ginger or 1.25 cm (½") fresh root ginger peeled and chopped
- 2 garlic cloves, crushed
- 1 onion, chopped
- 225 g (8 oz/1 cup) firm tofu, cubed
- 4 tbsp water
- 450 g (1 lb/2 cups) purple sprouting broccoli, chopped

1 Cook rice following instructions on packet.
2 Dissolve sugar in tamari. Set aside.
3 Heat oil in pan. Stir-fry ginger and garlic for one minute.
4 Add onion and cook until soft.
5 Add tofu and water and cook for 2 minutes.
6 Add broccoli and cook until just soft. Add the sugar and tamari.
7 Serve hot with the Jasmine rice.

RADISH AND BEETROOT SLAW
(Serves 2-4)

- 2 medium beetroot, peeled and grated
- 10-15 radishes, chopped
- 1 tsp sesame oil
- 2 tsp olive oil
- 1 tsp white wine vinegar

- Salt and black pepper

1 Put grated beetroot and radish in a bowl.
2 Add rest of ingredients and stir well.
3 Refrigerate before serving.

RADISH, CARROT AND ORANGE SALAD
(Serves 4)

- 175 g (6 oz/¾ cup) radishes, thinly sliced
- 450 g (1 lb/2 cups) carrots, peeled and grated
- 1 large onion, chopped
- 3 tbsp olive oil
- 2 tbsp lemon juice
- 2 tbsp orange juice
- Pinch of cinnamon
- Bunch parsley, chopped
- Salt and black pepper

1 Put radishes, carrots and onion in a bowl.

2 Whisk together olive oil, lemon juice, orange juice, cinnamon, parsley, salt and pepper. Pour over salad.
3 Cover and chill.
4 Serve with warm pitta bread.

RADISH AND FETA SALAD WITH GARLIC VINAIGRETTE
(Serves 4)
For the vinaigrette
- *150 ml (¼ pint/5 fl oz) olive oil*
- *150 ml (¼ pint/5 fl oz) white wine vinegar*
- *1 tsp Dijon mustard*
- *½ tsp herbs, such as dill or basil, can be dried or fresh*
- *2 cloves garlic, crushed*
- *Juice of ½ lemon*
- *Salt and black pepper*

For the salad
- *225 g (8 oz/1 cup) radishes, thinly sliced*
- *225 g (8 oz/1 cup)*

crumbled Feta cheese
- *225 g (8 oz/1 cup) black olives, pitted*
- *3 spring onions, finely chopped*

1 Place all ingredients for the vinaigrette in a jar with a lid and shake vigorously to mix well.
2 Put salad ingredients in a bowl, mix well.
3 Add vinaigrette and refrigerate before serving.

RHUBARB BREAD FOR BREAD MAKING MACHINE
(Makes 1½ lb loaf)
- *225 g (8 oz/1 cup) rhubarb, chopped*
- *225 ml (8 fl oz/1 cup) water*
- *½ tsp orange peel, finely grated*
- *225 g (8 oz/2 cups) wholemeal flour*
- *125 g (4 oz/1 cup) white bread flour*

- *25 g (1 oz) butter or margarine*
- *3 tbsp brown sugar*
- *¾ tsp salt*
- *½ tsp ground cinnamon*
- *1 tsp active dry yeast*

1 Combine rhubarb and water in a pan. Bring to boil, reduce heat and simmer, uncovered until rhubarb is tender.
2 Measure rhubarb and add water, if necessary, to equal 350 ml (12 fl oz). Cool slightly.
3 Add ingredients to bread machine according to manufacturer's directions.

Sprout snippet: *Six rhubarb plants will provide enough rhubarb for a family of four. Chinese doctors use rhubarb as a laxative, to reduce fever, and cleanse the body.*

RHUBARB AND OATMEAL BARS
(Makes about 12 bars)
Crumble mixture for base and top
- *175 g (6 oz/1½ cups) plain flour*
- *225 g (8 oz/2 cups) oatmeal*
- *90g (3 oz) brown sugar*
- *175 g (6 oz) butter or margarine, melted*

Filling
- *450 g (1 lb/2 cups) rhubarb, cut into 1.25 cm (½") pieces*
- *150 g (5 oz/¾ cup) brown sugar*
- *1½ tbsp plain flour*
- *¼ tsp ground nutmeg*
- *25 g (1 oz) butter or margarine, softened*
- *1 egg, beaten*

1 Preheat oven 180°C (350°F/Gas 4).
2 For the base and top, mix flour, oatmeal, brown

sugar and butter or margarine together until crumbly.

3   Press half of the crumble mixture into a greased 24 cm (9½") square baking tin.
4   Add rhubarb.
5   Mix sugar, flour, nutmeg and butter or margarine together, add egg. Beat until smooth.
6   Pour over the rhubarb.
7   Top with the other half of the crumble mixture and press down lightly.
8   Bake in oven for about 35 minutes.
9   Refrigerate and cut into bars.

RHUBARB TART
(Serves 6-8)
Crumble mixture for the base
- *125 g (4 oz/1 cup) plain flour*
- *90 g (3 oz/½ cup) icing sugar*
- *90 g (3 oz) butter or margarine*

Filling
- *225 g (8 oz/1 cup) brown sugar*
- *4 tbsp plain flour*
- *1 tsp vanilla essence*
- *2 eggs, beaten*
- *700 g (1½ lb/3 cups) rhubarb, finely chopped*

1   Preheat oven 180ºC (350ºF/Gas 4).
2   In a bowl combine flour and icing sugar. Rub in the butter or margarine until mixture resembles fine breadcrumbs.
3   Put crumble mixture into the bottom of a square 24 cm (9½") baking tin. Press down firmly, lightly bake for about 10 minutes. Do not brown.

4   In a bowl mix together sugar, flour and vanilla essence. Beat in the eggs until smooth.
5   Stir in rhubarb.
6   Pour over warm crumble mixture in baking tin.
7   Return to oven and bake for about 35 minutes.
8   Cool or refrigerate before slicing.

SPINACH WITH CORIANDER AND YOGHURT
(Serves 4)
- *2 tsp ground cumin*
- *2 tbsp fresh coriander or 2 tsp ground coriander*
- *900 g (2 lb/4 cups) spinach, washed and chopped*
- *2 cloves garlic, crushed*
- *150 ml (¼ pint/5 fl oz) yoghurt*
- *Pinch ground nutmeg*

- *Salt and black pepper*

1   Heat frying pan and toast cumin and ground coriander for about one minute. If using fresh coriander, do not toast.
2   Add spinach, fresh coriander (if used) and garlic. Stir continuously until spinach has wilted.
3   Put in serving dish, stir in yoghurt and nutmeg. Season.
4   Serve immediately.

SPINACH BAKE WITH CREAM CHEESE, BASIL AND PARSLEY
(Serves 4)
- *900 g (2 lb/4 cups) spinach, washed*
- *2 onions, finely chopped*
- *120 g (4 oz) cream cheese*
- *1 tbsp basil, chopped*
- *2 tbsp parsley, chopped*

- *1 egg*
- *Salt and black pepper*

1. Place spinach in a pan with no extra water, sprinkle with a little salt, cover and cook for about 10 minutes, shaking the pan occasionally. Drain well.
2. Combine spinach, onion, cream cheese, basil, parsley, egg together and season.
3. Put mixture into a greased baking dish and bake for about 30 minutes or until cooked.

SPINACH WITH GREEN PEPPER AND PEANUT BUTTER

(Serves 4)

- *1 tbsp olive oil*
- *1 onion, chopped*
- *1 medium green pepper, deseeded and chopped*
- *1 tomato, chopped*
- *450 g (1 lb/2 cups) spinach, washed and chopped*
- *50 g (2 oz/¼ cup) peanut butter*
- *Salt and black pepper*

1. Heat oil in pan and cook onion and green pepper until onion is tender.
2. Add tomato and spinach, cover and simmer until spinach is tender, about 5 minutes.
3. Stir in peanut butter, season, and heat gently.
4. Serve immediately.

Purple Sprouting Broccoli

FARMING NEWS FOR JUNE

*M*ore Brassica planting, planting, planting! Subscribers also join Mathis to weed the beetroot, carrots, chicory, leeks, onions, and parsnips, getting together for what turns out to be a social event as well. These work shifts and the regular festivals that EarthShare arranges are great opportunities for the subscribers to get together and network. The diverse backgrounds and skills of subscribers often lead to useful contacts being made.

At around the time of almost continuous daylight of the Summer Solstice, 21/22 June, all subscribers are invited to the Summer Tea Party which celebrates the crops of summer. It is a chance to view the gardens of Cullerne and see the salad crops and delicacies growing. Garden staff conduct tours, musicians play, there is singing, and the children play games. Teas of cucumber sandwiches with strawberries and cream follow to complete an enjoyable afternoon.

EarthShare has the use of two big Clydesdale horses, owned by Nicky Molnar. The horses assist in preparing and manuring the land before brassica planting as part of the rotation process. They are used for inter-row cultivation of potatoes and then heaping up again ie tattie row ridging. They work all times of the year doing general harrowing of bare land – when new land is broken to fight the couch grass – and for the springtime harvesting. Nicky is a farming assistant and is Mathis' right-hand man. He will be in charge of the fields from November to February, when Mathis is farming his olive groves in Spain.

HARVESTING

What harvesting? Slim pickings. Subscribers live on salad crops from Cullerne: parsley, basil, new carrots, lettuce  and spinach, with Rhubarb from Rafford for puddings. Pick elderflowers to make fritters, cordial and champagne.

MAINTENANCE AND MACHINERY

Machines take a back seat as the land gets maintained – by hand weeding.

PLANTING

In Cullerne Garden, fortnightly planting of lettuces continues.

PESTS AND DISEASES

The cabbage root fly tries – and often succeeds – to lay eggs on brassica seedlings. Mathis' battle with the bug begins in earnest.

WEATHER

June often catches us out with a cold snap, even a light frost on occasion. At least the month is usually dry, allowing access to the weeding

Elderflower

JUNE
RECIPES

JUNE RECIPES

CARROTS WITH CASHEW NUTS
(Serves 4-6)

- *700 g (1½ lb/3 cups) carrots, scrubbed and grated*
- *2 tbsp cashew nuts, toasted and chopped*
- *1 tbsp fresh basil, chopped*
- *2 tbsp lime juice*
- *½ tbsp maple syrup*

1 Place carrots in a bowl.
2 Toast cashew nuts by putting them in a hot, dry pan. Cook, watching constantly, stirring frequently until the cashew nuts start to brown and they smell toasted, about 5 minutes.
3 Add cashew nuts and basil to carrots. Mix well.
4 Blend together the lime juice and maple syrup.
5 Pour over carrots and mix well.

CARROTS IN A MUSTARD AND LEMON DRESSING
(Serves 4)

- *Juice of one lemon*
- *2 tsp Dijon mustard*
- *1 tsp sugar*
- *1 onion, finely chopped*
- *5 tbsp olive oil*
- *1 tbsp fresh basil, chopped*
- *Salt and black pepper*
- *450 g (1 lb/2 cups) carrots, scrubbed and cut into thin strips, or grated*

1 In a jar with a lid, combine lemon juice, mustard, sugar, onion, olive oil, basil, salt and pepper. Shake vigorously until blended.
2 Put carrots into a salad bowl. Pour dressing over and mix well.
3 Chill before serving.

ELDERFLOWER CHAMPAGNE
Everyone loves this champagne! Elderflowers are easy to find and pick all over Britain in June. It makes a great day out collecting them.

- *4 litres (7¼ pints) water*
- *450 g (1 lb) sugar*
- *2 lemons, sliced*
- *2 tbsp white wine vinegar*
- *7 large elderflower heads*

1 Boil the water.
2 Put sugar in a large container and pour the boiled water over the sugar. Stir to dissolve.
3 Leave to cool.
4 Add the lemons, white wine vinegar and flower heads.
5 Leave for 24-36 hours.
6 Sterilise 4-5 one-litre glass bottles with screw tops.
7 To sterilise the bottles, wash them in soapy water, then rinse in hot clean water. Put them into an oven at 120°C for 20 minutes.
8 Strain the liquid through muslin, or fine sieve, and bottle.
9 Leave for 7-10 days until fizzy. The time varies, depending on the weather.

ELDERFLOWER CORDIAL

- *25 good elderflower heads, stalks removed*
- *3 large lemons, thinly sliced*
- *1.5 L (2¾ pints) boiling water*

- 1.4 Kg (3 lbs) granulated sugar
- 50 gm (2 oz) citric acid (available from chemists)

1 Place elderflowers and lemons in a stainless steel, pottery, or plastic container.

2 In another pan, pour boiling water over the sugar and stir over heat until sugar is dissolved. Add the citric acid.

3 Leave to cool until luke-warm and pour the liquid over the elderflowers and lemon.

4 Leave to stand for 48 hours, stirring occasionally.

5 Strain through muslin or a fine sieve.

6 Pour into sterilised bottles.

7 To sterilise bottles, wash them in soapy water. Then rinse in hot clean water. Put the glass bottles into an oven at 120°C for about 20 minutes.

ELDERFLOWER FRITTERS
(Serves 4)
For the batter
- 125 g (4 oz) plain flour
- Pinch of salt
- 1 tbsp vegetable oil
- 150 ml (¼ pint/5 fl oz) water
- 1 egg white

Oil for frying
- 8 elderflower heads
- Sugar for coating cooked fritters

1 Sift flour and salt together in a bowl.

2 Make a well in the centre, add the oil and water, beating until smooth. Allow the batter to rest for about one hour.

3 Whisk egg white until stiff, then fold evenly into the batter with a metal spoon.

4 Heat oil in a pan.

5 Dip one elderflower head into the batter and add to hot oil. Deep fry for about 2 minutes or until the batter is cooked.

6 Remove and place on a kitchen paper towel to drain.

7 Dredge in sugar before serving.

8 Repeat until all of the elderflower heads are used.

LETTUCE AND WALNUT LOAF
- 350 g (12 oz/1½ cups) sugar
- 175 ml (6 fl oz/¾ cup) vegetable oil
- 1½ tbsp lemon juice
- 4 eggs
- 350 g (12 oz/3 cups) plain flour
- 2 tsp baking powder
- 1½ tsp bicarbonate of soda
- ¼ tsp cinnamon
- 1 tsp salt
- 450 g (1 lb/2 cups) lettuce, finely chopped
- 125 g (4 oz/¾ cup) walnuts, chopped

1 Preheat oven 180°C (350°F/Gas 4).

2 Whisk sugar and oil together.

3 Add lemon juice and eggs and beat well.

4 Fold in the flour, baking powder, bicarbonate of soda, cinnamon and salt.

5 Stir in lettuce and walnuts.

6 Pour into a greased loaf tin.

7 Bake for about 50 minutes, or until a knife inserted into the centre of loaf comes out clean.

LETTUCE AND COCONUT CHUTNEY

- 425 ml (¾ pint/15 fl oz) hot water
- 175 g (6 oz/¾ cup) desiccated coconut
- 1 large lettuce, washed and roughly chopped
- ½ tsp of dried chilli powder (according to taste)
- 1 tsp tamarind paste
- ½ tsp salt
- ½ tsp ground cumin

1 Pour half the water and all of the coconut into a pan. Bring to the boil and simmer for about 1 minute.

2 Stir and add the remaining water.

3 Spread the lettuce leaves on top of the liquid evenly, cover, bring back to the boil and cook gently for about 3 minutes.

4 Remove from the heat, stir in the rest of the ingredients and let stand for 5 minutes with the lid on the pan.

5 Uncover and allow to cool for 15-20 minutes.

6 Put the mixture into a food processor and roughly blend.

7 Put into jars.

LETTUCE, FRIED
(Serves 4)

- 1 large lettuce, washed and trimmed
- 1 tbsp olive oil
- 2 garlic cloves, crushed
- 1 tsp soy sauce
- Salt and black pepper

1 Cut lettuce into four.

2 Heat oil in a pan and fry the lettuce for about one minute.

3 Add the garlic, soy sauce and mix well.

Cook for another minute.

4 Season to taste.

LETTUCE AND HAZELNUT SOUP
(Serves 4)

- 1 tbsp olive oil
- 1 onion, finely chopped
- 50 g (2 oz) hazelnuts
- 2 medium potatoes, peeled and finely diced
- 725 ml (1¼ pint/24 fl oz) vegetable stock
- 2 large or 4 small lettuce, roughly chopped
- 75 ml (3 fl oz) double cream
- ¼ tsp nutmeg, grated
- Salt and black pepper

1 Heat oil in a large pan and fry the onion and ¾ of the hazelnuts until the onions are tender, about 5 minutes.

2 Add the diced potato and stock, bring to the boil, reduce heat and simmer until potato is cooked.

3 Add the lettuce and cook for a further 2 minutes.

4 Pour the soup into a food processor and blend until smooth.

5 Add 4 tablespoons of cream and adjust with a little water if the soup is too thick.

6 Add the nutmeg and season to taste.

7 Serve hot or cold with rest of cream drizzled over the soup and rest of hazelnuts.

LETTUCE RISOTTO
(Serves 5-6)

- *1 L (1¾ pints/4½ cups) vegetable stock*
- *3 tbsp olive oil*
- *2 shallots, finely chopped*
- *2 cloves garlic, chopped*
- *350 g (12 oz) Arborio rice*
- *2–4 mixed lettuce, depending on size, washed and roughly shredded*
- *125 g (4 oz) fresh garden peas, shelled*
- *12 spring onions, cut diagonally into 1 cm (½") pieces*

To finish:
- *Knob of butter or margarine*
- *25 g (1 oz) fresh Parmesan, grated*

1 Bring the stock to the boil, then turn down the heat to simmering point.

2 Heat olive oil in a pan, add shallots and cook without browning, then add garlic and cook for a further 2 minutes.

3 Add rice to the pan and stir well to coat rice with oil.

4 Pour in the first ladleful of hot stock.

5 Stir the risotto until the stock has been absorbed. Continue to add stock in this way until all has been used.

6 When rice is almost done, after about 15 minutes, add lettuce, peas and spring onions.

7 Stir gently to mix vegetables through the rice. It may seem that you have added too much lettuce, but it will soon wilt and the rice will absorb its juices.

8 The risotto is ready when all the liquid has been absorbed, the peas are tender and the rice is cooked, about 3 minutes after adding the lettuce. The texture should be creamy rather than dry.

9 Stir in a knob of butter or margarine and sprinkle with Parmesan.

POTATOES WITH LEMON TAHINI SAUCE
(Serves 4)

- *1 tsp olive oil*
- *¼ tsp toasted sesame oil*
- *1 onion, chopped*
- *1-2 gloves garlic, crushed*
- *700 g (1½ lb/3 cups) potatoes, peeled and diced*
- *1 tsp basil, chopped*

Lemon tahini sauce
- *2 garlic cloves, crushed*
- *2 tbsp tahini*
- *Juice of one lemon*
- *1 tbsp fresh parsley, chopped*
- *Water to thin*
- *Salt and black pepper*

1 Heat oil in a pan and sauté onions and garlic until the onion is soft.

2 Add potatoes and basil to the pan and stir well. Sauté for about another 2-3 minutes.

3 Pour in 225 ml (8 fl oz/1 cup) boiling water. Bring to the boil, reduce heat and simmer until the potatoes are cooked and most of the liquid has been absorbed.

4 To make the sauce, mix together the garlic, tahini and

lemon juice. Slowly add water until the mixture becomes the texture of single cream. Add the parsley and season to taste.

5 Pour sauce over the potatoes, and heat gently until warmed through. Serve.

SALAD DRESSINGS

BASIL AND SESAME DRESSING

- 1 clove garlic, crushed
- 3 tsp white wine vinegar
- 1 tbsp lemon juice
- 2 tbsp Parmesan or mature cheddar cheese, grated
- ½ tsp dried basil
- 2–4 leaves fresh basil
- 2 tbsp parsley, chopped
- 150 ml (¼ pint/5 fl oz) olive oil
- ½ tsp sesame oil
- Salt and black pepper

1 Combine all ingredients in a blender and blend until smooth.
2 Chill and serve with a green salad.

BLUE CHEESE DRESSING

- 175 ml (6 fl oz/¾ cup) sour cream
- ½ tsp powdered mustard
- 2 cloves garlic, crushed
- 1 tsp Worcestershire sauce
- 8 tbsp mayonnaise
- 125 g (4 oz) blue cheese, crumbled
- Salt and black pepper

1 Place sour cream, mustard, garlic, Worcestershire sauce and mayonnaise into a food processor and pulse until blended.
2 Add crumbled cheese and blend again at low speed until blended.
3 Season to taste.

FRUITY DRESSING

- 150 ml (¼ pint/5 fl oz) orange juice
- ½ tsp orange zest, grated
- 75 g (3 oz) cream cheese
- 3 tbsp mayonnaise
- 1 tsp sugar
- ¼ tsp cayenne pepper

1 Put ingredients in a food processor and blend until smooth.

GARLIC, OLIVE OIL AND HERB DRESSING

- 8 tbsp olive oil
- 4 tbsp white wine vinegar
- 2 tsp English, French or Dijon mustard
- 2-3 garlic cloves, crushed
- ½ tsp salt
- ½ tsp black pepper
- 1 tbsp of any herbs or 1 tsp any dried herbs

1 Place ingredients in lidded jar, shake until blended.

94

GARLIC MAYONNAISE AND CUCUMBER DRESSING

- 2 garlic cloves, crushed
- 4 tbsp mayonnaise
- ½ cucumber, peeled and chopped
- 4 tbsp plain yoghurt
- 2 tbsp fresh parsley, chopped
- 1 tbsp fresh chives or spring onions, chopped

1 Mix together all ingredients.
2 Chill before serving.

GINGER AND LEMON DRESSING

- 1 tbsp fresh ginger root, grated
- Juice of ½ lemon
- 1 small onion, chopped
- 4 tbsp olive oil
- 2 tbsp rice wine vinegar or white wine vinegar
- 2 tbsp water
- 1 tbsp tomato purée
- 1 tbsp soy sauce
- Black pepper

1 Put ingredients into a food processor and blend until smooth.

HERBY VINAIGRETTE

- 150 ml (¼ pint/5 fl oz) olive oil
- 4 tbsp white wine vinegar
- 1 tbsp lemon juice
- 1 tsp mustard powder
- ½ tsp dried oregano
- ¼ tsp dried sage or coriander
- ¼ tsp ground cumin
- 1 clove garlic, crushed
- Salt and black pepper

1 Place all ingredients in a jar with a lid.
2 Shake until blended.
3 Chill before serving.

MAYONNAISE AND PARMESAN CHEESE DRESSING

- 8 tbsp mayonnaise
- 1 tbsp lemon juice
- 1 clove garlic, crushed
- 1 tbsp onion, finely chopped
- 4 tbsp Parmesan
- Salt and black pepper

1 Combine ingredients together, mix well.
2 Cover and refrigerate.

MUSTARD AND HONEY DRESSING
(Makes about 225 ml/1 cup)

- 6 tbsp olive oil
- 2 tbsp cider vinegar
- 2 tbsp honey
- 1 tbsp Dijon mustard
- 2 tbsp toasted sesame seeds
- 2 cloves garlic, crushed
- Salt and black pepper

1 Combine ingredients in food processor and blend until smooth.
2 Taste and adjust seasoning.
3 Store in the refrigerator.

PEANUT AND LIME DRESSING

This can be a little thick, so add more olive oil if necessary.

- Juice of 2 limes
- 2 tsp sugar
- 2 tbsp unsalted roasted peanuts
- 1 tbsp fresh ginger, chopped
- 4 cloves garlic, crushed
- 3 tbsp olive oil
- Salt and black pepper

1 Place all ingredients in a food processor, blend until smooth. Refrigerate.

TAHINI
(Home made)
- 450 g (1 lb/2 cups) sesame seeds
- 4-8 tbsp olive oil

1 Preheat oven 180°C (350°F/Gas 4).
2 Toast sesame seeds in a hot, dry frying pan, shaking frequently until fragrant, about 2-3 minutes. Do not brown. Cool.
3 Put sesame seeds in a food processor and gradually add the olive oil. Use enough oil to make a smooth paste of a thick pouring consistency.

TAHINI DRESSING
- 2 tbsp tahini (home-made or bought in a jar)
- About 4 tbsp water
- 1 tbsp fresh lemon juice
- 2-4 cloves garlic to taste, crushed
- Salt and black pepper

1 Put ingredients in a jar with a lid and shake vigorously until blended. The dressing should be the consistency of double cream.
2 Add more water if necessary.

TOMATO, HONEY AND HORSERADISH DRESSING
(Makes about 16 fl oz)
- 400 g tin tomatoes, mashed or thick tomato juice
- 150 ml (¼ pint/5 fl oz) olive oil
- 150 ml (¼ pint/5 fl oz) lemon juice
- 1 tbsp honey
- 1 tsp paprika
- 1 small onion, chopped
- 1 tsp creamed horseradish
- 1-2 cloves garlic
- Salt and black pepper

1 Put all ingredients in a food processor and blend until smooth.
2 Store in a sealed jar in the refrigerator.

VINEGAR AND HONEY DRESSING WITH HERBS
- 150 ml (¼ pint/5 fl oz) balsamic vinegar
- 2 tsp honey
- 1 tsp Dijon mustard
- 4 tsp cold water
- 6-8 tsp olive oil
- ½ tsp dried dill or basil
- Salt and black pepper

1 Warm vinegar and honey in a pan until honey dissolves.
2 Transfer to a jar with a lid.
3 Add remaining ingredients, shake until blended.

WALNUT AND TARRAGON DRESSING
(Makes about ¼ pint/5 fl oz)
- ½ tsp mustard
- 2 tbsp white wine vinegar
- 3 tsp walnut oil
- 3 tbsp olive oil
- 1 tbsp fresh tarragon, chopped finely
- Salt and black pepper

1 Place all ingredients in a jar with a lid.
2 Shake vigorously until well blended.

SPINACH DIP
(Serves 6-8)
- 700 g (1½ lb/3 cups) spinach, washed
- 350 g (12 oz) mozzarella cheese, grated
- 150 ml (¼ pint/5 fl oz) sour cream
- 1-2 garlic cloves, crushed
- Salt and black pepper

1. Preheat oven 180ºC (350ºF/Gas 4).
2. Place spinach in a pan with no extra water, sprinkle with a little salt, cover and cook gently, shaking the pan occasionally for about 5 minutes. Drain well.
3. Transfer to a bowl.
4. Stir in mozzarella cheese, sour cream and garlic. Season to taste.
5. Pour mixture into a greased baking dish and bake for about 15 minutes, or until bubbly.
6. Serve with tortilla crisps or hot crusty French bread.

SPINACH WITH LEMON, YOGHURT AND BLACK PEPPER
(Serves 4)

- 2 tsp olive oil
- 2 garlic cloves, crushed
- 1 tsp cumin seeds
- 900 g (2 lb/4 cups) spinach, washed
- Zest and juice of one lemon
- ½ tsp sugar
- 4 tbsp plain yoghurt
- ¼ tsp black pepper
- Salt to taste

1. Heat oil in pan and add the garlic and cumin seeds and fry for one minute.
2. Add spinach and mix well with the garlic and cumin.
3. Add the lemon zest and juice and cook until the spinach has wilted.
4. Stir in sugar, yoghurt and season.
5. Serve immediately.

SPINACH AND PEAR SALAD WITH STILTON
(Serves 6)

- 125 g (4 oz/¾ cup) walnuts, hazelnuts, or almonds

Dressing

- 150 ml (¼ pint/5 fl oz) sherry or cider vinegar
- 150 ml (¼ pint/5 fl oz) olive oil
- 1 tbsp Dijon mustard

Salad

- 3 ripe pears
- 450 g (1 lb/2 cups) spinach, washed and chopped
- 225 g (8 oz/1 cup) Stilton or Gorgonzola cheese, crumbled
- 125 g (4 oz/½ cup) raisins
- Salt and black pepper

1. Cook nuts in a dry frying pan until golden, stirring often, about 5–10 minutes. Pour onto a paper towel and cool. Rub nuts in towel to remove any loose skins. Discard skins and roughly chop nuts.
2. Put dressing ingredients in a jar with a lid and shake vigorously until blended.
3. Cut pears lengthwise into quarters and core, then cut into thin slices.
4. In a large salad bowl, place pear slices, spinach and dressing. Stir well.
5. Sprinkle with cheese, raisins, nuts, season and mix gently.

SPINACH AND SAGE PESTO

(Makes 1 cup)

- 2 tbsp pine nuts, toasted
- 2 large garlic cloves, peeled
- 450 g (1 lb/2 cups) spinach, torn
- 225 g (8 oz/1 cup) fresh flat leaf parsley
- 125 g (4 oz/¼ cup) fresh sage leaves
- 2 tbsp Parmesan, grated
- 4 tsp lemon juice
- Salt and black pepper
- 3 tbsp olive oil

1 To toast pine nuts, put them in a hot, dry frying pan, shaking frequently until fragrant and just browned. Keep your eye on them so they do not burn.
2 Put pine nuts and garlic into a food processor and pulse until finely chopped.
3 Add remaining ingredients, except olive oil. Pulse again until finely chopped.
4 With processor on slow speed, add oil until well blended. You may need to add more olive oil. Adjust seasoning to taste.

Parsley

FARMING NEWS FOR JULY

HARVESTING

Fruit picking at Rafford begins this month. Blackcurrants, raspberries and strawberries appear in boxes, confirming that summer is here even if the weather isn't. It is also the time to begin picking the new potatoes and broad beans and from Cullerne: coriander, cucumber, lettuce, mange tout, parsley, peas and new carrots.

MAINTENANCE AND MACHINERY

Any machinery that has broken is fixed. It is a well-known fact that machines always break when you need them most!

PESTS AND DISEASES

Big fat wood pigeons feed on berry crops and anything else they fancy.

WEATHER

Statistically July is the wettest month in Scotland. Rain during this period can have a bad effect on the strawberries as they begin to rot before they can be picked. We are also prone to fog this month.

Broad Beans

Blackcurrants and Raspberries

JULY
RECIPES

JULY RECIPES

BLACKCURRANT PANCAKES
(Serves 4)

- *125 g (4 oz) plain flour*
- *Pinch of salt*
- *¼ tsp nutmeg*
- *1 egg, lightly beaten*
- *350 ml (12 fl oz) milk*
- *175 g (6 oz) blackcurrants*
- *Oil for frying*
- *Caster sugar for dredging*

1. Sift flour, salt and nutmeg into a bowl.
2. Make a hollow in the centre of the flour and drop in the egg.
3. Slowly pour in half the milk and gradually work the flour into the milk.
4. When all the flour is incorporated, beat until smooth.
5. Mix in the rest of the milk, beating continuously until the batter is bubbly and the consistency of double cream.
6. Add blackcurrants to the batter.
7. Heat a pan with oil and drop 2 tablespoons of the batter into the pan.
8. Cook for about 3 minutes, or until browned, turn and cook for a further 2-3 minutes on the other side.
9. Dredge in sugar.
10. Repeat until all the mixture is used.
11. Serve with yoghurt, fromage frais, fresh cream or ice cream.

BROAD BEAN AND CAULIFLOWER CURRY
(Serves 4)

- *350 g (12 oz/1½ cups) broad beans, shelled weight*
- *2 garlic cloves, chopped*
- *2 tbsp fresh ginger, chopped*
- *1 fresh green chilli, chopped*
- *1 tbsp olive oil*
- *1 medium onion, sliced*
- *1 large potato, diced*
- *25 g (1 oz) butter or margarine*
- *1 tsp curry powder*
- *1 cauliflower, broken into florets*
- *600 ml (1 pint/2½ cups/20 fl oz) vegetable stock*
- *2 tbsp creamed coconut*
- *Juice of ½ lemon*
- *Salt and black pepper*

To garnish:
- *Fresh coriander or parsley, chopped*

1. Put broad beans into boiling salted water, bring back to boil, reduce heat and simmer until tender, about 5-10 minutes. Drain.
2. Blend garlic, ginger, chilli and oil in a food processor until smooth.
3. In a pan, fry onion and potato in butter or margarine for about 5 minutes.
4. Stir in garlic, ginger, chilli and oil paste, curry powder and cook for 1 minute.
5. Add cauliflower and stir well.
6. Pour in stock. Bring to the boil and mix in coconut, stirring until melted. Season and cook uncovered until cauliflower is just tender.
7. Add broad beans and heat through.
8. Add lemon juice and season to taste.
9. Garnish and serve with rice.

BROAD BEAN GUACAMOLE
(Serves 4)

- 450 g (1 lb/2 cups) broad beans, shelled weight
- A small bunch of fresh coriander or parsley, chopped
- 3 garlic cloves, crushed
- ½ tsp ground cumin
- 1 onion, chopped
- 1 green or red chilli, de-seeded and chopped finely
- Juice of ½ lemon
- Salt and black pepper

1 Put broad beans in boiling salted water, bring back to boil, reduce heat and simmer until tender, about 10 minutes. Drain.
2 Put all ingredients in a food processor and blend to a rough paste.

CARROTS IN TARRAGON VINEGAR
(Serves 4)

- 450 g (1 lb/2 cups) carrots, scrubbed
- 1 tbsp butter or margarine
- 1 tbsp lemon juice
- 2 tbsp tarragon vinegar

1 Put carrots in salted water, bring to the boil, reduce heat and simmer until tender, about 10 minutes. Drain. Put in a serving dish.
2 Add butter to pan, stir until melted.
3 Add lemon juice and tarragon vinegar.
4 Pour over carrots and serve.

CARROTS GLAZED WITH CINNAMON AND CLOVES
(Serves 4)

- 450 g (1 lb/2 cups) carrots, scrubbed
- 25 g (1 oz) butter or margarine
- 1 tbsp brown sugar
- ¼ tsp cinnamon
- ¼ tsp ground cloves
- Salt and black pepper

1 Put carrots in salted water, bring to the boil, reduce heat and simmer until tender, about 10 minutes. Drain and keep warm.
2 In a small pan, melt butter, add brown sugar, cinnamon, cloves and season. Stir over heat until sugar has dissolved.
3 Pour glaze over carrots and stir well. Serve.

CORIANDER FETA DIP

- 225 ml (8 fl oz/1 cup) plain yoghurt
- 450 g (1 lb/2 cups) Feta cheese
- 2-3 garlic cloves, chopped
- 3 tbsp fresh coriander, chopped
- Salt and black pepper

1 Place yoghurt, Feta, garlic and coriander in a food processor and blend until smooth.
2 Season to taste.
3 Serve with mange tout, cucumber and new carrots.

CORIANDER, PARSLEY AND LIME PESTO

- 225 g (8 oz/1 cup) fresh coriander
- 125 g 4 oz/½ cup) parsley
- 50g (2 oz/¼ cup) walnuts, toasted and cooled
- 3 garlic cloves
- 125 ml (4 fl oz/1 cup) olive oil
- 3 tbsp Parmesan
- ½ tsp freshly grated lime zest
- Salt and black pepper

1 Place all ingredients in a food processor and blend until smooth. You may need to add a little more olive oil.

CORIANDER AND PARSLEY POTATOES
(Serves 4-6)
- *2-3 tbsp olive oil*
- *700 g (1½ lb/3 cups) potatoes, peeled and diced into 1.25 cm (½") cubes*
- *1 red chilli, seeds removed and chopped finely*
- *2 garlic cloves, crushed*
- *Salt and black pepper*
- *1 bunch coriander, finely chopped*
- *1 bunch parsley, finely chopped*

1 Heat oil in a pan, add the potatoes and fry until they are cooked and brown on all sides.
2 Add the chilli and garlic. Season to taste.
3 Continue to cook for about another 2-3 minutes.
4 Add the coriander and parsley and cook for about another 2 or 3 minutes.

CORIANDER RISOTTO OR NEXT DAY PATTIES
(Serves 4-6)
- *1 tbsp olive oil*
- *1 onion, finely chopped*
- *2 garlic cloves, crushed*
- *450 g (1 lb) Arborio rice*
- *150 ml (¼ pint/5 fl oz) white wine*
- *1 L (1¾ pints) vegetable stock*
- *1 large bunch fresh coriander, roughly chopped*
- *Salt and black pepper*

1 Heat oil in a pan and sauté onion and garlic until onion is soft, about 4 minutes.
2 Add the rice and stir to coat with the oil.
3 Add the wine and let it reduce by half.
4 Add the stock a little at a time, allowing the risotto to cook and the stock to be absorbed gradually.
5 Stir frequently until the rice is just cooked and the risotto is very thick.
6 Remove from heat and stir in the coriander. Season to taste. Serve as risotto.

Next day patties
7 Let the risotto cool. Refrigerate.
8 Shape the risotto into patties and fry in vegetable oil until golden brown on both sides.

9 Serve with roasted potatoes or green vegetables.

CORIANDER SAUCE WITH COCONUT AND DRY ROASTED PEANUTS
(Serves 4)
- *2 tbsp desiccated coconut*
- *1 onion, chopped*
- *1 tbsp olive oil*
- *2 tbsp dry roasted peanuts, roughly chopped*
- *1 tsp coriander seeds*
- *1 tsp ground turmeric*
- *3 tbsp coriander leaves, chopped*

1 Infuse coconut in 300 ml (10 fl oz/½ pint) of boiling water for about 20 minutes.
2 Sauté onion in oil until soft.
3 In a food processor,

add coconut and liquid, sautéed onions, peanuts, coriander seeds, turmeric and fresh coriander.

4   Put into a pan and heat gently.

5   Pour sauce over cooked vegetables or baked tomatoes.

COUSCOUS MOROCCAN STYLE
(Serves 4-6)

- *175 g (6 oz/¾ cup) couscous*
- *50 g (2 oz) raisins*
- *300 ml (10 fl oz/½ pint/1¼ cups) hot vegetable stock*
- *3 tbsp olive oil*
- *450 g (1 lb/2 cups) onions, chopped*
- *2 garlic cloves, crushed*
- *4 tomatoes, chopped*
- *2 tsp orange zest, grated*
- *Salt and black pepper*
- *1 bunch parsley, finely chopped*
- *3 tbsp fresh orange juice*
- *3 tbsp fresh lemon juice*

1   Place couscous and raisins in a bowl, and add boiling stock. Cover and let stand for 15 minutes.

2   Heat 2 tablespoons of olive oil in a pan and sauté onions and garlic, until onions are golden.

3   Add the tomatoes and orange peel, and cook for about 3-4 minutes, or until heated through. Season.

4   Uncover couscous and stir with a fork to fluff up.

5   Add to the pan with the vegetables and stir well. Add the parsley.

6   In a bowl, whisk together remaining oil, orange juice and lemon juice until blended. Add to the pan and stir well.

7   Spoon into a serving bowl and garnish with chopped parsley.

CUCUMBER AND ONION BAKE WITH HERB CRUST
(Serves 4)

- *2 cucumbers, sliced into medium slices*
- *2 medium onions, thinly sliced and separated into rings*
- *4 tbsp plain flour*
- *Salt and black pepper*
- *150 ml (¼ pint/5 fl oz) vegetable stock*
- *1 tbsp tomato purée or ketchup*

Crust

- *125 g (4 oz) breadcrumbs*
- *1 tbsp olive oil*
- *1 tbsp chopped fresh herbs such as coriander or parsley*

1   Preheat oven 180ºC (350ºF/Gas 4)

2   Alternate layers of cucumber and onions in a greased casserole dish.

3   Sprinkle each layer with flour, salt and pepper.

4   Mix together the vegetable stock and tomato purée or ketchup and pour over cucumber and onions.

5   Make the crust by mixing together breadcrumbs, and mixed herbs.

6   Sprinkle over the cucumber and onion and bake in oven for about 20 minutes or until brown.

CUCUMBER SALSA

- 1 cucumber, cut into medium slices
- 1 onion, chopped
- 2 tbsp parsley, chopped
- 2 tbsp coriander, chopped
- 1 chilli, seeded and chopped
- 1 garlic clove, crushed
- 2 tbsp lime juice
- 1 tbsp water
- Salt and black pepper

1 Combine cucumber, onion, parsley, coriander, chilli, garlic, lime juice and water together.
2 Season to taste.
3 Serve with tortilla chips.

CUCUMBER IN YOGHURT
(Serves 4)

- 1 cucumber
- Salt
- 150 ml (¼ pint/5 fl oz) plain yoghurt
- 3 tbsp fresh basil, chopped
- 2 tbsp fresh mint, chopped
- 1 onion, chopped
- 1 clove garlic, crushed
- Salt and black pepper

1 Place cucumber into a colander and sprinkle with salt. Leave for about 30 minutes.
2 Rinse cucumber and pat dry.
3 Combine yoghurt, basil, mint, onion, and garlic in a bowl.
4 Stir cucumber into yoghurt mixture and season to taste.

LETTUCE AND POTATO SOUP
(Serves 4)

- 450 g (1 lb/2 cups) potatoes, peeled and chopped
- 1 onion, chopped
- 2 lettuce, chopped
- 1 litre (35 fl oz/1¾ pints/4 cups) vegetable stock
- 2 egg yolks
- 150 ml (¼ pint/5 fl oz) double cream
- Salt and black pepper

1 Place the potatoes, onion, lettuce and vegetable stock into a large pan.
2 Bring to the boil, reduce heat and simmer for about 10 minutes, or until potatoes are cooked.
3 Liquidise and return to the pan.
4 Mix the egg yolks and cream in a bowl. Whisk in about 8 fl oz/1 cup of the hot soup.
5 Gently whisk the egg mixture into the soup.
6 Season to taste and serve.
7 Make meringue shell with egg whites.

Meringue no fail - *Make a* **meringue shell** *from the two egg whites. This recipe was given to us by Jacqui's mum, Joan Pettit, who says it never fails. Put egg whites in a bowl, add 175 g (6 oz) caster sugar, 2 tbsp warm water, 2 tsp of cornflour, ½ tsp vanilla essence and ½ tsp of any vinegar. Use an electric whisk and whisk for about 10 minutes until stiff. (We know this sounds a long time, but it is really worth it.) Shape meringue into a circle with a well in the middle, on a baking tray lined with grease-proof paper. Bake at 120°C (250°F/Gas ½) for about an hour or until firm to the touch. Once cooked switch the oven off and leave in overnight, or cool on wire rack. Fill with fruit and cream.*

MANGE TOUT WITH CARROTS AND SOY SAUCE
(Serves 4)

- 450 g (1 lb/2 cups) baby carrots, scrubbed
- 350 g (12 oz/1½ cups) mange tout, trimmed
- 2 tbsp soy sauce
- 1 garlic clove, crushed
- 1.25 cm (½") fresh root ginger, peeled and grated
- Freshly ground black pepper

To garnish:
- 25 g (1 oz) toasted sunflower seeds

1   Put carrots into boiling, salted water, return to boil, and simmer until just tender, about 10 minutes. Drain and keep warm.
2   Put mange tout into boiling, salted water, return to boil reduce heat and simmer until just tender, about 2-3 minutes. Drain and keep warm.
3   Blend soy sauce, garlic, ginger and pepper together.
4   Put vegetables and soy sauce mixture in a pan and stir for one minute over a low heat until mixed.
5   Transfer to a serving dish, sprinkle with toasted sunflower seeds.

MANGE TOUT WITH GARLIC AND PARMESAN
(Serves 4)

- 225 g (8 oz/1 cup) mange tout, cut into bite-size pieces
- 2 tbsp olive oil
- 1 small onion, sliced
- 2 garlic cloves, crushed
- Salt and black pepper
- 5 tbsp single cream
- 225 g (8 oz) pasta
- 1 tbsp Parmesan, grated

1   Put mange tout into boiling, salted water, return to boil, reduce heat and simmer until tender, but still crisp, about 2-3 minutes. Drain and set aside.
2   Heat oil in a pan. Sauté onion and garlic until onion is transparent.
3   Stir in the cooked mange tout, and season to taste.
4   Add the cream and heat through gently, without boiling.
5   Cook pasta following instructions on the packet. Serve mange tout on top of pasta and sprinkle with Parmesan.

PARSLEY AND GRUYÈRE CHEESE OMELETTE
(Makes 2)

- 4 large eggs
- 3 tbsp fresh parsley, chopped
- 2 tsp water
- Salt and black pepper
- 25 g (1 oz/¼ stick) butter or margarine
- 125 g (4 oz) Gruyère cheese, grated

1   In a bowl beat eggs, 2 tbsp parsley, water, and seasoning.
2   Melt half the butter in a pan and add half the egg mixture.
3   Cook until the eggs are just set in the centre. Lift the edge of the omelette with a spatula and tilt the pan so that any uncooked mixture flows underneath, about 2 minutes.
4   Add half the cheese.

Using spatula, fold other half of the omelette over cheese. Slide out onto plate.

5   Repeat 2 and 3 above to make the second omelette.

6   Garnish omelettes with remaining parsley.

PARSLEY AND POTATO SOUP
(Serves 4)

- 1 onion, chopped
- 1 tsp olive oil
- 450 g (1 lb/2 cups) potatoes, peeled and chopped
- 950 ml (32 fl oz/1¾ pints) vegetable stock
- Salt and black pepper
- 2 tbsp parsley, chopped

1   In a large pan sauté the onion in the oil until onion is soft. Add potatoes, and vegetable stock.

2   Bring to the boil, reduce heat and simmer for about 20 minutes or until potatoes are cooked.

3   Liquidise. Season.

4   Stir in parsley and serve.

POTATOES WITH CARDAMOM AND YOGHURT
(Serves 4)

- 450 g (1 lb) new potatoes, washed
- 150 ml (¼ pint/5 fl oz) plain yoghurt
- 3 cardamom pods, seeded
- Salt and black pepper

To garnish:
- Coriander or parsley, chopped

1   Put new potatoes in a pan with salted water, bring to the boil, reduce heat and simmer until tender. Drain.

2   Mix yoghurt, with the seeds from the cardamom pods and season.

3   Combine with the hot potatoes.

4   Transfer to a serving dish, sprinkle with parsley or coriander and serve.

RHUBARB AND STRAWBERRY FOOL

- 450 g (1 lb) rhubarb, chopped
- 450 g (1 lb) strawberries
- 125 g (4 oz) sugar (to taste)
- 36 g (2 tbsp) custard powder
- 18 g (1 tbsp) sugar
- 20 fl oz (1 pint/2½ cups) milk
- ½ pint fresh single cream (to taste)

1   Stew the rhubarb by putting it into a pan with 2 tablespoons of water. Bring to the boil reduce heat and simmer until just tender.

2   Add strawberries, reheat until fruit is soft.

3   Add sugar to taste and allow to cool a little.

4   Meanwhile, put the custard powder and sugar into a bowl. Mix to form a paste with a little of the milk.

5   Heat remaining milk to just under boiling point and pour onto the custard mix, stirring continuously.

6   Return to the pan, bring to the boil over a gentle heat stirring continuously until thick. Cool for a few minutes, stirring if necessary, to prevent a skin forming.

7   Blend custard with the stewed fruit and most of the cream.

8   Pour into a serving

dish, or individual bowls, and cool in the fridge.

9 Serve with a swirl of cream on the top.

STRAWBERRIES WITH RASPBERRY SAUCE

- *900 g (2 lb) strawberries*
- *225 g (8 oz) raspberries*
- *1 tbsp orange juice*
- *1 tbsp maple syrup*

1 Put strawberries in a serving bowl.
2 In another bowl, press raspberries with the back of a fork to mash them. Stir in orange juice and maple syrup.
3 Pour raspberry mixture over the strawberries, mix gently.
4 Serve with fresh cream or ice cream.

STRAWBERRY AND YOGHURT PARFAIT WITH GRANOLA

- *225 g (8 oz) granola*
- *225 g plain yoghurt*
- *450 g (1 lb) strawberries, washed and sliced*
- *4 tsp runny honey*
- *4 tall parfait or sundae glasses*

1 Layer ingredients. Place a tablespoon of granola at the bottom of each glass.
2 Next a tablespoon of yoghurt.
3 Now place a layer of strawberries over the yoghurt.
4 Now a layer of honey.
5 Repeat the process until layers reach the top of the glass.
6 Top with a dollop of yoghurt, honey and a whole strawberry.

Mange Tout

108

FARMING NEWS FOR AUGUST

HARVESTING

Delicious early potatoes and broad beans, and the first onions with green tops. Calabrese and cauliflowers are picked, beetroot cropped. Garlic harvest also starts at Rafford this month, where the picking of blackcurrants and raspberries continue. At Cullerne new carrots, lettuce, courgettes, cucumbers, French beans, parsley, peas and tomatoes are picked.

MAINTENANCE AND MACHINERY

General maintenance of machinery.

PLANTING

The new strawberry plants go in for next year's crop. Spring cabbage sown for next year.

WEATHER

Temperate rather than sweltering.

Garlic ready for hanging-up

French Beans

AUGUST
RECIPES

AUGUST RECIPES

BEETROOT AND CABBAGE SALAD WITH GINGER AND CHERRIES
(Serves 6-8)

- 450 g (1 lb/2 cups) beetroot, trimmed and peeled
- 450 g (1 lb/2 cups) cabbage
- 1 onion, diced
- 450 g (1 lb/2 cups) sweet red cherries, pitted
- 60g (2 oz/¼ cup) crystallized ginger, chopped finely
- 4 tbsp olive oil
- 5 tbsp red wine vinegar
- 2 tbsp parsley, chopped
- Salt and black pepper

Garnish:
- Parsley sprigs

1 Grate beetroot and cabbage. Transfer to a mixing bowl.

2 Add onion, cherries, ginger, oil, red wine vinegar and parsley. Mix well. Season.

3 Garnish with parsley sprigs and serve.

BEETROOT, COCONUT AND LIME SALAD WITH CORIANDER
(Serves 4)

- 450 g (1 lb/2 cups) beetroot, scrubbed, but not topped or tailed
- 175 g (6 oz) yoghurt
- 50 g (2 oz/¼ cup) desiccated coconut
- Finely grated zest and juice of 1 lime
- ½ tsp ground coriander
- Salt and black pepper
- 4 large lettuce leaves, washed

1 Put beetroot in salted water, bring to boil and simmer for about one hour or until tender. Drain, peel and cool.

2 Cut into cubes.

3 Put beetroot into mixing bowl.

4 Stir in yoghurt, coconut, lime zest, juice and coriander. Season.

5 Arrange lettuce leaves on a serving dish, spoon beetroot over the top and serve.

BEETROOT DIP
(Serves 4)

- 450 g (1 lb/2 cups) beetroot, scrubbed
- 125 g (4 oz) soft tofu, drained
- 1–2 tbsp cider vinegar
- 2 tbsp shallots
- ½ tsp powdered mustard
- ½ tsp dried thyme
- ½ tsp dried tarragon
- Salt and black pepper

1 Put beetroot in salted water, bring to boil and simmer for about one hour or until tender. Drain, allow to cool, peel and cut into chunks.

2 Put beetroot and rest of ingredients (with one tablespoon of the cider vinegar) in a food processor and blend until smooth.

3 Adjust seasonings, adding more vinegar and salt to taste. Serve immediately or refrigerate for up to 3 days.

BEETROOT TANGY SALAD
(Serves 4-6)

- 700 g (1½ lb/3 cups) beetroot, trimmed and peeled
- 1 onion, chopped
- Salt and black pepper

Dressing
- 150 ml (¼ pint/5 fl oz) olive oil
- 150 ml (¼ pint/5 fl oz) cider vinegar
- 1 tsp Dijon mustard

- 1 tsp celery seeds
- Salt and black pepper

1. Grate beetroot finely and put in a bowl.
2. Add onion, season and set aside.
3. Put dressing ingredients in a jar with a lid and shake to combine.
4. Pour dressing over beetroot and toss to coat. Cool and serve.

BROAD BEAN AND COURGETTE PASTA SAUCE
(Serves 4)

- 250 g (8 oz/1 cup) broad beans, shelled
- 2 garlic cloves, crushed
- 1 onion, chopped
- 1-2 tbsp olive oil
- 2 courgettes cut into 1 cm (½") slices
- 300 ml (½ pint) single cream
- 1 x 400 g tin tomatoes or 400 g (14 oz) fresh tomatoes
- 100 g (4 oz) mozzarella cheese
- 1 tsp dried oregano
- Salt and black pepper
- Penne pasta for 4

1. Put broad beans in boiling salted water, bring back to the boil, reduce heat and simmer for about 5-10 minutes until just tender. Drain and set aside.
2. Sauté garlic and onion in oil until the onion is transparent.
3. Add sliced courgettes and cook for about another 5 minutes.
4. Stir in the cream and broad beans.
5. Add the tomatoes, sliced mozzarella, oregano and heat gently. Season.
6. Serve with pasta.

BROAD BEAN PÂTÉ (1)
(Serves 4-6)

- 900 g (2 lb/4 cups) broad beans, shelled
- 2 tsp ground coriander
- 2 tsp ground cumin
- 2 tsp turmeric
- Juice of one lemon
- 2 cloves garlic, crushed
- 4 tbsp olive oil
- Salt and black pepper

1. Cook the beans in boiling, salted water until tender, about 5-10 minutes. Drain and reserve liquid.
2. Place the beans, coriander, cumin, and turmeric in a liquidiser and blend until smooth.
3. Add lemon juice and garlic, plus some of the reserved liquid to form a thick purée.
4. Gradually add olive oil until the desired thickness of pâté is reached.
5. Season to taste.
6. Put into a serving bowl and sprinkle a little turmeric over the top.

BROAD BEAN PÂTÉ (2)
(Serves 4-6)

- 2 tbsp olive oil
- 1 onion, chopped
- 225g (8 oz) broad beans, shelled
- Grated zest and juice of an orange
- 4 tbsp Greek yoghurt
- 3 tbsp mint, chopped
- Salt and black pepper

1. If using frozen beans, defrost. If using fresh pod them.
2. Heat oil in a frying pan, add the onion and cook for 3–4 minutes until soft.
3. Add beans, orange zest and juice and 4 tbsp water.
4. Cover, simmer for 20 minutes or until

beans are tender.

5 Transfer to a food processor, add the yoghurt and pulse until smooth.

6 Season and chill.

BROAD BEANS WITH SWEET AND SOUR SAUCE
(Serves 4)

- *450 g (1 lb/2 cups) broad beans, shelled*

Sweet and sour sauce

- *1 tbsp soy sauce*
- *3 tbsp pineapple juice*
- *2 tbsp tomato purée*
- *2 tbsp white wine vinegar*
- *2 tbsp vegetable oil*
- *2 tbsp brown sugar*

Sauté

- *1 tbsp olive oil*
- *2 cloves garlic, crushed*
- *1 tsp fresh ginger, grated*
- *1 bunch spring onions, chopped*
- *1 red pepper,*

seeded and chopped

Thickening

- *1 tbsp cornflour*
- *1 tbsp water*

1 Put broad beans in boiling salted water, bring back to the boil, reduce heat and simmer until tender. Drain.

2 For the sauce, put ingredients in pan. Heat gently until the sugar has dissolved. Set aside.

3 Heat oil in a pan, add garlic, ginger, spring onions and red pepper. Sauté for 2 minutes.

4 Add sauce and make a paste with the cornflour and water.

5 Stir paste into the pan, heat, stirring continuously until sauce thickens.

6 Add broad beans and serve.

CALABRESE AND GREEN PEPPERS WITH CHEESE
(Serves 4-6)

- *Green peppers, de-seeded and quartered*
- *450 g (1 lb) calabrese, roughly chopped*
- *225 g (8 oz) Cheddar cheese, grated*
- *4 tbsp plain flour*
- *½ tsp powdered mustard*
- *350 ml (12 fl oz/1½ cups) milk*
- *2 eggs, beaten*
- *Salt and black pepper*

1 Preheat oven 180ºC (350ºF/Gas 4).

2 Place peppers on a lightly greased baking dish.

3 Put calabrese into boiling salted water. Return to the boil, reduce heat and simmer until crisp-tender, about 8-10 minutes. Drain.

4 Place calabrese on top of peppers and top with cheese.

5 Beat together flour, mustard, milk and eggs until smooth. Season.

6 Pour over vegetables and bake for about 30 minutes or until cheese is bubbly and top is brown.

CARROT AND COCONUT SALAD
(Serves 4)

- *4 carrots, peeled and grated*
- *2 tbsp desiccated coconut*
- *2 tbsp onion, finely grated*
- *1 tbsp lemon juice*
- *2 tbsp fresh coriander or parsley, chopped*
- *1 fresh green chilli pepper, seeded and chopped*
- *Salt and black pepper*

1 Mix all ingredients together in a bowl.
2 Refrigerate before serving.

CARROT AND COCONUT RELISH
- 5 carrots, peeled and diced
- 2 medium cucumbers, chopped
- 2 green peppers, de-seeded and chopped
- 350 ml (12 fl oz/1½ cups) malt vinegar
- 225 ml (8 fl oz) water
- 575 g (1¼ lb/1½ cups) granulated sugar
- 1 tsp salt
- 1 tbsp celery seed
- 2 tbsp flour
- ½ tbsp powdered English mustard
- ½ tbsp turmeric

1 Put carrots in salted water, bring to the boil, reduce heat and simmer until just tender, about 10 minutes. Drain.
2 Add cucumbers and peppers.
3 Combine vinegar, water, sugar, salt, celery seed, flour, mustard and turmeric.
4 Add vegetables to liquid and cook until slightly thick.
5 Put into sterilised jars and seal.

CARROT AND SWEDE SALAD
(Serves 4)
- 450 g (1 lb/2 cups) carrots, peeled and grated
- 125 g (4 oz) swede, peeled and finely grated
- 50 g (2 oz) raisins

Dressing
- 150 ml (¼ pint/ fl oz) plain yoghurt
- 3 tbsp mayonnaise
- 2 tsp English mustard

- 2-3 level tbsp mango chutney
- 25 g (1 oz) flaked almonds, toasted

1 Put carrots, swede and raisins in a bowl.
2 Mix the mayonnaise, yoghurt, mustard and chutney together.
3 Add to the vegetables and raisins.
4 Transfer to serving dish and sprinkle over flaked almonds before serving.

CAULIFLOWER, APPLE AND COCONUT SOUP
(Serves 6)
- 2 tbsp olive oil
- 1 onion, chopped
- 1 large carrot, diced
- 225 g (8 oz/1 cup) cauliflower florets
- 1 cooking apple, peeled, cored and diced
- ½ tsp ground cumin

- ½ tsp coriander
- ½ tsp ginger
- ½ tsp turmeric
- ¼ tsp chilli powder
- 1 L (1¾ pints) vegetable stock
- 1 x 400 g (14 oz) can butter beans
- 50 g (2 oz) creamed coconut
- Salt and black pepper

1 Heat oil in a pan and sauté the onion and carrot until onion is soft.
2 Add cauliflower, apple, cumin, coriander, ginger, turmeric and chilli powder and cook for 1–2 minutes, stirring continuously.
3 Add the stock, bring to the boil, cover and simmer for about 20 minutes or until vegetables are cooked.
4 Add butter beans, creamed coconut

and simmer gently until beans are heated through and the coconut has melted. Season.

5 Serve with fresh crusty bread.

CAULIFLOWER, CALABRESE AND CARROT FLAN WITH CORNFLAKE CRUMB
(Serves 4)

- 1 small-medium cauliflower, broken into florets
- 1 head calabrese, chopped
- 3 medium carrots, sliced
- 1 tbsp olive oil
- 1 onion, chopped
- 1 clove garlic
- Salt and black pepper
- 2 eggs, beaten
- 125 g (4 oz) cornflakes, broken into crumbs

1 Preheat oven 180°C (350°F/Gas 4).
2 Put the cauliflower, calabrese and carrots into boiling salted water. Bring back to boil, reduce heat and simmer until carrots are crisp-tender
3 Drain and place in a mixing bowl.
4 Heat oil and sauté onion and garlic until onion is soft. Season and add to the vegetables.
5 Add the eggs and mix well.
6 Grease a baking dish and coat with half the cornflake crumbs.
7 Spoon vegetable mixture onto this layer, and top with remaining cornflake crumbs.
8 Bake in oven until heated through and browned.

COURGETTE AND BLUE CHEESE SOUP
(Serves 4)

- 1 tbsp olive oil
- 1 onion, chopped
- 2 cloves garlic, chopped
- 900 g (2 lb/4 cups) courgettes, chopped
- 425 ml (15 fl oz/¾ pint) vegetable stock
- 425 ml (15 fl oz/¾ pint) milk
- 250 g (9 oz) blue cheese, Stilton or Roquefort, crumbled
- Salt and black pepper
- 5 tbsp (3 fl oz/75 ml) single cream

1 Heat oil in a pan and sauté onion and garlic until soft.
2 Add the courgettes and cook over a low heat for about 10 minutes.
3 Add stock and milk and bring to the boil.
4 Simmer for 10–15 minutes.
5 Remove from heat and allow to cool.
6 Pour into a food processor and blend until smooth.
7 Return to the heat. Crumble the cheese into the soup and gently heat until melted.
8 Season to taste.
9 Stir in the cream just before serving.

COURGETTES WITH FRESH MINT, GARLIC, PINE NUTS, AND CURRANTS
(Serves 4)

- 2 tbsp olive oil
- 2 garlic cloves, chopped
- 4 courgettes, sliced
- Sprig of mint, chopped
- 2 tbsp pine nuts
- 50 g (2 oz) currants
- Salt and black pepper

To garnish:

- *1 spring onion, chopped*

1 Heat oil in a pan and sauté garlic for about 1 minute.
2 Add courgettes and mint, and cook until courgettes are just starting to brown.
3 Add pine nuts and currants. Season and cook for about another minute.
4 Put into serving dish and garnish with spring onion.

COURGETTE PANCAKES
(Serves 4)

- *2 eggs, separate yolk from white*
- *450 g (1 lb/2 cups) courgettes, grated*
- *1 tsp baking powder*
- *1 tbsp plain flour*
- *1 small onion or onion top, chopped*
- *125 g (4 oz) Feta cheese, diced*

- *Salt and black pepper*
- *1 tbsp oil for frying*

1 Beat the white of the eggs until stiff. Set aside.
2 Mix rest of the ingredients together.
3 Fold in egg white.
4 Heat oil in frying pan and fry mixture until browned on one side, turn and brown on other side. Cut into 4.

COURGETTE PASTY
(Serves 4)

- *1 medium onion, finely chopped*
- *1 tbsp olive oil*
- *450 g (1 lb/2 cups) courgettes, grated*
- *Salt and black pepper*
- *450 g (1 lb) shortcrust pastry*
- *50 g (2 oz) pine nuts*
- *175 g (6 oz) Feta cheese, crumbled*
- *2 tbsp milk for brushing*

1 Preheat oven 190ºC (375ºF/Gas 5).
2 Sauté the onions in the oil until just browned.
3 Add the courgettes, mix well and season to taste.
4 Roll out pastry into a rectangle.
5 Cover the central one-third with pine nuts.
6 Place onions and courgettes on top of the pine nuts.
7 Put Feta cheese on top of onions and courgettes.
8 Brush the edges of the pastry with milk.
9 Bring two sides of pastry up into the middle and pinch together. Now pinch together the sides, sealing the pastry.
10 Brush with milk and bake in until pastry is browned.
11 Serve with salad.

COURGETTE PIZZA
(Serves 4)
For the base

- *450 g (1 lb/2 cups) courgettes, grated*
- *450 g (1 lb/2 cups) potatoes, grated*
- *Salt and black pepper*

Toppings

- *Tomatoes, green or red pepper, grated cheese, parsley or any herbs*

1 Preheat oven 180ºC (350ºF/Gas 4).
2 Mix courgettes, potatoes, salt and pepper together.
3 Press into a pizza tin or baking tray to form the base of your pizza. Thickness according to taste.
4 Top with sliced tomatoes, green pepper, grated cheese and parsley or any other herb.
5 Bake for 20 minutes or until browned.

116

COURGETTE, POTATO AND CORIANDER PIE

Slice the potatoes thinly or they may not cook.

(Serves 4)

- 3 tbsp coriander, chopped
- 1 clove garlic, chopped
- 1 cm (½") fresh root ginger, peeled and chopped
- 150 g (5 oz) Cheddar cheese, grated
- 350 g (12 oz/1½ cups) potatoes, peeled and thinly sliced
- 175 g (6 oz) courgettes, thinly sliced
- 1 large onion, thinly sliced
- 4 tbsp white wine, cider, beer or stock.

1 Preheat oven 190ºC (375ºF/Gas 5).
2 Mix the coriander, garlic, ginger and cheese in a bowl.
3 Line a dish with half the potatoes and cover with half the courgettes and half the sliced onion.
4 Spoon on half the coriander, garlic, ginger and cheese mixture.
5 Continue with a second layer of the remaining potato, courgette and onion. Reserve the remaining cheese mixture until later.
6 Pour on the white wine, cider, beer or stock and cover with foil.
7 Bake in the oven for about an hour or until tender.
8 Top with remaining cheese and finish off under the grill.

COURGETTE PURÉE

(Serves 4)

- 3 tbsp olive oil
- 225 g (8 oz/1 cup) onion, chopped
- 3 cloves garlic, chopped
- ¼ tsp ground turmeric
- 1.25 Kg (2¾ lb) courgettes, diced
- 1 tsp salt
- 1 tsp ground cumin
- ¼ tsp cayenne pepper
- ¼ tsp black pepper
- ½ tsp tomato purée

1 Heat oil in pan and sauté onion and garlic until soft.
2 Add turmeric and stir. Remove one third of the onions and set aside.
3 Add courgettes and salt to the pan.
4 Cook until courgettes begin to release a little liquid. Cover, simmer and cook until courgettes are soft.
5 Add the cumin, cayenne pepper, black pepper and tomato purée.
6 Mash the courgette mixture with a potato masher while they are still cooking until the purée is coarse but well mixed.
7 Add the reserved onions and stir.
8 Serve hot, warm or chilled with breads, beans, split peas and yoghurt.

COURGETTE AND TOMATO BAKE

(Serves 4)

- 1 tbsp olive oil
- 1 onion, thinly sliced
- 3 cloves garlic, crushed
- 450 g (1 lb/2 cups) courgettes, thinly sliced
- 450 g (1 lb/2 cups) tomatoes, roughly chopped
- Salt and black pepper

Topping
- *125 g (4 oz) breadcrumbs*
- *1 tbsp parsley, chopped*
- *2 tbsp grated Parmesan*

1. Preheat oven 190ºC (375ºF/Gas 5).
2. Heat oil in a pan and sauté onion until transparent.
3. Add garlic, courgettes and tomatoes. Cook until courgettes are soft. Season to taste.
4. Transfer to a greased casserole dish.
5. Mix together breadcrumbs, parsley and Parmesan.
6. Sprinkle over the vegetable mixture.
7. Bake in oven for about 30 minutes or until golden.

GARLIC BAGUETTE WITH LEMON BUTTER
(Serves 6)
- *50 g (2 oz/½ stick) butter or margarine*
- *2 tbsp fresh parsley, chopped*
- *3 garlic cloves, crushed*
- *1 tsp lemon zest, grated*
- *Salt and black pepper*
- *French baguette, cut diagonally into 2.5 cm (1") pieces*

1. Preheat oven 160ºC (325ºF/Gas 3).
2. Mix butter or margarine, parsley, garlic and lemon zest together in a small bowl.
3. Season to taste.
4. Spread evenly over one side of each bread slice.
5. Reassemble the bread slices, wrap in foil and place on a baking sheet.
6. Bake until heated through, about 20 minutes.

GARLIC DIP
- *125 ml (4 fl oz) mayonnaise*
- *225 ml (8 fl oz) sour cream*
- *4-5 garlic cloves, crushed*
- *1½ tsp fresh parsley, finely chopped*
- *1 tsp dried dill*
- *2 tbsp white vinegar*
- *Milk to thin*
- *Salt and black pepper*

1. Preheat oven 180ºC (350ºF/Gas 4).
2. Mix together the mayonnaise, sour cream, garlic, dill, parsley, and white vinegar. Thin with milk to consistency of double cream.
3. Season to taste.
4. Use as a vegetable dip or on salad.

GARLIC PURÉE
- *4 large whole bulbs of garlic*
- *4 tbsp olive oil*
- *Salt and black pepper*
- *1 tbsp fresh lemon juice*

1. Chop off bottom of garlic bulbs and separate whole cloves, leaving outer covering intact.
2. Place cloves in a shallow baking dish, and drizzle with olive oil.
3. Bake until garlic is cooked, about 15 minutes.
4. Cool, remove skins.
5. Put garlic and lemon juice in food processor, blend until smooth. Season.
6. Use as a spread for buttered, toasted bread.

GARLIC WITH ROSEMARY, PARSLEY, WINE AND ROQUEFORT
(Serves 6)

- 6 whole bulbs of garlic
- 45 g (1½ oz) butter or margarine
- 4 tbsp olive oil
- 425 ml (15 fl oz/¾ pint) vegetable stock
- 4 tbsp dry white wine
- 2 tsp fresh rosemary, chopped
- 1 tsp parsley,
- chopped
- Black pepper
- 225g (8 oz) Roquefort cheese, crumbled

1. Preheat oven 190ºC (375º/Gas 5).
2. Cut off top of each garlic bulb 1.25 cm (½"), so that top of garlic cloves are exposed. Remove loose papery outer skin.
3. Place garlic, root side down on a greased baking dish. Top each bulb with butter or margarine. Pour olive oil over.
4. Mix vegetable stock and wine together and add to the dish. Sprinkle chopped rosemary and parsley over the garlic. Season with pepper to taste.
5. Bake uncovered for about 30 minutes or until garlic is cooked, basting regularly with pan juices. You may need to add more stock.
6. Sprinkle on the Roquefort and put back in the oven for about another 10 minutes or until cheese is melted.
7. Serve with hot, crusty bread.

LAVENDER AND ORANGE SORBET

- 1.2 L (2 pints/40 fl oz) orange juice
- 125 g (4 oz) sugar
- 1 tbsp lavender flowers

1. Put orange juice, sugar and lavender flowers in a pan.
2. Bring to the boil, reduce heat and simmer for about 15 minutes.
3. Cool and put in a freezer container.
4. Freeze until almost solid and serve with a lavender sprig on top.

Sprout snippet: If you burn yourself on the oven, or iron and the skin is not broken, put 2 drops of neat lavender essential oil directly on to the burn. This will remove the pain and will clear the burn up in no time. In many cases, it can prevent blistering and scarring.

LETTUCE AND COURGETTE SOUP
(Serves 4)

- 2 tsp olive oil
- 2 garlic cloves, crushed
- 1 onion, chopped
- 450 g (1 lb/2 cups) courgettes, sliced
- 600 ml (1 pint/20 fl oz) vegetable stock
- 1 lettuce, washed and chopped
- 2 sprigs parsley, chopped
- 300 ml (½ pint/10 fl oz) skimmed milk
- 1 tbsp cornflour, blended with a little water
- ¼ tsp nutmeg
- Salt and black pepper

1. Heat oil in pan, sauté garlic and onion until soft.
2. Add courgettes and cook until soft.
3. Add stock and bring to the boil.

4 Lower heat, add the lettuce and parsley.
5 Cover and simmer for about 20 minutes.
6 Liquidise soup until smooth. Return to pan, add milk, blended cornflour, nutmeg, salt and pepper.
7 Heat gently and stir until the soup has thickened.
8 This soup can also be served chilled.

ONION, APPLE AND TOMATO SAUCE WITH PASTA
(Serves 4)
- 2 tbsp olive oil
- 2 onions, chopped
- 1 apple, finely sliced or chopped
- 1 bay leaf
- 450 g (1 lb/2 cups) tomatoes, chopped
- Salt and black pepper

To serve: Pasta

1 In a pan heat oil, add onions, apple and bay leaf. Cover and simmer until apple and onion are soft.
2 Add tomatoes, salt and pepper. Simmer for about another 30 minutes. Remove bay leaf.
3 Cook pasta following instructions on packet and pour sauce over the pasta.

PASTA WITH ROASTED VEGETABLES AND GOAT'S CHEESE
(Serves 4)
- *Enough good quality pasta for 4 portions*
- *4 medium carrots, cut into slices, lengthways*
- *4 medium courgettes, cut into slices lengthways*
- *2 onions, thinly sliced*
- *2-4 tbsp olive oil*
- *1 tsp fresh thyme*
- *2-4 garlic cloves, chopped*
- *Salt and black pepper*
- *125 g (4 oz) mange tout*
- *125 g (4 oz) French beans, washed*
- *125 g goat's cheese, cut into cubes*

1 Preheat oven 200°C (400°F/Gas 6).
2 Boil pasta in salted water until tender. Drain and put in a ovenproof dish.
3 Put carrots, onions and courgettes in a roasting tin, coat with olive oil, fresh thyme, garlic, salt and pepper.
4 Roast until browned, about 20 minutes.
5 Steam the mange tout and French beans lightly.
6 Mix the vegetables in the ovenproof dish with the pasta.
7 Mix well,
8 Top with goat's cheese.
9 Put back in oven and cook until the goat's cheese begins to soften, but do not let it go crisp or brown.
10 Serve with a crisp green salad and a glass of good red wine.

POTATOES WITH COCONUT MILK AND BASIL
(Serves 4-6)
- *1 tbsp olive oil*
- *2 onions, chopped*
- *2 garlic cloves, crushed*
- *2 tsp coriander seeds, ground*
- *1 green pepper, de-seeded and chopped*
- *1 tbsp tamari or soy sauce*
- *700 g (1½ lb/3 cups) new potatoes, washed*

- 225 ml (8 fl oz/1 cup) coconut milk
- 2 tsp fresh basil

1. Heat oil in a pan and sauté onions, garlic and coriander seeds until onions are soft.
2. Add green pepper and tamari or soy sauce and cook for about a further 2 minutes.
3. Add potatoes and stir well.
4. Add coconut milk and chopped basil.
5. Cover and simmer for about 10-15 minutes, or until the potatoes are tender. Stir occasionally.
6. Serve.

POTATOES IN TANGY YOGHURT SAUCE

- 700 g (1½ lb) new potatoes, washed
- 275 g (10 oz/1¼ cups) yoghurt
- 300 ml (½ pint/10 fl oz) water
- 1 tsp turmeric
- ½ tsp chilli powder
- 1 tsp ground coriander
- ½ tsp ground cumin
- ½ tsp salt
- ½ tsp black pepper
- 1 tsp brown sugar
- 2 tbsp olive oil

1. Cook potatoes in their skins in boiling salted water until tender. Drain, keep warm and set aside.
2. Mix together yoghurt, water, turmeric, coriander, chilli, cumin, salt, pepper and sugar.
3. Heat oil in a pan, add the yoghurt mixture. Cook, stirring continuously for about 3 minutes.
4. Pour sauce over potatoes and serve.

SWEDE WITH PLUMS
(Serves 4)

- 450 g (1 lb/2 cups) swede, peeled and diced
- 225 g (8 oz/1 cup) plums
- 1 tbsp Dijon mustard
- Salt and black pepper
- 75 g (3 oz) sugar
- 150 ml (¼ pint/5 fl oz) vegetable stock
- 4 tbsp white wine vinegar
- 2 tbsp parsley, chopped

1. Put swede in salted water, bring to the boil, reduce heat and simmer until tender. Drain.
2. Remove stones from plums, discard and chop the flesh.
3. Place flesh into a bowl and add the mustard, salt and pepper.
4. In a pan, over a medium heat, caramelise the sugar by melting it until it reaches a light brown, syrupy consistency.
5. Add the vegetable stock, vinegar and simmer for about 5 minutes.
6. Add swede and plums and simmer for about another 5 minutes. Add the parsley and serve.

TOMATO BRUSCHETTA
(Serves 2)

- *4 ripe tomatoes*
- *1-2 tbsp olive oil*
- *1 tbsp balsamic vinegar*
- *1 tbsp basil, chopped*
- *4 slices bread thickly sliced (sourdough or ciabatta)*
- *2 large garlic cloves, lightly crushed*
- *Salt and black pepper*

1. Preheat oven 220ºC (425ºF/Gas 7).
2. Put the tomatoes in a baking dish and pour a little olive oil over them.
3. Roast in the oven until the skins start to blacken slightly in places.
4. Remove tomatoes from oven, cool a little and mix with balsamic vinegar and basil.
5. Season to taste.
6. Toast bread until golden on both sides, but still soft in the centre.
7. Rub the garlic cloves over the surface of the toast.
8. Pile the tomatoes on top of the toast and drizzle with more olive oil, salt and freshly ground black pepper and serve.

Cauliflower

FARMING NEWS FOR SEPTEMBER

 HARVESTING

Beetroot, calabrese, cabbage, carrots, cauliflower and remaining garlic are harvested. Cullerne provides courgette, cucumber. French beans, lettuce, small leaf greens and tomatoes.

It is also the month to lift the onions; a major job and, if it is a wet month, that proves very difficult. Onions last better if they are harvested in dry weather and stored in dry, airy conditions. Any damp leads to rot and mildew, and an early composting for the onion.

Mathis has used various methods to meet these exacting demands over the years. One year he used a fan trained on them to dry them, but it remained a problem to store them properly in bulk. One solution has been to pass the complete year's supply to the subscribers between September and Christmas.

Subscribers are advised on stringing methods to dry them but some simply put them on windowsills. It seems to work.

One of the best methods is that of subscriber, John Scott. He strings the onions and puts them in a tree for three or four weeks, after which they are stored in a wooden shed. The fir tree environment appears to have sufficient wind and at the same time shelter from the rain to dry them out. As most people do not have fir trees, we look forward to any suggestions!

 MAINTENANCE AND MACHINERY

Ongoing maintenance. The tattie harvester serviced and repaired ready for the big event next month.

 PLANTING

Strawberries planted out and sowing of oriental greens and winter lettuce in polytunnels.

WEATHER

Can be a little cold and wet, but generally mild and sunny.

Success! Marianne Rosenbusch with a fresh string of onions

Cucumbers growing in Cullerne polytunnel

SEPTEMBER
RECIPES

SEPTEMBER RECIPES

BEETROOT AND HORSERADISH SALSA
(Serves 4)

- 3 beetroot, peeled and grated
- 3 spring onions, chopped
- 1 apple, peeled, cored and grated
- Juice of 1 lemon
- 6 tbsp olive oil
- 1 tbsp creamed horseradish
- Salt and black pepper
- 4 dill sprigs or 2 tsp dill weed

1 Mix beetroot and onion together in a bowl.
2 In another bowl, stir apple into the lemon juice.
3 Add oil, horseradish and seasoning. and mix well to blend.
4 Add to the beetroot and onion.

5 Stir dill into the mixture.
6 Cover and chill for 30 minutes before serving.

BEETROOT AND TOMATO ROGAN JOSH
(Serves 4-6)

- 2 tbsp olive oil
- 2 onions, sliced
- 2 garlic cloves, crushed
- 2.5 cm (1") root ginger, grated
- 2 tbsp Rogan josh curry paste
- 225 g (8 oz) beetroot, peeled and diced
- 450 g (1 lb) tomatoes, chopped
- 4 tbsp water
- 125 g (4 oz) frozen peas or courgettes, sliced
- Handful of fresh mint, chopped
- Salt and black pepper

1 Heat oil in a pan.
2 Add onions and sauté until golden.
3 Add garlic, ginger and sauté for about 2 minutes.
4 Stir in Rogan josh curry paste.
5 Add beetroot and stir well.
6 Add tomatoes and water, bring to the boil, reduce heat, cover and simmer for about 30 minutes or until beetroot is cooked.
7 Add frozen peas or courgettes and mint. Cover and simmer until vegetables are tender.
8 Season to taste and serve with rice.

CABBAGE WITH CARAWAY SEED
(Serves 4)

- 450 g (1 lb/2 cups) cabbage, finely sliced into strips

- 50 g (2 oz/½ stick) butter or margarine
- 2-3 tsp caraway seeds

1 Put cabbage into boiling, salted water, bring back to the boil, reduce heat and simmer until crisp-tender, about 5-10 minutes.
2 Drain and set aside.
3 In the same pan, melt the butter or margarine, and add the caraway seeds. Fry them for about 1-minute stirring continuously. Remove from heat.
4 Add cabbage to pan, stir and serve.

CABBAGE WITH POTATOES, CHEDDAR AND FETA CHEESE
(Serves 6)

- 450 g (1 lb/2 cups) potatoes, peeled and cut into chunks

- 25 g (1 oz) butter or margarine
- 4 tbsp milk
- Salt and black pepper
- 1 tbsp olive oil
- 2 garlic cloves, crushed
- 450 g (1 lb/2 cups) cabbage, cut into thin strips
- Freshly ground black pepper
- 125 g (4 oz) Cheddar cheese
- 75 g (3 oz) Feta cheese
- ½ tsp paprika

1 Preheat oven 180ºC (350ºF/Gas 4).
2 Put potatoes into salted water, bring to the boil, reduce heat and simmer until tender, about 15 minutes.
3 Drain and mash with butter or margarine, milk and season.
4 In a pan heat the olive oil and sauté the garlic for 1-2 minutes, or until just browned.
5 Add the cabbage and sauté until just wilted, not soft. Add freshly ground black pepper.
6 Grease a baking dish and cover with the mashed potato.
7 Top with cabbage. Add Cheddar and Feta cheese.
8 Sprinkle with a little paprika.
9 Bake for 20-25 minutes until hot and the cheese has melted.

CABBAGE SPICY SOUP
(Serves 4)
- 2 tbsp olive oil
- 2 garlic cloves, chopped
- 1 onion, chopped
- 1 red chilli, chopped
- 225 g (8 oz) cabbage, shredded
- 40 fl oz (2 pints) vegetable stock
- 400 g (14 oz) can cannellini beans
- Salt and black pepper

1 Heat oil in a pan and sauté garlic, onion and chilli, for about 2 minutes.
2 Add cabbage and vegetable stock.
3 Bring to the boil, reduce heat, and simmer until cabbage is cooked.
4 Add cannellini beans drained and heat for 3 minutes.
5 Season to taste and serve with fresh, crusty bread.

CALABRESE IN BATTER
(Serves 4)
- 2 egg yolks
- 200 ml (7 fl oz) cold water
- 125 g (4 oz) plain flour
- A little flour for dusting
- Pinch of salt
- 450 g (1lb) calabrese, broken into florets
- Vegetable oil

1 For the batter, place egg yolks in a bowl. Add the cold water and mix lightly. Do not beat.
2 Add flour and salt and mix lightly. The batter will be very lumpy.
3 Dust calabrese with the extra flour.
4 Heat oil in a pan until very hot.
5 Dip individual florets of the calabrese in the batter and place in the hot oil, frying only a few at a time.
6 Deep fry for about 3 minutes until golden.
7 Drain on kitchen paper roll.

8 Continue until all calabrese is used.

9 Serve with mayonnaise, dips and condiments.

CALABRESE WITH COCONUT, GINGER AND SOY SAUCE
(Serves 4)

- *450 g (1 lb) calabrese, roughly chopped*
- *2 tbsp olive oil*
- *1 tsp sesame oil*
- *1 red chilli, seeded and sliced*
- *1.25 cm (½") piece fresh root ginger, peeled and finely chopped*
- *2 spring onions, finely chopped*
- *25 g (1 oz) desiccated coconut*
- *1 tbsp soy sauce*
- *1 tsp white wine vinegar*
- *Black pepper*

1 Put the calabrese into boiling, salted water, return to boil, reduce heat and simmer until crisp-tender. Drain.

2 Heat one tablespoon of olive oil and the sesame oil in a pan and fry the chilli, ginger, and onion until soft.

3 Add the coconut and fry over a medium heat for about 3-4 minutes, stirring frequently, until coconut is golden.

4 Add the calabrese, remaining oil, soy sauce, vinegar and pepper. Stir well and serve.

CARROT, CASHEW NUT AND RED LENTIL PATTIES
(Serves 4)

- *350 g (12 oz) red lentils*
- *900 ml (1½ pints/30 fl oz) vegetable stock*
- *2 tbsp olive oil*
- *2 garlic cloves, crushed*
- *225 g (8 oz/1 cup) carrots, grated*
- *1 onion, chopped*
- *3 tbsp mango chutney*
- *125 g (4 oz) cashew nuts, chopped*
- *Salt and black pepper*

1 Put lentils and stock in a pan, bring to the boil, reduce heat and simmer for 15-20 minutes, until lentils are soft and stock is absorbed.

2 Heat half the oil in a pan, sauté garlic, carrots and onion until the carrots are tender.

3 Add mango chutney, cashew nuts, lentils and season.

4 Set aside to cool slightly.

5 Using floured hands, shape the mixture into 8 patties.

6 Heat the remaining oil in a pan and sauté the patties for 4 minutes on each side until golden.

CAULIFLOWER, GREEN PEPPER AND SMALL LEAF GREEN SALAD WITH TAHINI
(Serves 4)

- *1 cauliflower, broken into florets*
- *1 green pepper, de-seeded and finely chopped*
- *A generous handful of any small leaf greens, chopped*
- *1-2 garlic cloves, crushed*
- *3 tbsp tahini*
- *3 tbsp water*
- *Juice of one lemon*
- *Salt and black pepper*

To garnish:

- *Fresh parsley, chopped*

1 Put cauliflower into boiling salted water.

2   Bring back to the boil, reduce heat and simmer until al dente, about 3-5 minutes. Drain and cool.
3   Mix the cauliflower with the pepper and small leaf greens.
4   Blend together the garlic, tahini, water, lemon juice, salt and pepper so that it has a creamy consistency.
5   More water may be needed.
6   Pour the dressing over the vegetables and stir well.
7   Garnish with chopped parsley.
8   Refrigerate before serving.

CAULIFLOWER AND SPINACH WITH TOFU AND DIJON MUSTARD
(Serves 4-6)
- *1 large cauliflower,*
- *broken into florets*
- *350 g (12 oz) spinach, chopped and washed*
- *125 g (4 oz/½ cup) breadcrumbs*
- *1 tbsp olive oil*
- *350 g (12 oz) tofu*
- *2 tbsp Dijon mustard*
- *Salt and black pepper*
- *¼ tsp cayenne pepper*
- *75 g (3 oz) Parmesan*

1   Preheat oven 190ºC (375ºF/Gas 5).
2   Grease a baking dish.
3   Put cauliflower into boiling salted water, bring back to the boil, reduce heat and simmer until tender. Drain and rinse under cold water. Set aside.
4   Cook spinach in pan with just rinsing water clinging to the leaves, stirring often, until just wilted, about 3-5 minutes. Drain and rinse under cold water. Add to cauliflower.
5   In a bowl, mix the breadcrumbs with olive oil. Stir well. Set aside.
6   In a food processor, add tofu, mustard, salt, pepper, and cayenne pepper and process until smooth and creamy.
7   Add Parmesan and blend until just mixed in.
8   Add tofu mixture to cauliflower and spinach, stir well to coat vegetables with the sauce.
9   Transfer to greased baking dish, sprinkle breadcrumbs over the top.
10 Bake until heated through and top is golden brown, about 25-35 minutes.

CAULIFLOWER WITH TOMATOES AND FETA
(Serves 4)
- *1 large cauliflower, broken into florets*
- *2 tbsp olive oil*
- *1 onion, thinly sliced*
- *2 garlic cloves, crushed*
- *1 tsp dried oregano*
- *2 pinches of ground cinnamon*
- *4-6 tomatoes, chopped*
- *1 tsp honey*
- *Salt and black pepper*
- *Juice of one lemon*
- *75 g (3 oz) Feta cheese, crumbled*

To garnish:
- *Parsley, chopped*

1   Preheat oven 180ºC (350ºF/Gas 4).
2   Put cauliflower into boiling salted water, bring back to the boil, reduce heat and simmer until just tender. Drain and place in a

greased baking dish.

3 Heat oil in a pan, add onion, garlic, oregano, cinnamon, and sauté until the onion is soft.

4 Add tomatoes and cook for about 5 more minutes. Add honey, salt and pepper.

5 Pour over cauliflower.

6 Squeeze lemon juice over the top and add Feta.

7 Bake until the sauce is bubbly and the cheese is browned, about 20 minutes.

8 Garnish with chopped parsley.

COURGETTES WITH GARLIC, LEMON JUICE AND PEANUTS
(Serves 4)

- *1 tbsp olive oil*
- *700 g (½ lb/ cups) courgettes, sliced*
- *2 garlic cloves, crushed*
- *1 tbsp lemon juice*
- *25 g (1 oz/¼ stick) butter or margarine*
- *Salt and black pepper*
- *350 g (12 oz/1½ cups) peanuts, toasted and coarsely chopped*

1 Heat oil in pan, add courgettes and fry until just softening.

2 Add garlic, lemon juice, butter or margarine. Season.

3 Mash ingredients and add more lemon juice if required.

4 Transfer courgettes to a serving dish and sprinkle with toasted peanuts.

5 Serve with rice or millet.

COURGETTE CURRY PANCAKES
(Serves 4)

- *450 g (1 lb/2 cups) courgettes, trimmed and grated*
- *2 spring onions, finely chopped*
- *1-2 cloves garlic, crushed*
- *½ tsp curry powder*
- *½ tsp dried thyme*
- *Salt and black pepper*
- *1 egg, beaten*
- *75 ml (3 fl oz) milk*
- *140 g (5 oz/1¼ cups) plain flour*
- *1½ tsp baking powder*
- *Vegetable oil for frying*

1 Place courgettes in a colander and sprinkle with salt. Mix well. Leave for 20 minutes.

2 Squeeze the courgettes between your hands to extract the water. Put in a bowl.

3 Add onions, garlic, curry powder, thyme and seasoning.

4 Mix in egg and milk.

5 Add the flour and baking powder and mix well.

6 Heat oil in a pan and fry a tablespoon of the mixture for 3 minutes on one side and 1 minute on the other.

7 Repeat until mixture is used up.

COURGETTE PÂTÉ
(Serves 4)

- *2 tbsp olive oil*
- *450 g (1 lb/2 cups) courgettes, sliced*
- *2 spring onions,*
- *finely chopped*
- *2 eggs*
- *¼ tsp marjoram*
- *¼ tsp thyme*
- *Salt and black pepper*

1 Heat 1 tbsp oil in pan and add the courgettes. Cook gently for about 10 minutes or until just cooked.

2 Transfer courgettes to a food processor,

but do not blend yet.

3 Add remaining oil to the pan and fry the onion until just soft.
4 Add eggs, stir and scramble them until just cooked.
5 Add marjoram and thyme. Season well.
6 Add the egg mixture to the courgettes in the food processor and blend until roughly mixed.
7 Refrigerate before serving.

DAIKON, CARROT AND FRENCH BEAN STIR-FRY
(Serves 4)

- 2 tbsp olive oil
- 1 medium onion, thinly sliced
- 2 cloves garlic, crushed
- 2.5 cm (1") piece of ginger, grated
- 225 g (8 oz) daikon, peeled and cut into thin strips
- 225 g (8 oz) carrots, peeled and cut into thin strips
- 225 g (8 oz) French beans, cut into 2.5 cm (1") lengths
- Juice and zest of 1 lime
- 2 tsp miso
- 6 tbsp hot water
- 4 tbsp soy sauce
- 1 tbsp cornflour
- 4 tbsp dry sherry

1 Heat oil in pan and stir-fry onions, garlic, and ginger for 1 minute over a high heat.
2 Add daikon, carrots and French beans. Fry for a further minute. Add the lime juice and zest.
3 Mix together miso, hot water and soy sauce.
4 Mix cornflour into a paste with sherry and stir into the miso mix.

5 Pour over vegetables and continue to stir-fry until the liquid has evaporated or the vegetables are crisp-tender.
6 Serve with rice.

DAIKON, CARROT AND MISO SOUP
(Serves 4)

- 1 tbsp olive oil
- ½ tsp ginger root, sliced
- 2 tsp sesame oil
- 225 g (8 oz) carrots, peeled and cut into thin strips
- 225 g (8 oz) daikon, peeled and cut into thin strips
- 600 ml (1 pint/20 fl oz) vegetable stock
- 2 tbsp soy sauce
- 1 tbsp miso

1 Heat olive oil in pan and sauté ginger for 2-3 minutes.
2 Add sesame oil, carrots and daikon.

Cover and simmer for 15 minutes.
3 Add stock, soy sauce and miso.
4 Bring to the boil, reduce heat and simmer for about 10 minutes.
5 Serve with crusty bread.

ELDERBERRY PIE

- 8 oz shortcrust pastry
- 700 g (1½ lb) elderberries, washed
- 125 g (4 oz) sugar
- 1 pinch salt
- 3 tbsp lemon juice
- 2 tbsp plain flour
- 25 g (1 oz) butter or margarine

1 Preheat oven 180ºC (350ºF/Gas 4).
2 Line a pie dish with half of the pastry.
3 Mix elderberries, sugar, salt and lemon juice together.

130

4   Put into the lined pie dish.
5   Sprinkle with flour and dot with butter or margarine.
6   Cover the top with remaining pastry.
7   Bake in the oven for about 30 minutes or until brown.
8   Serve warm with a scoop of ice cream.

Sprout snippet: Elderberries are ripe when the clusters turn upside down, around the middle of September. Make sure you do not use the green unripe berries - unripe elderberries contain cyanide and can cause severe diarrhoea. Wash the berries well. You can add them to other fruit to make a rich fruit salad Try steeping them overnight in red wine – yum. The Russians believe that elder trees ward off evil spirits and it is considered good luck to plant some near the house.

LETTUCE SOUP
(Serves 4)
- *225 g (8 oz) lettuce, washed and chopped*
- *1 tbsp olive oil*
- *1 small onion, finely chopped*
- *425 ml (¾ pint/15 fl oz) vegetable stock*
- *Salt and black pepper*
- *1 pinch sugar*
- *¼ tsp grated nutmeg*
- *300 ml (½ pint/10 fl oz) milk*

To garnish:
- *Croutons or toast*

1   Pour boiling water over lettuce leaves, add salt and let stand for 2 minutes. Drain and set aside.
2   Heat oil in a pan and sauté onion until soft.
3   Add lettuce and stock. Heat until boiling, add salt, pepper, sugar and nutmeg. Allow the soup to cool slightly and liquidise.
4   Return to pan, add milk and reheat gently.
5   Ladle into bowls and serve with croutons or toast.

ONION RINGS, DEEP FRIED
(Serves 4)
- *Vegetable oil for frying*
- *2 egg whites*
- *3-4 medium onions, peeled and sliced into rings*
- *25 g (1 oz) plain flour, seasoned*

1   Heat oil in a large pan until very hot.
2   Whisk the egg whites to soft peaks.
3   Toss onion rings in the seasoned flour.
4   Dip in egg white and fry in the hot oil for 1-2 minutes until crisp and golden.
5   Drain and keep hot.
6   Repeat until all onion has been cooked.
7   Serve with dips or mayonnaise.

POTATOES, MUSHROOMS AND SMALL LEAF GREENS WITH BALSAMIC VINEGAR
(Serves 4)
- *450 g (1 lb) small potatoes, scrubbed*
- *2 tbsp olive oil*
- *2 garlic cloves, crushed*
- *225 g (8 oz) mushrooms, sliced*
- *2-3 tbsp balsamic vinegar (to taste)*
- *1 spring onion, sliced*
- *Small leaf greens*

1   Boil potatoes whole until cooked, about 20 minutes.
2   Drain, cut in half and allow to cool.

3   Heat oil in a pan, sauté the garlic and mushrooms, stirring occasionally until golden.
4   Remove from heat. Toss with potatoes, balsamic vinegar, spring onion and small leaf greens.
5   Serve warm.

SMALL LEAF GREENS, PAK CHOI, OR SWISS CHARD STIR-FRY
(Serves 4)
- *2 tbsp olive oil*
- *2 garlic cloves, crushed*
- *450 g (1 lb) of any mixed greens*
- *Salt and black pepper*
- *Juice and zest of ½ lime*

1   Heat the oil in a pan and stir-fry garlic for 1 minute.
2   Add the greens, stir to coat in the olive oil and season.
3   Cook until wilted, add lime juice and stir for 1 more minute. Serve.

TOMATO, PESTO, CHEESE AND ROSEMARY SLICES
(Serves 4-6)
- *225g (8 oz) plain flour*
- *125 g (4 oz) butter, diced*
- *125 g (4 oz) Cheddar cheese, grated*
- *3 tbsp pesto*
- *2-3 tbsp cold water*
- *450 g (1 lb) tomatoes, halved*
- *1 tbsp rosemary, chopped*
- *Salt and black pepper*

1   Preheat oven 200ºC (400ºF/Gas 6).
2   Put flour in a bowl, rub in the butter until it resembles fine breadcrumbs.
3   Stir in 75 g (3 oz) of the cheese and half the pesto with the water to form a firm dough.
4   Roll dough out on a lightly floured surface until about ¼"- ½" thick and line a baking tray with dough.
5   Prick all over with a fork and bake for 20 minutes until crisp and golden.
6   Preheat the grill.
7   Spread remaining pesto sauce over the pastry, add the tomatoes, rosemary, seasoning and remaining cheese to cover.
8   Grill for 5-6 minutes until cheese has melted and tomatoes are hot.
9   Cut into squares and serve.

RUNNER BEAN PICKLE
- *1.8–2.3 Kg (4 lb-5 lb) runner beans, sliced*
- *1½ pints malt vinegar*
- *450 g (1lb) brown sugar*
- *1 tbsp celery seed*

For paste
- *50 g (2 oz) plain flour*
- *50 g (2 oz) mustard powder*
- *1 tbsp turmeric*
- *4 tbsp malt vinegar*

1   Put runner beans into boiling salted water and cook until tender, about 10 minutes. Drain.
2   Put malt vinegar, brown sugar and celery seed in a pan and boil for about 5 minutes.
3   Meanwhile mix flour, mustard, turmeric and vinegar together to form a paste.

132

4 Add paste to boiling vinegar and boil together for 3-5 minutes.
5 Add the runner beans.
6 Put pickle into sterilised jars.

VICTORIA SPONGE

- *225 g (8 oz) butter or margarine*
- *225 g (8 oz) caster sugar*
- *225 g (8 oz) self-raising flour*
- *1 tsp baking powder*
- *4 eggs, beaten*

1 Preheat oven 190°C (375°F/Gas) 5).
2 Cream butter or margarine and sugar together in a bowl with a fork until the butter goes pale and the mixture is light and fluffy.
3 Sieve flour and baking powder into the creamed mixture, add the eggs, and fold in gently, turning the bowl quarter of a turn with each fold.
4 Grease and flour two 17 cm (7") sponge tins.
5 Spoon the mixture equally between the two tins.
6 Bake in oven for about 20 minutes until the top is firm and the sponge is golden brown.
7 Cool on wire rack.
8 Layer the two cakes with jam and/or cream. Dust the top with icing sugar.

The formula of this sponge allows you to make a mixture for 8 or 80. The number of eggs is the secret. The formula is a 1:2 ratio. That is one egg to 2 oz of butter, sugar and flour. 8 eggs, 16 oz of butter sugar and flour and so on. For the baking powder you need one teaspoon per 8 oz of flour. This formula only works when using imperial measurements.

Sprout Snippet: *This cake mixture is very useful as a basic recipe. The key is to fold dry ingredients in lightly and gently as if you were caressing your loved one!*

Courgette

FARMING NEWS FOR OCTOBER

*P*otatoes have always featured strongly in the Scottish agricultural – and cultural – calendar. In years gone by the 'tattie harvest' in Scotland required everyone to muck in, and schools would close for the two weeks it took to gather the crops in.

Although today the harvest is done by machine and a few workers, schools still close for the two-week period in October, which is just as well for the EarthShare subscribers. Another of the big harvesting events of the year for EarthShare, the tattie harvest is the time when the subscribers complete their work shifts if they are some hours short. Potatoes are lifted and if – like onions – they are stored properly they form the backbone of the year's boxes. So it's important to get it right. The Clydesdale horses have been used to harvest some of the potatoes. Subscribers love the horses which keep tradition alive and make the work shifts fun. At one tattie harvest, the horses pulled the children around the fields in a cart, to their delight.

When the tattie harvest is complete, it is time to celebrate another growing year coming to a close with a bonfire party. A huge circle of subscribers gather around a fire. They make music, sing, dance, eat and drink, chat with friends old and new – many made through being a member of EarthShare.

One of EarthShare's big expenses is buying in seed potatoes. Buying in new seed potatoes avoids the viruses that are transmitted via the aphids, which diminish the vigour of the plants. The Irish potato famine resulted from just such conditions. EarthShare buy them in from a certified source to prove that they are disease free. The seed potatoes they buy in come from Northern Scotland and the company they buy from provides seed potatoes all over Britain. The climate in this part of Scotland is windy and the seed potatoes are less prone to aphids.

🗒 HARVESTING

EarthShare harvests about 30 tons of potatoes during this month. The pigs complete the potato harvesting by finding all the little tubers and eating them so they do not grow in the middle of the different crops that are planted in their place next year. The first winter cabbage is also harvested, along with cauliflower, red cabbage, carrots, parsnips and leeks and from Cullerne: courgettes, cucumbers, tomatoes and spinach. The first pumpkins from Rafford are lifted out too.

🌿 PLANTING

Garlic is planted at Rafford and winter lettuce and Oriental greens in the polytunnels at Cullerne.

☁ WEATHER

Anything from freezing cold to very mild and sunny for this time of year.

Clydesdale horses

Leeks

OCTOBER
RECIPES

OCTOBER RECIPES

BEETROOT, CARROT AND CUCUMBER SALAD WITH LIME VINAIGRETTE
(Serves 4)

- *2 medium beetroot, scrubbed but not topped and tailed*
- *3-4 medium carrots, peeled and cut into slices, diagonally*
- *1 cucumber, sliced*

Dressing
- *6 tbsp olive oil*
- *Juice of 2 freshly squeezed limes*
- *1 tsp dried mixed herbs*
- *2 garlic cloves, crushed*
- *½ tsp ground cumin*
- *Salt and black pepper*

1 Put beetroot into salted water and bring to the boil. Reduce heat and simmer for about 1 hour, or until tender. Drain, cool, peel and cut into bite-size pieces.

2 Put carrots into salted water and bring to the boil. Reduce heat and simmer until tender. Drain and cool.

3 In a bowl, mix beetroot, carrots and cucumber together.

4 Put dressing ingredients in a jar with a lid.

5 Shake vigorously to blend.

6 Pour dressing over vegetables and stir well. Refrigerate before serving.

CABBAGE AND LEEKS IN A CREAMY SAUCE
(Serves 4)

- *1 tbsp olive oil*
- *½ cabbage, finely sliced into strips*
- *3 medium leeks, washed and sliced*
- *2 garlic cloves, crushed*
- *2 tbsp dry white wine or sherry*

For the creamy sauce
- *25 g (1 oz/¼ stick) butter or margarine*
- *25 g (1 oz) plain flour*
- *300 ml (10 fl oz/½ pint/1¼ cups) milk*
- *¼ tsp grated nutmeg*
- *1 tsp Dijon mustard*
- *Salt and black pepper*

1 Heat oil in a large pan and add the cabbage, leeks and garlic. Sauté until vegetables are just soft.

2 Add white wine or sherry and cook for about 2 minutes.

3 To make the sauce, melt the butter or margarine in a pan, blend in the flour and cook over a low heat for 2-3 minutes, stirring continuously, with a wooden spoon or whisk. *(Sauce is less likely to become lumpy if you use a whisk).*

4 Gradually add the milk to the mixture, beating or whisking vigorously between each addition of milk. It will be very thick initially.

5 When all the milk has been added, bring to the boil and simmer gently for about 2 minutes, stirring frequently.

6 Add the nutmeg, mustard and season to taste.

7 Pour the sauce over vegetables and stir well. Serve.

CARROTS, FRIED
(Serves 4)

- *2 tbsp olive oil*
- *2 garlic cloves, chopped*
- *4 carrots, grated*

- *2 tbsp tamari or soy sauce*
- *¼ tsp fresh ginger, grated*
- *Freshly ground black pepper*

1 Heat oil in a pan and sauté garlic for one minute.
2 Stir in the carrots, tamari or soy sauce, ginger and pepper.
3 Stir-fry for a few minutes until carrots are tender.

CARROT FRITTERS WITH BEER BATTER
(Serves 4)
For the batter
- *125 g (4 oz) plain flour*
- *¼ tsp salt*
- *1 egg yolk, slightly beaten*
- *1 tbsp vegetable oil*
- *150 ml (¼ pint/5 fl oz) flat beer*
- *1 tsp curry powder*
- *1 egg white,*

- *whisked until stiff*
- *225 g (8 oz/1 cup) carrots, peeled and coarsely grated*
- *Vegetable oil for frying*

1 Combine flour, salt, egg yolk, vegetable oil and beer and beat to make a smooth batter.
2 Fold in curry powder and whisked egg white.
3 Gently fold in the carrots.
4 Drop large spoonfuls of mixture in hot vegetable oil and cook for about one minute on each side. The oil does not need to be more than 2.5 cm (1") deep.
5 Remove fritters with slotted spoon and let them drain on paper towels.

CAULIFLOWER AND CRUNCHY CABBAGE SALAD
(Serves 4-6)
- *450 g (1 lb/2 cups) cauliflower florets, sliced*
- *450 g (1 lb/2 cups) cabbage, finely shredded*
- *1 onion, thinly sliced*
- *225 g (8 oz) mayonnaise*
- *225 g (8 oz) sour cream*
- *1 tsp sugar*
- *1 tbsp white vinegar*
- *1 dash Worcester-shire sauce*
- *Salt and black pepper*

1 In a large bowl mix cauliflower, cabbage and onion together.
2 Mix together the sour cream, mayonnaise, sugar, vinegar, and Worcestershire sauce and season to taste.
3 Pour over vegetables and mix well.

CAULIFLOWER WITH GINGER AND CORIANDER
(Serves 4)
- *4 tbsp olive oil*
- *1.25 cm (½") piece of fresh root ginger, finely chopped*
- *1 large cauliflower, cut into florets*
- *Salt and black pepper*
- *4 tbsp coriander, finely chopped*
- *Juice of one lemon*

1 Heat oil in a pan and add ginger. Stir for about 10 seconds.
2 Add cauliflower and season well.
3 Cover and cook for about 2-3 minutes, or until cauliflower is tender, but still crisp.
4 Uncover and add the coriander and lemon juice. Mix well.

137

CAULIFLOWER WITH SPICY TOMATOES AND POTATOES
(Serves 4-6)

- 2 tbsp olive oil
- 1 onion, finely chopped
- 2-3 cloves garlic, crushed
- 2.5 cm (1") piece fresh root ginger, finely chopped
- 2-3 tomatoes,
- ¼ tsp turmeric
- ½ tsp garam masala
- 150 ml (¼ pint/5 fl oz) water
- 1 medium-large cauliflower, broken into florets
- 2 medium potatoes, peeled and cubed
- Salt and black pepper

1. Heat oil in a pan, sauté onion, garlic, ginger and tomatoes until onion is soft.
2. Add turmeric, garam masala and cook for about 2-3 minutes.
3. Add water.
4. Add cauliflower and potatoes. Season.
5. Cover and simmer for about 10 minutes, stirring occasionally, until vegetables are tender. Add more water if necessary.

COURGETTE AND CABBAGE CRUMBLE
(Serves 4)

- 225 g (8 oz/1 cup) rice
- 1 tbsp olive oil
- 3 medium courgettes, sliced thinly
- 225 g (8 oz/1 cup) cabbage, grated
- 1 egg
- 150 ml (¼ pint/5 fl oz) milk
- Salt and black pepper
- 125 g (4 oz) Cheddar cheese
- 2-3 slices wholemeal bread, made into breadcrumbs

1. Preheat oven 180°C (350°F/Gas 4).
2. Cook rice according to instructions on the packet. Drain.
3. Heat oil in a pan and sauté the courgettes and cabbage until soft.
4. Stir the courgettes and cabbage into the rice.
5. Add the egg, milk, seasoning and half the cheese.
6. Put in an ovenproof dish.
7. Mix breadcrumbs with remaining cheese and sprinkle on top of rice. Bake in oven for about 30 minutes or until crust is crisp.

COURGETTE CHUTNEY
(Makes approximately 3 x 450 g (1lb) jars)

- 700 g (1½ lb/3 cups) courgettes, medium sliced
- 1½ tbsp salt (to taste)
- 225 g (8 oz/1 cup) onion, chopped
- 3 garlic cloves, chopped
- 350 g (12 oz) Muscovado sugar
- 900 ml (30 fl oz/1½ pints/3¾ cups) red wine vinegar
- 225 g (8 oz) raisins
- 1 tbsp coriander seeds, crushed
- 2 tbsp brown mustard seeds
- 1 tbsp fresh root ginger, peeled and finely chopped
- 2 dried chillies

1. Mix the courgettes with ½ tablespoon of the salt and leave to drain in a colander for about an hour. Rinse, drain and pat dry.
2. Put courgettes in a hot pan, add onion,

garlic, remaining salt, sugar, and red wine vinegar. Bring to the boil, simmer gently until sugar has dissolved and vegetables are soft.

3 Add raisins, coriander seeds, mustard seeds, ginger and chillies. Check seasoning.

4 Mix well and simmer for about another 35 minutes or until chutney is thick, stirring frequently.

5 Cool slightly and put into warm, dry sterilised jars.

COURGETTE WITH TAGLIATELLE, WHITE WINE AND RICOTTA CHEESE
(Serves 4)

- *4 tbsp olive oil*
- *1 onion, thinly sliced*
- *2 cloves garlic, crushed*
- *450g (1 lb) courgettes,* thinly sliced
- *4 tbsp white wine*
- *450 g (1 lb) tagliatelle*
- *3 tbsp Ricotta cheese*
- *3 tbsp Parmesan, grated*
- *2 tsp balsamic vinegar*
- *Salt and black pepper*

1 Heat oil in a pan, sauté onion and garlic for about 3-4 minutes.

2 Add courgettes and sauté until they are just cooked.

3 Add wine, boil off the alcohol, cover and simmer until courgettes are soft.

4 Put tagliatelle into boiling salted water, bring back to the boil, reduce heat and simmer until cooked. Drain and return to the pan.

5 Add courgettes, Ricotta, Parmesan and stir over heat

for a couple of minutes, then add balsamic vinegar.

6 Season and serve.

LEEK, POTATO AND CHEESE PIE WITH FILO PASTRY
(Serves 6)

- *1-2 tbsp olive oil*
- *700 g (1½ lb/3 cups) leeks, washed and sliced*
- *1 onion, chopped*
- *2 medium potatoes, peeled and thinly sliced*
- *Salt and black pepper*
- *6 sheets frozen filo pastry, defrosted*
- *50 g butter or margarine, melted*
- *50 g (2 oz/½ cup) walnuts, toasted and chopped*
- *175 g (6 oz) grated Gorgonzola cheese or Cheddar cheese*

1 Preheat oven 200ºC (400ºF/Gas 6).

2 Heat some of the oil in pan. Add leeks and onion and sauté, stirring occasionally, until softened. Remove from the pan and set aside.

3 Heat oil in pan, add potatoes. Sauté on each side until the potatoes are crisp. Season and add to leeks and onions.

4 Place 2 sheets of filo pastry on a 24 cm (9½") greased baking tray, allowing the pastry sheets to extend over the edge. Brush with a little melted butter or margarine.

5 Add two more layers with the 4 remaining sheets of filo pastry brushing each layer with a little melted butter or margarine.

6 Layer leek, potatoes, walnuts and cheese in the centre of the pastry.
7 Gather the filo pastry up over the centre of the pie to cover top and pinch together to seal.
8 Brush with melted butter or margarine and bake in the oven for about 20 minutes or until the pastry is crisp and golden.

LEEKS AND POTATOES WITH WHITE WINE AND ROSEMARY
(Serves 6)
- 2 tbsp olive oil
- 50 g (2 oz/½ stick) butter or margarine
- 900 g (2 lbs/4 cups) potatoes, peeled and thinly sliced
- 350 g (12 oz/1½ cups) leeks, washed and chopped
- 225 ml (8 fl oz/1 cup) vegetable stock
- 225 ml (8 fl oz/1 cup) dry white wine
- 1 tbsp fresh rosemary or 1 tsp dried
- Salt and black pepper

1 Heat oil and butter or margarine in a pan. Add potatoes and leeks and cook for about 8 minutes, stirring occasionally, turning potato slices until translucent.
2 Add vegetable stock, wine and rosemary.
3 Season to taste.
4 Bring to the boil, reduce heat and simmer until potatoes are tender.
5 Uncover and cook until most of the liquid is absorbed.
6 Serve.

ONION AND LIME SOUP WITH HERB DUMPLINGS
(Serves 4-6)
- 2 tbsp olive oil
- 900 g (2 lb/4 cups) onions, peeled and thinly sliced
- 2-5 garlic cloves, crushed
- 1 green chilli, seeded, and finely chopped
- 1 large tomato, chopped
- 1 L (1¾ pints) vegetable stock
- Juice and zest of a fresh lime
- Salt and black pepper

Dumplings
- 4 oz self-raising flour
- ¼ level tsp salt
- ½ tsp dried mixed herbs
- 50 g (2 oz) shredded vegetable suet
- About 4 tbsp water

1 Heat oil in a pan. Add the onions and cook them slowly for about 20 minutes, stirring frequently.
2 Increase the heat slightly and add the garlic and chilli. Sauté for about 2 minutes.
3 Add the tomato and stir for about 1 minute.
4 Add stock, lime juice and zest.
5 Season to taste.
6 Bring the soup to the boil, reduce heat and simmer gently, uncovered for about 25 minutes.
7 For the dumplings, sieve the flour and salt in a bowl and add mixed herbs and suet. Using a knife, stir in the water to form light, elastic dough. Gently knead the dough.

8   Divide the dough into 8 and shape into balls.
9   When the soup has simmered uncovered for 25 minutes, drop the dumplings gently into the soup.
10 Cover the pan with a tight-fitting lid and simmer gently for about 15 minutes or until cooked.
11 Serve in bowls.

ONION AND ORANGE RICE
(Serves 6)

- *3 tbsp water*
- *2 garlic cloves, crushed*
- *1 onion, finely chopped*
- *450 ml (16 fl oz/2 cups) orange juice*
- *450 ml (16 fl oz/2 cups) water*
- *450 g (1 lb/2 cups) long-grain white rice*
- *1 tsp dried oregano*
- *½ tsp cinnamon*
- *Salt and black pepper*

1   Heat 3 tablespoons of water in a pan and cook garlic and onion until just tender, about 3-4 minutes.
2   Add orange juice, water, rice, oregano, and cinnamon.
3   Season.
4   Bring to the boil, reduce heat and simmer until the liquid is absorbed, about 20 minutes.
5   Serve.

Marco Solari, is a professional chef and he gave us these recipes. His parents are Italian, and he grew up in London. He was always in the kitchen with his mum and grandparents who are all wonderful cooks. Marco says, "I believe that cooking and celebrating good food is truly an act of love".

POTATO BREAD FROM CERETO
Starter dough

- *2-3 medium potatoes (floury variety), boiled in their skins, peeled and mashed*
- *About 3 tbsp strong white flour*
- *25 g (1 oz) fresh yeast, diluted in a little warm water*

Bread dough

- *1250 g (2¾ lb) strong white flour*
- *1½ tbsp salt*
- *750-850 ml (1½ pints/30 fl oz) warm water*

1   Preheat oven 220ºC (425ºF/Gas 7).
2   For the **starter dough**, combine the slightly warm mashed potato with about 2 tablespoons of flour to form a dumpling-like dough.
3   Add diluted yeast and about 1 tablespoon of flour and mix thoroughly to form a soft, slightly wet dough.
4   Put the starter dough in a warm place, covered with a tea towel for 2 hours.
5   For the **bread dough**, combine the flour, salt and warm water with the starter dough.
6   Knead until you have a smooth elastic dough.
7   Return dough to a lightly floured bowl and cover with a tea towel. Leave to rise until it has doubled in size.
8   Knock air out of the dough and divide into 4 equal pieces.
9   Form into loaves, and place on trays lined with grease-proof paper.

10 **NOTE:** *set them well apart for loaves to grow.*

11 Bake for 30-40 minutes.

12 Transfer bread onto a cooling rack.

POTATO GNOCCHI WITH TOMATO AND BASIL
(Serves 4)
Tomato Sauce
- 1 medium onion, finely sliced
- 2 garlic cloves, finely sliced
- 8 tbsp olive oil
- 80 g (3 oz) butter
- 500 g carton of good quality Passata
- Salt to taste

Gnocchi
- 1 Kg (2.2 lbs) potatoes (floury potatoes are best), scrubbed
- 500 g (1 lb 2 oz) plain white flour (additional flour may be needed)
- A good pinch of salt

To finish
- Fresh basil leaves, chopped
- Parmigiano Reggiano (Parmesan) cheese, grated

1 For the **tomato sauce**, cook the onion and garlic in olive oil and butter until tender.

2 Add Passata and salt, bring to boil, reduce heat and simmer for 30 minutes.

3 Adjust seasoning and remove from heat.

4 For the **gnocchi**, cook potatoes with their skins in boiling water until tender. Cool slightly, remove skins and mash.

5 Mix the flour into the warm potatoes using your hands and work the dough on a well-floured work surface until you have a nice firm and smooth dough. It should not be too sticky.

6 On floured work surface, roll dough into long sausage like shapes and cut uniform little pieces of about 3 cm (1¼") x 2 cm (¾") in size.

7 Roll the gnocchi gently but firmly over the inside of a fork to obtain a pattern (optional).

8 Cook the gnocchi in plenty of boiling salted water. When they float to the surface of the water continue cooking for one minute.

9 Lift gnocchi out of the water with a slotted spoon and combine with the tomato sauce, fresh basil and cheese.

10 Serve and enjoy!

POTATO TART
(Makes 2 x 26 cm (10½") tarts)
Pasta
- 225 g (8 oz) strong white flour
- 150 g (5 oz) semolina
- A pinch of salt
- 2 medium eggs
- 110 ml–150 ml (¼ pint/4-5 fl oz) cold water

Filling
- 8-9 medium potatoes, scrubbed (dry variety are good for this recipe)
- 2 small-medium onions, finely sliced
- 2 garlic cloves, finely sliced
- 3-4 fresh rosemary sprigs
- 6-7 tbsp olive oil
- 70 g (2½ oz) butter
- 1½ tbsp tomato purée
- 120 g (4 oz) grated Parmesan cheese
- 200 ml (7 fl oz) milk

1 Preheat oven 190ºC (375ºF/Gas 5).
2 **To make the pasta**
3 Place flour, semolina and a pinch of salt into a large bowl.
4 Add the eggs and the water and whisk ingredients together with a fork.
5 Turn out onto a work surface and knead until you have a pliable dough. You may have to adjust the consistency by adding some extra flour or water.
6 Return this dough to the lightly floured bowl, cover and place in the fridge to rest for at least 30 minutes before using.

For the filling
7 Place potatoes in a large pot. Cover with water and quickly bring to the boil. Reduce heat and simmer until they are cooked. Drain and set aside.
8 While the potatoes are cooking, sauté the onion, garlic and rosemary in the olive oil and butter thoroughly for at least 15 minutes.
9 Add the tomato purée and continue cooking for a further 2-3 minutes, then set aside.
10 Peel the skins off the potatoes and mash them to a smooth consistency.
11 Remove and disregard the rosemary sprigs from the onion and garlic mixture.
12 Add mixture to the potatoes along with the cheese. Adjust seasoning with salt. You can add a little hot milk to enrich and slightly soften but the mixture should not be too soft.

To assemble
13 Grease a tart case with olive oil.
14 Roll out the pasta evenly until very thin, using a rolling pin or pasta machine.
15 Line tart case with pasta, leaving an overhang of 3 cm - 5 cm (1"–2").
16 Fill with potato making sure not to overfill - 2 cm (¾") height maximum.
17 Fold in overhang, and cover top with another sheet of pasta. Use water to stick pasta sheets together.
18 With a fork, pierce surface of tart all over, then brush with olive oil or beaten egg and bake for about 40 minutes. Turn over half-way through cooking to brown both sides evenly.

The tart is delicious eaten warm or cold the next day. Ideally store on a wooden board covered with a teacloth.

PUMPKIN STUFFED WITH PARSNIP AND POTATO
Looks spectacular served on Halloween night.

(Serves 8)
- *1 small-medium pumpkin*
- *Salt and black pepper*
- *1.4 Kg (3 lb/6 cups) parsnips, peeled and diced*
- *450 g (1 lb/2 cups) potatoes, peeled and diced*
- *50 g (2 oz) butter or margarine*
- *½ tsp ground nutmeg*
- *1 tsp mixed herbs*

1 Preheat oven 190ºC (375ºF/Gas 5).
2 Cut top off pumpkin and save.
3 Scoop out seeds and coarse inner fibres.
4 Season cavity with salt and pepper.
5 Place the pumpkin upright in an oven-proof dish with the top next to it.
6 Bake until tender, but firm enough to support filling, about 45 minutes.
7 Remove from oven and keep warm.
8 While pumpkin is cooking, boil the parsnips and potatoes together in salted water until tender, about 10-15 minutes. Drain and mash.
9 Add butter or margarine, nutmeg, and season to taste.
10 Fold in one tsp mixed dried herbs.
11 Place pumpkin shell on a serving dish. Fill with the mashed vegetables and replace the top.
12 To serve, spoon out the vegetables and scoop out a little of the baked pumpkin.

RED CABBAGE WITH APPLES AND DILL
(Serves 4)

- *2 tbsp olive oil*
- *1 onion, thinly sliced*
- *1 garlic clove, crushed*
- *1 medium head red cabbage, grated or cut into fine strips*
- *2 medium green apples, quartered, cored and thinly sliced*
- *2 tbsp white wine vinegar*
- *1 tbsp sugar*
- *2 tbsp fresh chopped dill or ¾ tsp dried dill*
- *Salt and black pepper*

1 Heat oil in a pan, add onion and cook until onion is soft.
2 Add garlic and cook for another minute.
3 Stir in the cabbage, cover and cook until cabbage has wilted.
4 Add apples, wine vinegar, sugar and dill. Season to taste.
5 Stir and continue to cook until apples are tender, about 10 minutes.
6 Serve.

RED CABBAGE, GREEN PEPPER AND CUCUMBER SALAD

- *450 g (1 lb/2 cups) red cabbage, grated*
- *1 medium onion, finely chopped*
- *1 green pepper, de-seeded and chopped*
- *1 cucumber, diced*
- *4 tbsp olive oil*
- *4 tbsp fresh lemon juice*
- *½ tsp Dijon mustard*
- *1 tsp caraway seeds*
- *½ tsp oregano*
- *Salt and black pepper*

1 In a bowl, combine red cabbage, onion, green pepper and cucumber. Mix well.
2 In a jar with a lid, add olive oil, lemon juice, mustard, caraway seeds, oregano, and seasoning. Shake vigorously until blended.
3 Pour dressing over vegetables and mix well.

VEGGIES IN THE HOLE
(Serves 4)

- *1 courgette, sliced*
- *1 medium parsnip, peeled cut into sticks*
- *2-3 medium carrots, cut into sticks*
- *1 green pepper, de-seeded and chopped*
- *1-2 tbsp olive oil*

Batter

- *125 g (4 oz) plain flour*
- *Pinch of salt*
- *1 egg, lightly beaten*
- *300 ml (10 fl oz/½ pint/1¼ cups) milk*

1. Preheat oven 220ºC (425ºF/Gas 7).
2. In a roasting tin, coat the vegetables with the oil.
3. Put in the oven and bake for about 10-12 minutes. Turn once during cooking and continue until they are slightly browned.
4. To make the **batter,** put flour and salt into a large bowl. Make the hollow in the centre with a wooden spoon and drop in the egg.
5. Slowly pour half the milk into the centre with the egg and beat until smooth.
6. Add the rest of the milk, beating continuously, until the batter is bubbly and has the consistency of single cream.
7. Pour batter over the roasted vegetables and bake for about 15 minutes or until golden in colour.
8. Cut into slices and serve.

Potato 'Tattie' Harvesting

FARMING NEWS FOR NOVEMBER

*P*otato grading or dressing weekly.

HARVESTING

Beetroot is harvested, netted in sacks and buried in furrows – an old-fashioned form of clamping. This is usually done by hand. The chicory is pulled, its green tops are taken off the root which are then shortened to 6 inches and planted at Cullerne in a polytunnel under 8 inches of soil. By January or February, chicory will have grown for winter salads.

From the fields come green cabbage, curly kale, red cabbage, beetroot, carrots, kohlrabi, parsnips swede, onions and leeks. Cullerne's last month provides green tomatoes, lettuce, oriental greens and spinach.

MAINTENANCE AND MACHINERY

At Cullerne, the wind-break hedges are weeded and mulched.

WEATHER

The weather – as wet as ever this month – hampers harvesting.

Curly Kale

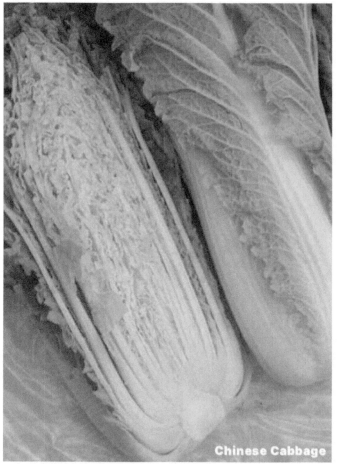

Chinese Cabbage

NOVEMBER
RECIPES

BEETROOT WITH MOODY BLUE CHEESE AND WALNUT
(Serves 6-8)

- *900 g (2 lb/4 cups) beetroot, scrubbed but not topped and tailed*
- *50 g (2 oz/4 tbsp) chopped walnuts*
- *1 tbsp olive oil*
- *2 medium onions, chopped*
- *50 g (2 oz/1 tbsp) brown sugar*
- *1-2 tbsp balsamic vinegar*
- *125 g (4 oz/½ cup) crumbled blue cheese*

1 Place beetroot in a pan with cold, salted water. Bring to the boil, cover the pan and return to the boil. Reduce heat and simmer until cooked, about one hour. Drain, rinse under cold water, rub off skins and cut into wedges. Set aside.

2 Place walnuts in a hot, dry frying pan until toasted, about 4 minutes, stirring frequently. Remove from pan and set aside.

3 Heat oil in frying pan, add onion and cook until soft but not browned. Add beetroot and stir.

4 Combine sugar and vinegar.

5 Add to frying pan and cook for about 2 minutes until the beetroot is glazed.

6 Either stir in toasted walnuts and blue cheese, or put the beetroot into a dish and sprinkle the walnuts and blue cheese on top.

7 Serve with rice.

BEETROOT AND CARROT SOUP
(Serves 6-8)

- *2 tbsp olive oil*
- *1 onion, chopped*
- *1 medium potato, peeled and sliced*
- *450 g (1 lb) beetroot, peeled and diced*
- *450 g (1 lb) carrots, sliced*
- *1 litre (1¾ pints) vegetable stock*
- *1 pinch of nutmeg*
- *Salt and black pepper*

To garnish:
- *Sour cream*

1 Heat oil in a pan and sauté onion and potato for about 10 minutes, stirring occasionally.

2 Add beetroot and carrots, cover and cook gently for a further 20 minutes.

3 Add stock, nutmeg, and bring to the boil, reduce heat and simmer for a further 10 minutes.

4 Liquidise, season and ladle into bowls with a swirl of sour cream over the top.

BEETROOT ROASTED WITH GARLIC
(Serves 4)

- *2 tbsp olive oil*
- *700 g (1½ lb/3 cups) beetroot, scrubbed, topped, tailed and quartered*
- *Salt and black pepper*
- *1½ large bulbs of garlic, peeled*
- *1 tbsp balsamic vinegar*
- *2 tbsp raspberry or red wine vinegar*
- *2 tbsp dry red wine*
- *1 clove*
- *1 tbsp sugar*
- *1 tbsp softened butter or margarine*

1 Preheat oven 190ºC (375ºF/Gas 5).

2 Mix olive oil and beetroot together. Season.

3 Place in a baking dish and bake for about 30 minutes.

4 Add garlic cloves to pan, mix and bake for about another 15 minutes or until beetroot is tender.

5 Place in a blender and add remaining ingredients. Purée until smooth. Adjust seasoning.

6 Serve with mashed potatoes.

BEETROOT WITH HONEY
(Serves 4)
- *450 g (1 lb/2 cups) beetroot, scrubbed but not topped and tailed*
- *1 tbsp vinegar*
- *1 tsp salt*
- *1 onion, chopped*
- *50 g (2 oz) margarine or butter*
- *2 tbsp honey*
- *1 tbsp lemon juice*
- *½ tsp salt*
- *¼ tsp cinnamon*
- *1 tbsp chopped parsley*

1 Place beetroot in a pan with water, vinegar and salt. Bring to the boil, cover and return to the boil. Reduce heat and simmer until cooked, about one hour.

2 Peel beetroot and cut into strips.

3 Sauté onion in pan with margarine or butter until onion is soft.

4 Stir in the beetroot, honey, lemon juice, salt and cinnamon and cook until hot, about five minutes.

5 Place in serving dish and sprinkle with chopped parsley.

CABBAGE STRUDEL
(Serves 6)
- *1 tbsp olive oil*
- *700 g (1½ lb/3 cups) cabbage, finely chopped*
- *1 medium onion, chopped*
- *350 g (12 oz) apples, peeled, cored and diced*
- *125 g (4 oz) pitted dates, chopped*
- *6 tbsp low fat sour cream or yoghurt*
- *1 tsp mustard*
- *8 sheets frozen filo pastry, thawed*
- *4 tbsp vegetable oil or melted margarine for brushing pastry*

1 Preheat oven 200ºC (400ºF/Gas 6).

2 Heat olive oil in pan, add cabbage and onion. Cover and cook for 5 minutes.

3 Place apples and dates in a bowl, add cabbage mixture.

4 Combine sour cream or yoghurt and mustard and mix well. Add to cabbage mixture and set aside.

5 Working with one filo pastry sheet at a time, brush each sheet with vegetable oil or melted margarine, placing one on top of the other, forming a stack.

6 Spoon cabbage mixture lengthwise down one-third of filo stack, leaving a 2.5 cm (1") border on longest sides and 1.85 cm (¾") on shortest sides.

7 Starting with the longest side, roll up stack like a Swiss roll and place seam side down on a greased baking tray. Tuck shortest ends under and brush

with melted margarine or vegetable oil.

8 Diagonally cut slits across the top.

9 Bake for about 25–40 minutes or until browned.

CABBAGE WEDGES IN CHEESE SAUCE
(Serves 4)

- *450 g (1 lb/2 cups) cabbage, cut into wedges*
- *1 medium onion, peeled and chopped*
- *1 green or red pepper, with seeds removed, chopped*
- *50 g (2 oz) butter or margarine*
- *50 g (2 oz/½ cup) plain flour*
- *425 ml (¾ pint) milk*
- *125 g (4 oz/½ cup) Cheddar cheese, grated*
- *1 tsp mustard*
- *¼ tsp nutmeg*

- *Salt and black pepper*

1 Preheat oven 180ºC (350ºF/Gas 4).

2 Place cabbage wedges and onion in boiling salted water and cook until just tender, about 10 minutes. Drain and place in baking dish with green or red pepper.

Cheese sauce:

3 Melt butter or margarine in pan, add flour and stir for one minute. Gradually add milk, stirring continuously, until sauce thickens.

4 Add grated cheese and stir until melted.

5 Add mustard and nutmeg. Season to taste.

6 Pour cheese sauce over vegetables and bake in the oven until browned and bubbly.

7 You can add extra breadcrumbs or cheese as a topping if you wish.

CARROT COOKIES WITH HONEY
(Makes about 30 cookies)

- *125 g (4 oz) butter or margarine*
- *225 g (8 oz/1 cup) sugar*
- *2 eggs, beaten*
- *3 tbsp honey*
- *1 tsp vanilla essence*
- *275 g (10 oz/2¼ cups) plain flour*
- *2 tsp bicarbonate of soda*
- *½ tsp freshly grated nutmeg*
- *¼ tsp salt*
- *125 g (4 oz) carrots, grated*

1 Preheat oven 160ºC (325ºF/Gas 3).

2 Beat together the butter or margarine and sugar until light and creamy.

3 Add eggs, honey and vanilla essence

4 Combine the flour, bicarbonate of soda, nutmeg and salt.

5 Fold dry ingredients into butter or margarine mixture.

6 Fold in carrot.

7 Using well-floured hands, shape rounded teaspoons of mixture into balls.

8 Grease a baking tray and place the cookies 5 cm (2") apart and bake for 12-15 minutes, or until edges are lightly browned.

9 Place on a wire rack to cool.

CARROTS WITH LEEKS AND DILL
(Serves 4)

- 450 g (1 lb/2 cups) carrots, peeled and cut into 0.6 cm (¼") thick pieces
- ½ tsp dill weed
- 1 tbsp olive oil
- 2 medium leeks, cut in half lengthwise, and then each half into very thin, long slivers. Wash well
- 1 tbsp olive oil
- 1 tsp cider vinegar
- Salt and black pepper

1 Place carrots and dill in a pan with cold, salted water. Bring to the boil, reduce heat and simmer until tender, about 10 minutes. Drain.
2 Heat oil in pan and sauté leeks until soft. Add carrots, oil, vinegar, salt and pepper.
3 Heat and serve.

CARROTS WITH LENTILS AND MARJORAM
(Serves 4)

- 2 tbsp olive oil
- 1 onion, chopped
- 2 garlic cloves, crushed
- 450 g (1 lb/2 cups) carrots, sliced into rounds 0.6 cm (¼") thick
- 225 g (8 oz/1 cup) red lentils
- 450 ml (16 fl oz/2 cups) stock
- 1 tsp dried marjoram
- Salt and black pepper

1 Heat oil in a pan. Add onion, garlic and sauté until soft, about five minutes.
2 Add carrots, lentils and stock. Cover, simmer until lentils are just tender and liquid absorbed, about 20 minutes. More liquid may be needed.
3 Mix in marjoram and season to taste.

CURLY KALE AND CHEESE BAKE
(Serves 4)

- 2 tbsp olive oil
- 1 onion, chopped
- 1 red or green pepper, de-seeded and chopped
- 450 g (1 lb/2 cups) curly kale, cut into thin strips
- Salt and black pepper
- 175 g (6 oz) Cheddar cheese, grated
- 2 tbsp Parmesan, grated

1 Preheat oven 180ºC (350ºF/Gas 4).
2 Heat oil in pan. Add onion and pepper and cook for about 5 minutes.
3 Add curly kale and cook until wilted, about 5 minutes. Season to taste.
4 Add the Cheddar cheese, stir well, and transfer to a baking dish.
5 Sprinkle Parmesan over the top, cover and bake for about 20 minutes.
6 Uncover and bake for about a further 10 minutes, until cheese is brown and bubbly.

CURLY KALE STIR FRY WITH LENTILS
(Serves 4)

- 450 g (1 lb/2 cups) curly kale, chopped
- 2 tbsp olive oil
- 1-2 tsp sesame oil
- 1 green pepper, de-seeded and chopped
- 1 onion, chopped
- 1.25 cm (½") piece of fresh root ginger, peeled and finely chopped
- 2 garlic cloves, crushed
- 2 tbsp sesame seeds

- 425 g (15 oz) red lentils, cooked
- 1 tsp soy sauce
- 3 tbsp water
- 1 tsp fresh lime juice
- Black pepper

1 Put kale into boiling, salted water. Bring back to boil, reduce heat and simmer until kale is tender. Drain.
2 Heat olive oil and sesame oil in a pan. Stir-fry the pepper, onion, ginger, garlic and sesame seeds over a high heat for about 3 minutes.
3 Add the kale, lentils, soy sauce, water and lime juice.
4 Season to taste.
5 Stir well, cover and simmer for about 5 minutes or until the vegetables are tender.

GREEN TOMATO CAKE
- 450 g (1 lb/2 cups) green tomatoes, skinned and chopped
- 225 ml (8 fl oz/1 cup) vegetable oil
- 400 g (14 oz/1¾ cups) sugar
- 3 eggs
- 1 tsp vanilla essence
- 350 g (12 oz/3 cups) plain flour
- 1 tsp baking powder
- 1 tsp bicarbonate of soda
- Pinch of salt
- ½ tsp cinnamon
- ½ tsp ginger
- 225 g (8 oz/1 cup) raisins
- 175 g (6 oz/1 cup) walnuts, chopped

1 Preheat oven 180ºC (350ºF/Gas 4).
2 Place tomatoes in a bowl of boiling water, leave for 2-3 minutes, remove skin and chop.
3 Beat together oil, sugar, eggs and vanilla essence until light and creamy.
4 Add the sieved flour, baking powder, bicarbonate of soda, salt, cinnamon and ginger. Mix well.
5 Add tomatoes, raisins and walnuts to cake mixture.
6 Pour mixture into a greased loaf or cake tin and bake for about 1 hour or until cooked. A knife inserted into the middle of the cake should come out clean when the cake is cooked.

GREEN TOMATO PIE
(Serves 6)
Pastry
- 150 g (5 oz) soft margarine
- 225 g (8 oz) plain flour
- 2 tbsp water

Sugar mixture
- 125 g (4 oz/½ cup) sugar
- 2 tsp plain flour
- Grated rind of one lemon
- ¼ tsp ground allspice
- ¼ tsp salt

Green tomato layer
- 900 g (2 lb/4 cups) green tomatoes, sliced
- 1 tsp lemon juice
- 25 g (1 oz) butter or margarine

1 Preheat oven 180ºC (350ºF/Gas 4).
To make the pastry
2 Put margarine with 2 tablespoons of flour and the water into a bowl. Cream with a fork until well mixed.
3 Still using the fork, work in the rest of the flour to form a manageable dough.
4 Turn onto a floured board and knead lightly until smooth.

152

5   Roll out and line a pie dish with two-thirds of the pastry.

Sugar mixture

6   Blend sugar, flour, lemon rind, allspice and salt together. Sprinkle a little of this on top of the pastry.

7   Arrange the tomato slices, a layer at a time, and put some sugar mixture, lemon juice and a dot of butter or margarine between each layer.

8   Keep layering until all tomatoes and sugar mixture are used.

9   Roll out remaining pastry, cut into strips and make a lattice top.

10 Bake for about 30 minutes, or until tomatoes are cooked and pastry is golden brown.

KOHLRABI WITH APPLES
(Serves 4)

- *50 g (2 oz/½ stick) butter or margarine*
- *450 g (1 lb/2 cups) kohlrabi, peeled and cut into thin slices*
- *225 g (8 oz/1 cup) cooking apples, peeled, cored and cut into thin wedges*
- *Salt and black pepper*

1   Melt butter or margarine in a pan and add kohlrabi slices. Sauté until just soft and starting to brown, stirring frequently.

2   Add apple wedges, salt and pepper to taste and continue to sauté until the apple is cooked, stirring frequently.

3   Serve.

KOHLRABI AND CARROT SALAD WITH PAPRIKA AND HORSERADISH
(Serves 4-6)

- *3 tbsp white wine vinegar*
- *1 tbsp paprika*
- *150 ml (¼ pint/5 fl oz) olive oil*
- *2 tsp creamed horseradish*
- *1½ tsp sugar*
- *Salt and black pepper*
- *450 g (1 lb/2 cups) kohlrabi, peeled and grated*
- *225 g (8 oz/1 cup) carrots, peeled and grated*

1   Put paprika, vinegar and oil in a bowl. Whisk until blended.

2   Mix in the creamed horseradish, sugar and season to taste.

3   Place kohlrabi and carrot in a bowl. Add dressing and stir well. Serve.

KOHLRABI WITH CINNAMON AND HERBS
(Serves 4-6)

- *700 g (1½ lb/3 cups) kohlrabi, peeled and diced*
- *1 onion, chopped*
- *1 tsp cinnamon*
- *1 tbsp vegetable oil*
- *1 tsp dried mixed herbs*
- *Salt and black pepper*
- *125 g (4 oz) fresh breadcrumbs*
- *25 g (1 oz) butter or margarine*

1   Preheat oven 180ºC (350ºF/Gas 4).

2   Place kohlrabi in a saucepan with salted water. Bring to the boil, cover the pan and quickly return to the boil. Reduce heat and simmer until just tender, about 15 minutes. Drain and cool.

153

3 Place kohlrabi in a bowl, add onion, cinnamon, oil, mixed herbs and season to taste.
4 Put into a greased baking dish.
5 Mix breadcrumbs with butter or margarine and sprinkle over top.
6 Bake in oven until golden, about 15-20 minutes.

LEEK AND POTATO SOUFFLÉ
(Serves 4)
- 50 g (2 oz) fresh breadcrumbs
- 450 g (1 lb/2 cups) potatoes, peeled and quartered
- 350 g (12 oz/11/2 cups) leeks, sliced and washed well
- 1 tbsp olive oil
- 2 garlic cloves, crushed
- ½ tsp dried oregano
- ½ tsp dried parsley
- 120 g (4 oz) Parmesan, grated
- 4 eggs, separated
- Salt and black pepper

1 Preheat oven 180ºC (350ºF/Gas 4).
2 Place potatoes in a pan with salted water. Bring to the boil, cover the pan and return to the boil. Reduce heat and simmer until cooked, about 15 minutes.
3 Drain, mash and keep warm.
4 Put leeks into boiling salted water and cook until tender, about 10 minutes. Drain and finely chop.
5 Heat olive oil, add garlic and cook for about 2 minutes, but do not brown.
6 Add leeks, oregano and parsley and cook for 2 more minutes. Take off heat.
7 Mix together leek mixture, potatoes, Parmesan, egg yolks and seasoning.
8 Beat egg whites until stiff and fold into leek mixture.
9 Spoon mixture into 30 cm (12") round baking dish and smooth out. Top with breadcrumbs mixed with a little olive oil and bake until golden, about 30 minutes.
10 Serve immediately.

LETTUCE, LEEK AND TARRAGON SOUP
(Serves 6)
- 50 g (2 oz/½ stick) butter or margarine
- 700 g (1½ lb/3 cups) leeks, sliced and washed well
- 1 garlic clove, crushed
- 950 ml (32 fl oz/1¾ pints/4 cups) vegetable stock
- 1 head of lettuce, washed and sliced into 2.5 cm (1") strips
- 1½ tsp dried tarragon
- Salt and black pepper

To garnish:
- Crème fraîche, sour cream or double cream

1 Melt butter or margarine in a pan. Add leeks and garlic. Sauté until soft and starting to turn golden, about 10 minutes.
2 Add stock, bring to the boil, reduce heat and simmer for about 15 minutes.
3 Stir in lettuce. Cook uncovered until lettuce has wilted, about 5 minutes.
4 Stir in tarragon and season to taste.
5 The soup can be

served like this or liquidised.

6 Put soup into individual bowls and swirl a little crème fraîche, sour cream or double cream over the top.

ONIONS CURRIED AND BAKED
(Serves 6)

- *700 g (1½ lb/3 cups) onions, sliced*
- *25 g (1 oz) butter or margarine*
- *2 tbsp plain flour*
- *¼ tsp cayenne pepper*
- *½ tsp curry powder*
- *¼ tsp paprika*
- *2 tsp bouillon*
- *225 ml (8 fl oz/1 cup) milk*
- *75 g (3 oz) mature Cheddar cheese, grated*
- *6 slices wholemeal bread, cut in triangles and toasted*

1 Preheat oven 180ºC (350ºF/Gas 4).

2 Place onions in a pan with enough water to cover them. Bring to the boil, reduce heat and simmer for about 10 minutes or until onions are soft. Drain.

3 Melt the butter or margarine in a pan. Over a gentle heat, stir in the flour with a wooden spoon until it makes a thick paste.

4 Add the cayenne, curry powder and paprika. Add the bouillon and stir in the milk gradually until you have a thick sauce.

5 Add the cheese, reserving 2 tablespoons for the top. Stir until the cheese has melted.

6 Place the toast in a buttered casserole dish. Cover with the drained onions.

7 Pour the sauce over them and sprinkle with remaining cheese.

8 Bake in the oven for 20 minutes or until the cheese is bubbly and browned.

PARSNIP CHIPS (FRENCH FRIES)
(Serves 4-6)

- *900 g (2 lb/4 cups) parsnips, peeled and cut into chips*
- *Vegetable oil for frying*
- *1 tbsp celery salt*
- *1½ tsp dried dill*
- *½ tsp black pepper*

1 Fry the parsnips in hot vegetable oil until golden brown. Transfer with a slotted spoon onto paper towels to drain.

2 In a small bowl mix celery salt, dill and pepper and sprinkle over parsnip chips.

PARSNIP CURRY WITH PEANUTS
(Serves 4)

- *1 onion, chopped*
- *1 tbsp olive oil*
- *½ tsp ground cumin*
- *½ –1 tsp chilli powder*
- *1½ tsp turmeric*
- *½ tsp cayenne pepper*
- *150 ml (¼ pint/5 fl oz) water*
- *Salt and black pepper*
- *450 g (1 lb/2 cups) parsnip, peeled and cubed*
- *125 g (4 oz/½ cup) peanuts*

To garnish:

- *1 medium green pepper, cut into thin strips*

1 Sauté onion in oil for about 5 minutes, or until golden.

2 Add cumin, chilli

powder, turmeric, and cayenne pepper. Cook, stirring, for one minute.

3 Add water, parsnips, salt and pepper and bring to the boil. Cover, and simmer for about 15–20 minutes until the parsnips are tender but not mushy. The sauce will become quite thick. Add more water if necessary.

4 Add peanuts and heat through.

5 Transfer to dish and garnish with strips of green pepper.

6 Serve with rice, chutneys and desiccated coconut.

PARSNIP AND POTATO GRATIN
(Serves 4-6)

- *450 g (1 lb/2 cups) parsnip, peeled and sliced*
- *450 g (1 lb/2 cups) potato, peeled and thinly sliced*
- *300 ml (½ pint/1¼ cups) double cream*
- *2 tsp creamed horseradish*
- *Salt and black pepper*
- *90 g (3 oz) grated Cheddar cheese*

1 Preheat oven 180ºC (350ºF/Gas 4).

2 Combine all ingredients except cheese in a heavy-bottomed saucepan. Bring liquid to boil, reduce heat and simmer gently for about 5 minutes.

3 Transfer mixture into baking dish.

4 Top with grated cheese and bake for about 30 minutes or until potatoes are tender.

PUMPKIN WITH LEMONY LENTILS
(Serves 4-6)

- *600 ml (1 pint/ 2½ cups) vegetable stock*
- *1 medium onion, chopped*
- *225 g (8 oz/1 cup) lentils*
- *350 g (12 oz/1½ cups) pumpkin, peeled and diced*
- *3 tbsp lemon juice*
- *½ tsp dried parsley*
- *¾ tsp ground ginger*
- *¼ tsp ground cumin*
- *Salt and black pepper*

1 Put stock in a pan, add onion and lentils. Bring to the boil, reduce heat, cover and simmer for about 15 minutes, stirring occasionally.

2 Add pumpkin, lemon juice, parsley, ginger, cumin, salt and pepper. Stir and cook until pumpkin is tender, about 20 minutes.

3 Serve with herb roasted potatoes.

PUMPKIN SWEET AND SOUR
(Serves 6-8)

- *1 x 1.4 Kg (3 lb) pumpkin, peeled, seeded and cut into 2.5 cm (1") cubes*
- *1 tsp dried mint*
- *4 tbsp water*
- *1 medium onion, chopped*
- *3 tbsp cider vinegar*
- *2 tbsp brown sugar*
- *Salt and black pepper*

1 Preheat oven 180ºC (350ºF/Gas 4).

2 In a bowl, mix all ingredients together.

3 Transfer to a 5 cm (2") deep baking dish. Cover, put in the oven and bake for 30 minutes.

4 Remove from the oven and uncover. If

mixture seems dry, add a little more water, re-cover and return to oven.

5 If it seems watery, return to the oven uncovered. Continue to cook until pumpkin is tender, about 15 minutes. Taste for seasoning.

6 Serve with crunchy roast potatoes and green vegetables.

RED CABBAGE WITH RED WINE
(Serves 6)

- *1 onion, peeled and sliced*
- *900 g (2 lb/4 cups) red cabbage, sliced finely*
- *900 g (2 lb/4 cups) apples, unpeeled, cored and sliced*
- *225 ml (8 fl oz/1 cup) vegetable stock*
- *4 tbsp red wine*
- *4 tbsp red wine vinegar*
- *4 tbsp brown sugar*
- *Salt and black pepper*

1 In a large pan, place onion, red cabbage, apples and stock, bring to the boil, cover, reduce heat and simmer until cabbage is crisp-tender.

2 Add red wine, red wine vinegar, brown sugar and season to taste.

3 Cover and continue to simmer stirring occasionally until the vegetables are cooked.

SPINACH WITH CHEESY MASHED POTATOES
(Serves 6)

- *900 g (2 lb/4 cups) fresh spinach, washed*
- *1.4 Kg (3 lb/6 cups) potatoes, peeled and chopped*
- *120 g (4 oz/½ cup) butter or margarine*
- *300 ml (½ pint/1¼ cups) milk, warmed*
- *180 g (6 oz) Swiss cheese or Cheddar cheese*
- *Salt and black pepper*

1 Place washed spinach in a large pan with no extra water. Sprinkle with a little salt, cover and cook gently until it wilts, about 5 minutes. Drain and set aside.

2 Place potatoes in a pan with salted water. Bring to the boil, cover and return to the boil. Reduce heat and simmer until tender, about 15 minutes. Drain and return to pan.

3 Mash the potato and add the butter or margarine and milk gradually. Mix until smooth.

4 Add cheese and spinach, stirring until cheese melts. Season to taste.

SPINACH WITH COCONUT AND GINGER
(Serves 4)

- *1 tbsp olive oil*
- *1 tsp mustard seeds*
- *½ tsp whole cumin seeds*
- *1 tbsp brown sugar*
- *2 tsp grated fresh ginger or 1 tsp ground ginger*
- *900 g (2 lb/4 cups) spinach, washed*
- *125 g (4 oz/½ cup) desiccated coconut*
- *Salt and black pepper*
- *2 tbsp water*
- *Pinch of nutmeg*

To garnish:

- *Lemon wedges*

1 Heat oil in large pan. When hot, add

mustard seeds, cumin seeds and brown sugar. Fry until the seeds darken and the sugar caramelises.

2 Add the ginger, spinach, coconut, salt and pepper.

3 Cover, reduce heat to low and cook for about 10 minutes.

4 Uncover, stir and add a little water if necessary, and cook for a further 5- 10 minutes. Stir in the nutmeg.

5 Garnish with lemon wedges.

SPINACH AND RICE BAKE
(Serves 4)

- *700 g (1½ lb/3 cups) fresh spinach*
- *125 g (4 oz/½ cup) rice*
- *125 g (4 oz/½ cup) Cheddar cheese, grated*
- *2 eggs, beaten*
- *300 ml (½ pint/1¼ cups) milk*
- *50 g (2 oz) butter or margarine*
- *1 medium onion, chopped finely*
- *1 tbsp Worcestershire sauce*
- *1 tsp dried thyme or 1 tbsp fresh thyme*

1 Preheat oven 180ºC (350ºF/Gas 4).

2 Place washed spinach in a pan with no extra water. Sprinkle with a little salt, cover and cook gently, shaking the pan occasionally for about 5 minutes. Drain and set aside.

3 Put rice into boiling salted water. Boil rapidly until cooked. Drain rice and rinse it under hot water. Return to pan.

4 Combine spinach

with rice and rest of the ingredients in a large bowl.

5 Pour into a greased baking dish. Cover and bake for about 20 minutes.

6 Uncover and bake for 5 minutes more, or until browned.

SWEDE CURRY
(Serves 4)

- *3 tsp desiccated coconut*
- *3 tsp ground almonds*
- *3 tsp poppy seeds*
- *3 tsp coriander seeds*
- *150 ml (¼ pint/5 fl oz) plain yoghurt*
- *1 tsp ground ginger*
- *½-1 tsp chilli powder*
- *2 tbsp vegetable oil*
- *225 g (8 oz) onions, peeled and sliced*
- *3 garlic cloves, crushed*
- *450 g (1 lb/2 cups) swede, peeled and*

diced
- *4 tbsp water*
- *Salt and black pepper*

1 Dry roast coconut, almonds, poppy seeds, and coriander seeds in a hot frying pan and grind to a fine paste.

2 Add yoghurt, ground ginger and chilli powder. Set aside.

3 Heat oil, add onions and garlic and fry until light brown.

4 Add swede to the pan and fry until light brown.

5 Add yoghurt mixture and cook for about 5 minutes, stirring occasionally.

6 Add water, salt and pepper, cover and simmer gently for 15-20 minutes, or until the swede is tender and the sauce is thick.

SWEDE WITH POPPY SEEDS AND PAPRIKA

(Serves 4-6)

- 50 g (2 oz) butter or margarine
- 900 g (2 lb/4 cups) swede, peeled and diced
- 2 tbsp poppy seeds
- 1-2 tsp paprika
- 4 tbsp red wine vinegar
- Salt and black pepper

1. In a pan, heat the butter or margarine. Add swede and stir.
2. Add poppy seeds and sauté for about 10 minutes until light golden brown.
3. Add paprika, stir well.
4. Add vinegar, cook until evaporated, about 5 minutes, or until swede is soft. You may need to add a little water. Season to taste.
5. Serve.

Sprout Snippet: What is the difference between a pumpkin, a squash and a gourd?
They are all members of the cucurbit family.

Summer squash *is usually eaten as a vegetable and is picked when the rind is immature and soft, and the plant is still living.*
Zucchini, or courgette and crookneck squash *are in the summer squash group.*

Winter squash *is also eaten as a vegetable but is harvested after the plant has died and the rind has matured and become hard.* **Butternut** *and* **acorn squash** *are in this group..*

Pumpkins *have a hollow seed cavity and a thick rind. In the UK it is eaten as a vegetable and is also suitable for carving into Halloween lanterns. The pumpkin recipes in this book can also be used for winter squash.*

Gourds *have a much harder rind than winter squash or pumpkin and are used for their ornamental value and are often used to make bowls and oil lamps.*

Beetroot

Pumpkin and Squash

FARMING NEWS FOR DECEMBER

*E*arthShare is now settling into the winter routine. Part of this routine is potato grading or dressing.

☁ WEATHER

It is definitely going to be cold, with varying degrees of rain, snow and wind.

Latest farming news: *Mathis and Marianne Rosenbusch are starting a FruitShare Scheme in partnership with EarthShare. This is an unusual and creative response to the request from many subscribers for more fruit. The FruitShare box will contain oranges, tangerines, lemons, almonds, walnuts in shells and olives in brine, plus a surprise. This will be available to subscribers in early March.*

They are restoring a traditional Spanish farmhouse in the Alpujarra Valley, Andalucia, Spain, and are living and farming here between November and February. They have 10 acres of land with 130 black olive trees from which they are producing single farm virgin olive oil. Single farm virgin olive oil is the olive oil equivalent to single malt whisky.

Olives from their groves are picked, sometimes with the help of neighbours and taken to the local mill straight away. This ensures that they are pressed when freshly picked. Mathis stays at the mill while the oil is being pressed so that his olives are not mixed with those from other farms. Once pressed, it is poured into 25 litre cans. Because the oil is unfiltered from the press, it is left to settle for about 4-6 weeks before bottling.

The main benefit is that the olives are not rotting before they are pressed and this makes high quality oil. Mathis and Marianne believe that small-scale production results in a quality product. The fruit and nuts are grown on their own farm with some coming from their neighbours as they do not have enough trees yet.

 HARVESTING

From the fields, Brussels sprouts, red and white cabbage curly kale, carrots, parsnips, swede and kohlrabi are harvested.

⚙ MAINTENANCE AND MACHINERY

At EarthShare, general maintenance of machinery. At Cullerne, preservative stain is put on the wooden cold frames and doors of the tunnels. Christopher also plans next year's crops and orders seeds.

Parsnips

Brussels Sprouts

DECEMBER
RECIPES

BEETROOT WITH HORSERADISH
(Serves 4)

- *450 g (1 lb/2 cups) medium to small beetroot, scrubbed but not topped and tailed*
- *150 ml (¼ pint/5 fl oz) sour cream*
- *½ tbsp creamed horseradish*
- *1 tbsp chopped chives or parsley*
- *Coarsely ground black pepper*

1 Place beetroot in a saucepan with salted water. Bring to the boil, cover the pan and return to the boil. Reduce heat and simmer until cooked, about one hour depending on size. Drain and peel.

2 Mix sour cream and horseradish sauce together.

3 Place beetroot onto serving dish and make a deep cross-shaped cut into each beetroot and pour horseradish mixture over.

4 Garnish with chives or parsley and coarsely ground black pepper.

BEETROOT, ORANGE GLAZED
(Serves 4)

- *450 g (1 lb/2 cups) beetroot, scrubbed but not topped and tailed*
- *50 g (2 oz) butter or margarine*
- *1 tbsp flour*
- *2 tbsp brown sugar*
- *150 ml (¼ pint/5 fl oz) fresh orange juice*

1 Place beetroot in a pan with salted water. Bring to the boil, cover the pan and quickly return to the boil. Reduce heat and simmer until cooked, about one hour. Drain, peel and slice.

2 In a small pan melt butter or margarine, add flour and stir well. Add the brown sugar and gradually the orange juice. Stir until thickened.

3 Add the beetroot to the sauce and serve immediately.

BEETROOT AND ORANGE SOUP
(Serves 4)

- *450 g (1 lb/2 cups) beetroot with leaves*
- *1 litre (1¾ pints) vegetable stock*
- *2 tsp red wine vinegar*
- *½ tsp ground coriander*
- *Salt and black pepper*
- *225 ml (8 fl oz/1 cup) fresh orange juice*

To garnish:
- *Orange slices and fresh coriander*

1 Cut the leaves off the beetroot, wash and chop them and put them in a pan.

2 Scrub beetroot well. Finely grate in a food processor or grater.

3 Add beetroot to the pan with the leaves and vegetable stock.

4 Bring to the boil, cover and simmer for 25 minutes or until cooked

5 Add vinegar, coriander, orange juice and season.

6 Soup can be served like this or blended in a food processor until smooth.

To garnish:

7 Orange slices and fresh coriander.

BRUSSELS SPROUTS WITH CHESTNUTS
(Serves 6)

- *700 g (1½ lb/3 cups) Brussels sprouts, washed and trimmed*
- *225 g (8 oz) chestnuts*
- *1 tbsp olive oil*
- *½ tsp dried rosemary*
- *½ tsp dried tarragon*
- *½ tsp ground cumin*
- *1 tbsp cornflour*
- *275 ml (½ pint/1¼ cups) vegetable stock*
- *Salt and black pepper*

1 Preheat oven 180ºC (350ºF/Gas 4).
2 Bring salted water to the boil, add Brussels sprouts, cover the pan and return to the boil. Reduce heat and simmer for about 5 minutes until just cooked. Drain.
3 Take chestnuts, and with a sharp knife, make an X on the bottom of each one. Brush each chestnut with oil and bake in the oven for about 15 minutes or just cooked. Cool and shell.
4 Mix sprouts with chestnuts, rosemary, tarragon, and cumin, and transfer to a baking dish.
5 Mix the cornflour with a little stock to make a paste. Add to the rest of the stock and cook until it thickens, stirring frequently. Season to taste. Pour over the vegetables.
6 Bake in oven for about 20 minutes.

BRUSSELS SPROUTS WITH ORANGE LIQUEUR
(Serves 4)

- *450 g (1 lb/2 cups) Brussels sprouts, washed and trimmed*
- *25 g (1 oz) butter or margarine*
- *2 tbsp orange-flavoured liqueur (or use fresh orange juice)*
- *Salt and black pepper*

1 Bring salted water to the boil, add Brussels sprouts, cover the pan and return to the boil. Reduce heat and simmer until just tender, about 10 minutes. Drain into a serving dish and keep warm.
2 Heat butter or margarine in a small pan, add orange-flavoured liqueur or orange juice. Heat one minute longer. Season to taste.
3 Pour over Brussels sprouts. Serve.

BRUSSELS SPROUTS ORIENTAL STYLE
(Serves 6-8)

- *900 g (2 lb/4 cups) Brussels sprouts, washed and trimmed*
- *1 tsp soy sauce*
- *Black pepper*
- *25 g (1 oz) butter or margarine*
- *150 g (5 oz) tinned water chestnuts, drained and sliced*

1 Bring salted water to the boil, add Brussels sprouts, cover the pan and return to the boil. Reduce heat and simmer until just tender, about 10 minutes. Drain and return to pan.
2 Add other ingredients and heat through.
3 Transfer to serving dish.

CABBAGE AND CARROT BHAJI
(Serves 4)

- 1 tbsp coriander seeds, crushed
- ½ tsp cumin seeds
- 1-2 dried chillies or ½ tsp chilli powder
- 450 g (2 cups) cabbage, chopped finely or grated
- 225 g (8 oz/1 cup) carrots, diced
- 90 g (3½ oz) tomatoes, chopped
- ¼ tsp turmeric
- Salt and black pepper

1 Dry-fry coriander seeds, cumin seeds, chillies or chilli powder for about 1-2 minutes.
2 Add the cabbage, carrots, tomatoes and turmeric.
3 Mix thoroughly.
4 Season to taste.
5 Reduce heat, cover and simmer for 15-20 minutes.
6 Vegetables should be a little crunchy. You may need to add a little water.

CABBAGE, CARROT AND ONION CURRY
(Serves 4)

- 1 tbsp olive oil
- 2 large onions, peeled and cut into small pieces
- 2-4 garlic cloves, crushed
- ¼ tsp mustard seeds
- ½ tsp ground cumin
- ¼ tsp ground coriander
- ¼ tsp turmeric
- 450 g (1 lb/2 cups) carrots, cut into thin rounds
- 450 g (1 lb/2 cups) cabbage, cut into small pieces
- ¼ tsp chilli powder
- ¼ tsp cinnamon
- 1 tin (400 ml) coconut milk
- Salt and black pepper

1 In a pan, heat oil and sauté onion and garlic until soft.
2 Add mustard seeds, cumin, coriander and turmeric.
3 Add carrots to the pan and cook with the lid on for about 5 minutes.
4 Now add cabbage and mix well.
5 Add chilli powder, cinnamon, and coconut milk. Season to taste.
6 Put lid back on and cook for about 15 minutes or until cooked.
7 Serve hot with rice.

CABBAGE WITH GIN AND JUNIPER
(Serves 4)

- 450 g (1 lb/2 cups) cabbage, cut length-wise into 6 wedges, leaving core intact
- 2 shallots or one onion, chopped
- 50 g (2 oz) butter or margarine
- 1 tsp dried mixed herbs
- 6 juniper berries
- 75 ml (3 fl oz) gin
- Salt and black pepper

1 Bring 1 litre (1¾ pints) of salted water to the boil. Add cabbage, bring back to the boil. Reduce heat and simmer for 10 minutes or until just cooked. Drain and put aside.
2 In a hot pan, sauté shallots or onion in butter or margarine with mixed herbs and juniper berries, stirring occasionally, until soft.
3 Add the gin, salt and pepper to taste and cook for about one minute.
4 Add cabbage wedges, cut sides

down, and cook them for about 6 minutes, carefully turning once.

5   Transfer to a heated serving dish and pour the pan juices over it.

CARROT CHRISTMAS PUDDING
(Makes 2 puddings)

- *225 g (8 oz/1 cup) brown sugar*
- *120 g (4 oz/1 stick) butter or margarine*
- *1 egg*
- *225 g (8 oz/1 cup) carrots, peeled and grated*
- *225 g (8 oz/1 cup) potatoes, peeled and grated*
- *225 g (8 oz/1 cup) apples, cored and grated*
- *225 g (8 oz/1 cup) raisins*
- *225 g (8 oz/1 cup) currants*
- *150 g (5 oz/1¼ cups) plain flour*
- *1 tsp bicarbonate of soda*
- *1 tsp allspice*
- *1 tsp cinnamon*
- *½ tsp nutmeg, grated*
- *¼ tsp ground cloves*
- *½ tsp salt*

1   Cream together sugar, butter or margarine and add the egg.
2   Add carrots, potatoes, apples, raisins, and currants. Mix well.
3   Combine flour with bicarbonate of soda, allspice, cinnamon, nutmeg, cloves and salt.
4   Fold into creamed mixture.
5   Divide mixture into two buttered pudding bowls; leave at least 5 cm (2") at the top.
6   Cover with a double thickness of greaseproof paper and secure tightly with string around the outside of the bowl.
7   Place each pudding bowl in a pan of boiling water – fill up to the neck of the bowl.
8   Boil for 3 hours.

CARROTS WITH COCONUT
(Serves 4)

- *4 tbsp desiccated coconut*
- *450 g (1 lb/2 cups) carrots, cut cross-wise into slices*
- *50 g (2 oz) butter or margarine*
- *1 tsp salt*
- *½ tsp ground nutmeg*

1   Dry fry coconut in a hot pan until lightly browned and fragrant. Watch carefully so that the coconut does not burn. Set aside.
2   Put carrots in salted water in a pan, bring to the boil, reduce heat and simmer until soft.
3   Drain and put back into pan, add the butter or margarine and stir. Add salt and ground nutmeg.
4   Put carrots into serving dish, and sprinkle coconut over the top.

CARROT COINS
(Serves 4)

- *450 g (1 lb/2 cups) carrots, peeled and sliced into thin rounds or coins*
- *150 ml (¼ pint/5 fl oz) water*
- *2 tbsp brown sugar*
- *25 g (1 oz) butter or margarine*
- *1 tsp cider vinegar*
- *Salt and black pepper*

1. Place carrots in a pan with water. Bring to boil, then reduce heat. Cover and simmer for about 7 minutes, or until water has nearly evaporated and the carrots are soft.
2. Uncover carrots and add sugar, butter or margarine, and cider vinegar.
3. Turn up the heat and sauté, stirring for 2–3 minutes. A copper-coloured glaze will form over the carrots.
4. Season and serve.

CARROT AND HONEY CUSTARD
(Serves 4)
- 4 eggs
- 125 g (4 oz/½ cup) honey
- ¼ tsp salt
- 600 ml (1 pint/2½ cups) milk
- 175 g (6 oz/¾ cup) carrots, finely grated
- 2 tbsp sherry
- Grated orange peel
- ¼ tsp ground cinnamon

1. Preheat oven 180°C (350°F/Gas 4).
2. Beat eggs with honey and salt until frothy and light, then stir in milk.
3. Add carrots, sherry, and orange peel.
4. Pour mixture into greased baking dish and sprinkle top with cinnamon.
5. Put baking dish in a baking pan and add water to the pan so it is halfway up the baking dish.
6. Bake for about 40 minutes or until custard is firm.

CARROT AND ONION SOUFFLE
(Serves 4)
- 1 onion, chopped
- 225 g (8 oz/1 cup) carrots, grated
- 1 clove garlic, crushed
- 2 tbsp water
- 300 ml (½ pint/1¼ cups) skimmed milk
- 50 g (2 oz) oat bran
- 2 tbsp fresh parsley, chopped
- ¼ tsp ground nutmeg
- Salt and black pepper
- 4 eggs, separated
- 225 g (8 oz/1 cup) Cheddar cheese, grated

1. Preheat oven 160°C (325° F/Gas 3).
2. In a pan, add onion, carrots, garlic and water. Bring to boil, reduce heat. Cover, stir and simmer until vegetables are tender.
3. Do not drain.
4. Add milk, oat bran, parsley, nutmeg and seasoning.
5. Bring to boil, stirring constantly. Cook and stir for about 2 minutes. Stir in egg yolks and remove from heat.
6. Add cheese and stir until melted. Cool slightly.
7. In a large bowl, beat egg whites until stiff peaks form. Fold in the vegetable mixture.
8. Pour into a greased soufflé dish. Bake for 40–50 minutes or until top is brown and a knife inserted near the centre comes out clean.
9. Serve immediately.

CARROT, PARSNIP, POTATO AND SWEDE ROASTED WITH HERBS
(Serves 4-6)

- 125 g (4 oz) each of swede, carrots, parsnips, potatoes, peeled and cut into wedges
- 2 medium onions, peeled and cut into quarters
- 1–3 cloves garlic, chopped or crushed
- 3 tbsp olive oil
- 1 tbsp chopped, fresh mixed herbs or 1 tsp dried mixed herbs
- Salt and black pepper

1 Preheat oven 180°C (350°F/Gas 4).
2 Place vegetables in a large bowl, add garlic, olive oil, mixed herbs and seasoning. Mix until vegetables have a good coating of oil.
3 Place in oven and bake for about 25 minutes or until cooked. Stir at least once during cooking.

CARROT PÂTÉ
(Serves 4)

- 450 g (1 lb/2 cups) carrots, sliced
- 1 medium onion, chopped
- 1–3 garlic cloves, chopped
- ¼ tsp dill
- 2 tbsp olive oil
- 1 tbsp cornflour made into paste with 1 tbsp water
- 1 tbsp bouillon
- 1 tbsp tahini
- Salt and black pepper

1 In a pan, sauté the carrots, onion, garlic and dill in the olive oil for 2–3 minutes.
2 Add water, bring to the boil, reduce heat, cover, and simmer until carrots are tender, about 10-15 minutes.
3 Drain and purée the carrots in blender until smooth. Return to saucepan.
4 Combine cornflour, bouillon, tahini and seasoning together. Add this mixture to the puréed carrots.
5 Bring to a slow simmer, stirring constantly, and cook until the pâté detaches itself from the sides of the pan.
6 Remove from heat, turn pâté out onto a lightly oiled serving dish and let cool.
7 Serve with crackers, toast, or as a dip with crisp, raw vegetables.

CARROT PILAU WITH DATES
(Serves 4-6)

- 4 tbsp olive oil
- 225 g (8 oz/1 cup) carrots, diced
- 1 onion, sliced
- 2 cloves garlic, crushed
- 450 g (1 lb/2 cups) rice
- ½ tsp ground turmeric
- 3 tbsp dark raisins
- 12 pitted dates, chopped
- Freshly ground black pepper

1 Heat 1 tablespoon of oil in a pan and fry carrots, onion and garlic for about 3 minutes. Remove and set aside.
2 Put rice into boiling salted water. Boil rapidly until just cooked. Drain and rinse under cold water and add to carrots and onion.
3 Put 2 tablespoons of oil in a pan, add 2 tablespoons water

and turmeric. Stir.

4 Mix rice, carrots, onion, raisins and dates together and add to the oil and turmeric mixture.

5 Cover pan and cook over low heat for 5 minutes.

6 Sprinkle remaining oil over top. Cover and cook for 5–10 minutes.

7 Serve warm.

CARROTS, ROASTED WITH BALSAMIC VINEGAR
(Serves 4)

- 450 g (1 lb/2 cups) carrots, cut diagonally into 2.5 cm (1") pieces
- 4 tbsp balsamic vinegar
- 2 tsp olive oil
- Salt and black pepper

1 Preheat oven 180ºC (350ºF/Gas 4).

2 Combine carrots, balsamic vinegar, oil and seasoning in a bowl. Stir well.

3 Place onto a greased baking tray and bake for about 25 minutes until carrots are soft and browned. Stir once during cooking.

CLOOTIE DUMPLING

A clootie dumpling is made according to a very old traditional Scottish pudding recipe, dating back to pre-oven days when most food was cooked in a pot over an open fire. It is considered to exemplify a mother's love for her children.

It is tradition to wrap small silver coins and trinkets in greaseproof paper and place them in the mixture before cooking. Ingredients were placed in a floured cloth or 'cloot' – which is the old Scottish word for cloth – and boiled in water for several hours, hence the name, clootie dumpling. You may want to try this instead of traditional Christmas pudding.

(Serves 8-10)

- 2 eggs, beaten
- 2 tbsp black treacle
- 110g (4oz) wholemeal flour
- 170g (6oz) fine brown breadcrumbs
- 110g (4oz) vegetable suet, or butter
- 110g (4oz) sultanas
- 110g (4oz) currants
- 1 large cooking apple
- 1 lemon, juice and zest
- 1 tsp baking powder
- 1 tsp ground cinnamon
- 1 tsp ground ginger
- 1 tsp ground nutmeg
- 1 tsp ground cumin
- Fresh orange juice to mix

1 Boil a square of cotton or linen cloth, about 60 cm (24") square for a few minutes.

2 Spread it out on a table, sprinkle with a tablespoonful of wholemeal flour, tossing the flour to coat the main centre of the cloth quite thickly.

3 Place the eggs and treacle into a bowl, and beat lightly.

4 Add the remaining ingredients, mix to a stiff consistency, adding a little water, if needed.

5 Place mixture in the middle of the cloth.

6 Bring up the edges and tie with string, leaving a little space for expansion.

7 Hold tied ends of the cloth and gently pat the dumpling to produce a rounded shape.

8 Place the dumpling into a saucepan of boiling water, which should reach halfway up the side.

9 Cover and simmer gently for about 4

hours, checking occasionally and top up the water as needed.

10 Once cooked plunge into cold water for about one minute to release it from the cloth.

11 Put onto a plate and place the pudding into a hot oven for a few minutes to dry off the skin.

12 Serve hot with plenty of custard.

CURLY KALE AND SMOKED TOFU GRATIN
(Serves 4)

- *12 curly kale leaves, roughly torn into pieces*
- *1 tbsp olive oil*
- *1 onion, chopped*
- *225 g (8 oz) smoked tofu, sliced*
- *300ml (½ pint/10 fl oz/1¼ cup) double cream*
- *½ tsp Tabasco*
- *Freshly ground black pepper*
- *125 g (4 oz) Gruyère cheese, grated*

1 Plunge kale into boiling water just long enough for it to wilt.

2 Drain and refresh in cold water. Drain and squeeze out water, then lay on kitchen paper.

3 Heat oil in a pan and gently sauté the onion until soft, about 5 minutes. Transfer to a bowl.

4 In the same pan, fry the tofu until just beginning to brown.

5 Add to the onion.

6 In the same pan, boil the cream until it thickens.

7 Return onion and tofu to the pan and add the kale and Tabasco.

8 Season with black pepper. Stir over a low heat until mixed well.

9 Transfer to an oven-proof glass dish, sprinkle with cheese and brown under the grill.

CURLY KALE WITH GARLIC, PARSLEY AND PARMESAN
(Serves 4)

- *2 tbsp olive oil*
- *2 garlic cloves, crushed*
- *1 onion, finely chopped*
- *350 g (12 oz/1½ cups) curly kale, cut into fine strips*
- *1 tbsp parsley, chopped*
- *4 tbsp water*
- *Salt and black pepper*
- *50 g (2 oz) Parmesan, grated*

1 Heat oil in a pan and fry the garlic and onion for about 2 minutes.

2 Add curly kale and parsley. Stir for a few minutes to coat kale in oil.

3 Add 4 tablespoons of water. Bring to the boil, cover and simmer until kale is tender. Do not allow the pan to boil dry. Add a little more water if necessary.

4 Once the kale is cooked, bring the liquid to boil and allow the excess water to evaporate and stir in the Parmesan cheese. Season.

CURLY KALE AND POTATO SOUP
(Serves 4)

- *1 tbsp olive oil*
- *1 onion, chopped*
- *2 garlic cloves, crushed*
- *450 g (1 lb/2 cups) potatoes, peeled and sliced 0.6 cm (¼") thick*
- *1.5 L (2¾ pints/6 cups) vegetable stock*
- *225 g (8 oz/1 cup) curly kale, roughly chopped*
- *Salt and black pepper*

1. Heat oil in a pan. Add onion and garlic and cook for about 2 minutes.
2. Add potatoes and cook for a few minutes, stirring occasionally.
3. Add stock and bring to the boil. Reduce heat and simmer, covered, for about 20 minutes, or until the potatoes are just cooked.
4. Add curly kale, salt and pepper. Bring back to the boil and simmer until kale is cooked, about 5-10 minutes.
5. Serve.

CURLY KALE AND SOFT BLUE CHEESE PASTY
(Serves 4)

- *225 g (8 oz) flaky or shortcrust pastry*
- *175 g (6 oz) curly kale, cut into strips*
- *1 onion, finely chopped*
- *225 g (8 oz) Gorgonzola or other soft, mild, blue vein cheese*
- *Salt and black pepper*
- *1 egg, beaten*

1. Preheat oven 200ºC (400ºF/Gas 6).
2. Roll pastry into a long rectangle.
3. Combine curly kale, onion, cheese and season to taste.
4. Spoon mixture into centre of pastry.
5. Brush edges of the pastry with half the egg.
6. Bring edges of the pastry together and crimp shut. Brush with rest of the egg.
7. Place on a baking tray and bake in the oven for 40 minutes, or until golden.

KOHLRABI AND CARROTS ROASTED WITH CARDAMOM AND ORANGE GLAZE
(Serves 6-8)

- *700 g (1½ lb/3 cups) kohlrabi, peeled and cut into wedges*
- *700 g (1½ lb/3 cups) carrots, peeled and cut into chunks*
- *4 tbsp olive oil*
- *Finely grated zest of one orange*
- *Salt and black pepper*

For the glaze
- *4 tbsp sugar*
- *Juice of 4 oranges*
- *Seeds from 6–8 cardamom pods, crushed*

1. Preheat oven 190ºC (375ºF/Gas 5).
2. Put oil into roasting tin, place in oven until very hot.
3. Put vegetables into hot roasting tin. Sprinkle with orange zest, season and stir to coat vegetables in the oil.
4. Roast for about 25 minutes, turning once.
5. To make the glaze, heat the sugar and orange juice in a pan, stirring until sugar has dissolved.

6. Bring to boil and simmer for a few minutes until glaze is slightly syrupy and darker in colour.
7. Remove from the heat and stir in the cardamom seeds.
8. Pour glaze over the vegetables, roast for about 10 minutes more, stirring once making sure that the glaze doesn't burn.

KOHLRABI GRATIN WITH BUTTERY CRUST
(Serves 4 as a main dish, 6 as side dish)
- *900 g (2 lb/4 cups) kohlrabi, peeled, halved vertically and cut into thinly sliced semi-circles*
- *3 tbsp fresh parsley*
- *Finely grated zest of one lemon*
- *Salt and black pepper*
- *90 g (3 oz) butter or margarine*
- *300 ml (½ pint/10 fl oz) carton single cream or fromage frais*
- *90 g (3 oz) white breadcrumbs*
- *1–3 garlic cloves, finely chopped*
- *120g (4 oz) Gruyère or Edam cheese, grated*

1. Preheat oven 190ºC (375ºF/Gas 5).
2. Lightly grease a large gratin dish.
3. Arrange half the kohlrabi in the bottom of dish. Sprinkle with half the parsley and lemon zest. Season.
4. Dot kohlrabi with a little butter or margarine.
5. Make second layer with remaining kohlrabi, parsley and lemon zest, and season again.
6. Pour the cream or fromage frais over the mixture and dot another knob of butter or margarine over the top.
7. Loosely cover the gratin with foil and bake for about 40 minutes until kohlrabi is just tender.
8. Melt 50 g (2 oz) butter or margarine in frying pan, add breadcrumbs and garlic and fry for 2 minutes until crumbs are beginning to go crisp. Season.
9. Remove foil from gratin, sprinkle over cheese, and then breadcrumbs, and bake uncovered for about another 15 minutes.

PARSNIP AND CARROT WITH PEANUT DRESSING
(Serves 4)
- *1 litre (1¾ pints/4½ cups) water*
- *4 tsp red wine vinegar*
- *225 g (8 oz/1 cup) parsnips, peeled and cut into thin strips*
- *225 g (8 oz/1 cup) carrots, peeled and cut into thin strips*
- *1–2 tbsp peanut butter*
- *1 tbsp soy sauce*
- *¼ tsp sugar*
- *Season to taste*

1. In a pan, combine water, and one teaspoon of red wine vinegar. Bring to boil.
2. Add parsnips and carrots. Return to boil, reduce heat and simmer until vegetables are just tender. Drain.
3. In a bowl, combine

peanut butter, soy sauce, sugar, and remaining red wine vinegar. Add drained vegetables and toss until just combined.

PARSNIPS IN MUSTARD AND WHISKY SAUCE
(Serves 4)

- *450 g (1 lb/2 cups) medium parsnips, peeled and sliced diagonally*
- *45 g (1½ oz) butter or margarine*
- *2 tbsp Dijon mustard*
- *1 tsp honey*
- *3 tbsp whisky*
- *Season to taste*

1 Preheat oven 190ºC (375ºF/Gas 5).
2 Place parsnips in a pan with salted water. Bring to the boil, cover and return to the boil. Reduce heat and simmer until just tender, about 10 minutes. Drain.
3 Place parsnips in greased shallow baking dish.
4 Melt the butter or margarine in a pan and slowly add the mustard, honey and whisky. Cook gently for about 4 minutes.
5 Pour sauce over the parsnips, season to taste and bake for 10 minutes or until sauce is bubbly.

PARSNIP PIE
(Serves 4)

- *225 g (8 oz/1 cup) parsnips, peeled and sliced*
- *25 g (1 oz) butter*
- *Salt and black pepper*
- *2 eggs*
- *2 tbsp sugar*
- *½ tsp ground nutmeg*
- *225 ml (8 fl oz/1 cup) milk*
- *24 cm (9½") pie dish lined with shortcrust pastry*

1 Preheat oven 190ºC (375ºF/Gas 5).
2 Place parsnips in a pan with salted water. Bring to the boil, reduce heat and simmer until cooked, about 10 minutes. Drain and mash.
3 Add the butter, salt and pepper.
4 Beat eggs, add the sugar, nutmeg and milk.
5 Stir into mashed parsnip. Mix well.
6 Line the pie dish with pastry and pour in the parsnip mixture.
7 Sprinkle with nutmeg and bake for 30 minutes or until browned.

POTATOES BAKED WITH HERBS AND CHEESE
(Serves 4-6)

- *1 tbsp olive oil*
- *1 onion, finely chopped*
- *1 garlic clove, crushed*
- *2 eggs*
- *300 ml (½ pint/ 10 fl oz) crème fraîche or double cream*
- *125 g (4 oz) Gruyère cheese, grated*
- *700 g (1½ lb) potatoes, peeled and cut into matchsticks*
- *2 tsp dried mixed herbs*
- *¼ tsp grated nutmeg*
- *Salt and black pepper*

1 Preheat oven 190ºC (375ºF/Gas 5).
2 Grease an

ovenproof dish.

3   Heat oil in a pan and fry the onion and garlic until soft. Remove from heat.

4   In a large bowl, whisk together the eggs, crème fraîche or cream and half the cheese.

5   Stir in the onion mixture, potatoes, herbs, nutmeg and season to taste.

6   Put mixture into the ovenproof dish and sprinkle over the remaining cheese.

7   Bake for 50 minutes or until browned.

POTATOES ROASTED WITH LEMON AND HERBS
(Serves 6-8)
- *4 tbsp olive oil*
- *2 tbsp fresh lemon juice*
- *Salt and black pepper*
- *1 tsp fresh oregano or ½ tsp dried*
- *1 tsp fresh thyme or ½ tsp dried*
- *¼ tsp paprika*
- *900 g (2 lb/4 cups) potatoes, peeled and quartered*

1   Preheat oven 180°C (350°F/Gas 4).

2   Combine olive oil, lemon juice, salt, pepper, oregano, thyme and paprika together in a large bowl and mix well.

3   Add potatoes and toss.

4   Transfer to greased shallow roasting pan and bake for about 35 minutes until tender and well browned. Stir twice during cooking.

5   Excellent served with scrambled eggs, omelettes, or pumpkin and lemony lentils on <u>page 156.</u>

RED CABBAGE WITH CHESTNUTS AND RED WINE
(Serves 6)
- *900 g (2 lb/4 cups) chestnuts*
- *3 tbsp olive oil*
- *1 medium onion, finely chopped*
- *900 g (2 lb/4 cups) red cabbage, cored and cut into medium strips*
- *350 ml (12 fl oz/ 1½ cups) dry red wine*
- *350 ml (12 fl oz/1½ cups) vegetable stock*
- *2 tbsp red wine vinegar*
- *¼ tsp nutmeg*
- *Salt and black pepper*

1   Preheat oven 180°C (350°F/Gas 4).

2   Make a cross on the flat side of each chestnut with a sharp knife. Parboil in boiling water for 10 minutes, drain and remove outer and inner skins.

3   In a large pan, heat oil and sauté the onion for 5 minutes.

4   Stir in cabbage and cook for 10 minutes.

5   Add wine, vegetable stock, vinegar, nutmeg, chestnuts, salt and pepper.

6   Transfer to an oven dish. Cover and bake for about one hour. Check part way through the cooking and add more stock if needed.

SWEDE WITH BLUE CHEESE
(Serves 4)
- *450 g (1 lb/2 cups) swede, peeled and sliced paper thin*
- *1 medium onion, peeled and finely sliced*
- *4 tbsp olive oil*

- *150 ml (¼ pint/ 5 fl oz) whipping cream*
- *¼ tsp ground nutmeg*
- *Salt and black pepper*
- *125 g (4 oz/½ cup) Roquefort or Stilton or any blue cheese, crumbled*

1 Preheat oven 190ºC (375ºF/Gas 5).
2 Mix together swede, onion and oil and place in a baking dish. Cover and place in oven for about 30 minutes or until cooked.
3 In a pan, combine cream, nutmeg, salt and pepper. Bring to the boil and let cook for one minute.
4 Remove swede and onion from oven, remove cover and pour over cream mixture. Sprinkle with blue cheese

and return to the oven, uncovered.
5 Cook for about 15 minutes until cheese is melted, golden brown and crisp.

SWEDE WITH BUTTER BEANS
(Serves 4)

- *225 g (8 oz/1 cup) swede, peeled and sliced into 0.6 cm (¼") thick pieces*
- *400 g tin butter beans, drained*
- *1 tbsp olive oil*
- *1 medium onion, finely chopped*
- *1 tsp soy sauce*
- *50 g (2 oz) walnuts, chopped*
- *1 tsp dried mixed herbs*
- *4 tbsp water*
- *Salt and black pepper*

1 Preheat oven 190ºC (375ºF/Gas 5).
2 Place swede in a

pan with salted water. Bring to the boil, cover, reduce heat and simmer until tender. Drain.
3 Lightly grease a baking tray with oil.
4 Place swede onto baking tray.
5 Combine butter beans, oil, onion, soy sauce, walnuts, herbs, water and seasoning.
6 Spoon over swede.
7 Bake in the oven for about 15 minutes.

SWEDE AND BRUSSELS SPROUTS WITH HAZELNUTS
(Serves 6-8)

- *700 g (1½ lb/3 cups) Brussels sprouts, halved lengthwise*
- *550 g (1¼ lb/2½ cups) swede, peeled and cut into thin slices*
- *1 tbsp olive oil*

- *1 medium onion, chopped*
- *75 g (3 oz) hazelnuts, chopped*
- *1 tsp dried thyme*
- *3 garlic cloves, crushed*
- *Salt and black pepper*

1 Put Brussels sprouts into boiling salted water and cook until crisp-tender, about 5-10 minutes. Drain and keep warm.
2 Place swede in a pan with salted water. Bring to the boil, cover, reduce heat and simmer until tender, about 15 minutes. Drain and keep warm.
3 Heat oil in a pan. Add the onions, hazelnuts and sauté until nuts begin to brown.
4 Add thyme and the garlic.

5 Cook until nuts are golden, about 2 minutes.
6 Add Brussels sprouts and swede, cover and cook until heated through. Season.
7 Transfer to a bowl and serve.

Sprout Snippet: Kohlrabi is a member of the cabbage family but has a large edible bulb that resembles a turnip. However, kohlrabi is not a root vegetable. The bulb is actually part of the stem, not the root system. The inside flesh of kohlrabi is slightly sweet and crispy. It tastes similar to broccoli stems or cabbage heart, but sweeter. It can be eaten raw in salads or slaws or cooked.

Kohlrabi

Jacqui first made her own gifts many years ago when money was tight and imagination was rich. Fresh from studying art, she managed to create original Christmas gifts for her family and friends. Since then she has made many gifts, so the idea of making some from the EarthShare box was obvious to her.

This chapter shows how, with a bit of planning during the year, a sackful of original presents can be made to ease the strain on purse strings at Christmas, make bountiful birthdays, or just to say a special 'thank you'. Collect attractive jars and bottles, create your own labels and enjoy giving them to people.

BEETROOT, CARROT AND APPLE JUICE WITH GINGER

Make this delicious drink on the day you want to give it to someone. It will not keep for more than three days tightly sealed in the fridge.

- 1 medium beetroot, washed, topped and tailed and cut into pieces
- 2 carrots, washed and diced
- 1.25 cm (½") fresh root ginger, peeled
- 2 apples, unpeeled and cut into small pieces

1 Put the beetroot, carrots, ginger and apples in a juicer.

Enjoy the colour effects and the sweet, spicy taste

2 Pour into an attractive jar, label and refrigerate.

CARROT, LEMON AND CORIANDER MARMALADE
(Makes approx 5 x 450 g/1 lb jars)

- 700 g (1½ lb/3 cups) organic carrots
- 700 g (1½ lb/3 cups) organic lemons
- 900 ml (1½ pints/3¾ cups/30 fl oz) water
- 1.4 kg (3 lb/6 cups) organic sugar

- 1 small tsp freshly ground coriander

1 Peel carrots and medium-grate.
2 Peel zest off lemons with potato peeler and chop skin into thin strips, or medium-grate.
3 Cut lemons in half and squeeze juice.
4 Save pips and pith and tie in a muslin cloth.
5 Put carrots, lemon zest and juice, water and muslin cloth into a preserving pan and cook until softened (about ½ hour).
6 Add sugar and stir until dissolved.

7 Add freshly ground coriander and boil quickly until set. To check if set, put a teaspoonful of the marmalade onto a cold plate. After 2 minutes, push finger through sample and if it wrinkles, it is set.
8 Remove muslin cloth and squeeze excess liquid gently into pan (mind, it's hot!).
9 Skim the marmalade, then cool for about 30 minutes, stirring occasionally to distribute the zest evenly.
10 Pour into sterilised dry warm jars,

cover with paper discs, waxed side down, before putting the lid on.

CARROT AND RHUBARB PRESERVE

- *1 Kg (2.2 lb) carrots, peeled and sliced*
- *1 Kg (2.2 lb) rhubarb, sliced*
- *1 Kg (2.2 lb) granulated sugar*

1 Place carrots in a pan with enough water to just cover them.
2 Bring to the boil, reduce heat and simmer, covered, until tender. Drain reserving 125 ml (4 fl oz/½ cup) of liquid.
3 Purée carrots with reserved liquid.
4 Transfer to a large pot and add rhubarb and sugar.

5 Stir until sugar has dissolved.
6 Bring to a slow boil, reduce heat and simmer for about 20 minutes or until the preserve starts to thicken.
7 Remove from heat and pour into warm sterilised jars.
8 Seal and store in a cool place.

CASSIS (BLACKCURRANT LIQUEUR)

- *550 g (I lb 4 oz) fresh blackcurrants*
- *70 cl gin*
- *450 g (I lb) granulated sugar*
- *1 cm (½") piece cinnamon stick*
- *1 clove*

1 Place all of the ingredients into a glass container with a lid.
2 Shake gently once a day for the first few days or until the sugar has dissolved.
3 Store for one month.
4 Strain through double muslin, then bottle.
5 Label and date the bottle.
6 You can drink it straight away, but it improves with age.

This cassis tastes fabulous and is so simple to make. Drink it on its own or make Kir.

Traditional Kir combines cassis and white wine. Try a Kir Royale, which is a mixture of cassis and champagne. We tried it with a dry Spanish Cava and it tastes just as good as with champagne. Simply put 1 tbsp of cassis into the bottom of a tall tulip glass, add chilled white wine or champagne/Cava and stir gently to mix. Garnish with a twist of lemon zest.

ELDERBERRY KETCHUP

- *900 g (2 lb) elderberries*
- *Vinegar to cover*
- *225 g (8 oz) granulated sugar*
- *1 tbsp allspice*
- *1 tbsp cloves*
- *¼ tsp cayenne pepper*
- *½-1 tsp salt*
- *1 tsp cinnamon*

1 Cook elderberries in vinegar until the berries burst.
2 Sieve the berries and put the strained liquid in a pan.
3 Discard the berries.
4 Add sugar, allspice, cloves, cayenne pepper, salt and cinnamon to liquid.
5 Bring to the boil, reduce heat and simmer until thickened.
6 Pour in sterilised jars and seal.

Sprout snippet: Make sure you use ripe elderberries because unripe ones contain cyanide and can cause severe diarrhoea. The berries are ripe when the clusters begin to turn upside down, about the middle of September. Do not use any green berries.

HERB VINEGARS

Herb vinegar makes a great gift. It is also a way of using up fresh herbs from your vegetable box or garden. Many types of vinegar can be used such as white vinegar, cider vinegar, white wine vinegar, red wine vinegar or rice vinegar. They all work very well, although our preference is for white wine vinegar.

You can be creative and make up your own recipes.

The basic recipe below tells you to heat the vinegar and put into sterilised bottles.

Some cooks do not bother with this and use room temperature vinegar, sealing the bottles straight away without sterilising them, and say that this works just as well.

Once the herb vinegar is made, it can be stored for up to one year, but often lasts even longer.

1   Choose your herbs, and if you wash them, pat them between kitchen towels and let them dry thoroughly as any water left on the herbs will make your vinegar cloudy.
2   Heat vinegar in a glass or enamel pan, but do not boil.
3   Add the fresh herb sprigs to your sterilised bottles, then pour the heated vinegar over the top. Three to four sprigs per bottle are usually enough.
4   Let the vinegar cool and put the lid on.
5   Label, date, and decorate the bottle and store in a cool, dark place.
6   You can add multicoloured peppercorns, whole cloves of garlic and flower petals to the bottle. The following are some ideas.
7   Experiment a little and see.

- *Basil, bay leaf and marjoram in white wine vinegar*
- *Fennel leaves, parsley and garlic cloves in white wine vinegar*
- *Tarragon, marjoram and nasturtium flowers in white wine vinegar*
- *Sage, parsley, peppercorns and chives in red wine vinegar*
- *Rosemary, orange peel, raisins and garlic in red wine vinegar*
- *Garlic cloves, dill and nasturtium flowers in cider vinegar*
- *Garlic cloves, oregano and red chillies in cider vinegar*
- *Cardamom seeds, violet petals and lemon peel in white vinegar*
- *Rose petals, violet petals and orange peel in rice vinegar*
- *Lavender flowers (not stalks), rose petals and orange peel in rice vinegar*

LEMON ZEST LIQUEUR (LIMONCELLO)

- *Zest from 9 large lemons, scrubbed and dried*
- *1 Litre vodka*
- *1 Litres (1¾ pints) water*

- *500 g (1¼ lb/2¼ cups) granulated sugar*

1 Wash lemons well and dry.
2 Remove zest from lemons with a sharp vegetable peeler avoiding any white pith.
3 Put the vodka and the zest into a glass container with a lid, marinade for about 20 days until liquid turns yellow.
4 After 20 days boil water and add sugar. Stir until sugar has dissolved, then cool.
5 Strain the zest and vodka through muslin and add to the cooled sugar and water. Mix well.
6 Put into sterilised bottles and serve ice cold.

ONION MARMALADE
- *1 Kg (2.2 lb) onions, peeled and sliced*
- *4 tbsp olive oil*
- *125 g (4 oz/½ cup) caster sugar*
- *350 ml (12 fl oz/1½ cups) white vinegar*
- *3 cloves*
- *2 tbsp tomato paste*
- *¼ tsp cayenne pepper*
- *Salt and black pepper*

1 Sauté onions in the olive oil until soft.
2 Add the remaining ingredients, bring to the boil, reduce heat and simmer gently for about one hour or until mixture reaches a jam like consistency.
3 Remove from heat and pour off any surplus oil.
4 Put into hot sterilised jars and seal. Keeps for 3-4 months.

PUMPKIN JAM
- *2 Kg (4.4 lb) pumpkin, peeled, seeded and cut into thin slices*
- *2 lemons, washed and cut into thin slices*
- *1.5 Kg (3¼ lb) granulated sugar*

1 In a large bowl, alternate pumpkin, lemons and sugar.
2 Cover and put in the fridge overnight.
3 Next day, transfer pumpkin, lemon and sugar mixture to a pan, bring to the boil and simmer for about 40 minutes or until it starts to darken and slips off the spoon slowly.
4 Remove from heat, cool a little and pour into sterilised jars.
5 Put lids on when jam is still hot, as this helps to form a vacuum in the jar.
6 Label and store in a cool place.

RASPBERRY VODKA
- *300 g raspberries*
- *300 g sugar*
- *1 Litre vodka*
- *2 tbsp lemon juice*

1 Put ingredients into a preserving jar. Close lid tightly and shake gently until sugar dissolves.
2 Store in a cool, dark place. Shake once every day for first couple of weeks.
3 After 2-3 months, strain through a muslin cloth.
4 Pour into sterilised bottles and label.

SLOE OR DAMSON GIN

- 450 g (1 lb) sloes or damsons
- 70 cl gin
- 250 g (9 oz) granulated sugar

1 Wash the sloes or damsons and prick each one about 12 times.
2 Place in a lidded jar with the gin and sugar. Shake well and store in a cool, dark place.
3 Shake regularly for the first 2 weeks.
4 Leave for 2-3 months until it has matured and is a deep red colour.
5 Pour contents through muslin to strain it and put into clean bottles.
6 Label.

Sprout snippet: Pick sloes in September so that you will have some sloe gin ready for Christmas.

180

PLAYBACK THEATRE

Playback Theatre is an original form of improvisational theatre in which audience or group members tell stories from their lives and watch them enacted on the spot.

> *Playback Theatre affirms the importance and dignity of personal experience, enables people to view their lives in new ways, and draws people closer as they see their common humanity.*

First created in 1975, the form was developed by *JONATHAN FOX* and *JO SALAS*. The original Playback Theatre Company is in the Hudson Valley of New York.

The story of our friendship and the cookbook began when we met in the Universal Hall at the Findhorn Foundation in January 1999 when we attended the first of many Playback Theatre courses with trainers Veronica Needa and Anna Chesner. We went on to become founder members of the Findhorn Playback Theatre Company and became an active company along with four other members, Gwyneth Bowman, Mary Gillespie, Saille Mawson, and Francine Rietberg.

International Playback Theatre Network (IPTN) https://iptn.info/

This cookbook and Playback have gone hand in hand so much so that we ended up catering for a yearly 10-day Playback Theatre Practice in April 2001 in Findhorn. This cemented our commitment to the book and *we dedicate this chapter to Jo Salas and our fellow Playbackers.*

We took on the catering because we had a glut of vegetables from the box and garden and saw it as a golden opportunity to clear the back log and start researching recipes and trying them out. The connection between CSAs and Playback became apparent; *they both serve and enrich community.*

181

Playback Menus

STARTER
CURRIED PARSNIP SOUP

MAIN COURSE
BROCCOLI/MUSHROOM
STROGANOFF WITH RICE

DESSERT
CARROT CAKE

— MENU 2 —

STARTER
SAMBUSAK WITH
GREEN SALAD

MAIN COURSE
SWEET ONION & POTATO PIE
CARROT AND ORANGE SALAD

DESSERT
LEMON MERINGUE PIE AND
DUKE OF CAMBRIDGE TART

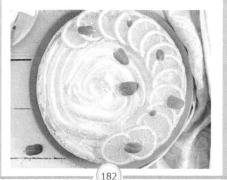

— MENU 3 —

STARTER
SPINACH & POTATO TORTILLA

MAIN COURSE
AFRICAN CHICKPEA, DATE
AND LIME STEW WITH
ROASTED HERB POTATOES

DESSERT
BOILED FRUIT CAKE
SELECTION OF WESTER
LAWRENCETON CHEESES
AND OATCAKES

PLAYBACK MENU 1

CURRIED PARSNIP SOUP
(Serves 4)
- 50 g (2 oz) margarine
- 1 medium onion, chopped
- 1 large garlic clove, crushed
- 450 g (1 lb) parsnips, peeled and sliced
- 1 small potato, peeled and diced
- 1 large dessert apple, peeled, cored and diced
- 1-2 tsp mild curry powder
- ¾ tsp turmeric
- 850 ml (1½ pints) vegetable stock
- Salt and black pepper

To garnish:
- Toasted croutons

1 Melt margarine in large pan.
2 Sauté onion, garlic, parsnip and potato for about 5 minutes, stirring frequently
3 Add apple, cook for a further 5 minutes until vegetables and apple are just soft.
4 Stir in curry powder, turmeric and sauté for about another minute.
5 Add stock, bring to the boil, reduce heat and simmer for about 15 minutes.
6 Leave to cool slightly. Purée in a food processor, return to the pan and reheat gently.
7 Add seasoning to taste and serve with croutons.

To make croutons
8 Remove crusts on 1.25 cm (½) thick slice of bread. Cut into cubes and toast or fry in butter until crisp, golden and sprinkle over soup.

MUSHROOM OR BROCCOLI STROGANOFF
(Serves 4)
- 50 g (2 oz) butter or margarine
- 2 tbsp olive oil
- 450 g (1 lb) mushrooms, or broccoli, chopped
- 1 tbsp brandy
- 1 red onion, finely chopped
- 1 tsp paprika
- 225 ml (8 fl oz) vegetable stock
- 50 g (2 oz) creamed coconut
- 150 ml (5 fl oz) crème fraîche
- 1 tbsp parsley, chopped

1 Heat half the butter and olive oil in a pan.
2 Sauté mushrooms or broccoli until soft.
3 Add brandy and ignite. Remove from pan and set aside.
4 Melt the rest of the butter and olive oil in pan, fry onion and paprika for 30 seconds.
5 Add stock and coconut.
6 Boil and reduce by one-third.
7 Add crème fraîche and thicken.
8 Add mushrooms or broccoli and simmer for 5 minutes until thick and creamy.
9 Sprinkle with parsley and serve with rice.

This recipe is from Joan's good friend Jan Ferguson who, with her husband Matthew, has run an award-winning bed and breakfast near Aviemore for 14 years.

CARROT CAKE

This is an American recipe measured in cups. As long as the same cup or mug is used throughout the recipe, it works. Everything goes in together and it is a great way of using up gluts of carrots and it can be frozen very successfully.

- 1½ cups sugar
- 1½ cups sunflower oil
- 4 large eggs
- 2 cups self-raising flour
- 2 tsp bicarbonate of soda
- 2 tsp ground cinnamon
- 1 tsp salt
- 3 cups carrots, grated
- ½ cup chopped mixed nuts
- 1 tsp vanilla essence

Topping:
- 200 g crème fraîche and 1 tbsp fresh orange juice

1 Preheat oven 180ºC (350ºF/Gas 4).
2 Mix together sugar and oil.
3 Add eggs and beat.
4 Add sifted dry ingredients and mix.
5 Add carrots, nuts and vanilla essence.
6 Line a large roasting tin 30 cm (11") square with foil and pour in mixture.
7 Bake for about 50 minutes until golden brown.
8 Topping: mix crème fraîche with orange juice and pour over cooled cake.

PLAYBACK MENU 2

SAMBUSAK
(Makes about 30 small sambusak)
Filling
- 450 g (1 lb) chick-peas, soaked overnight or 400 ml tin, drained
- 3 small onions
- 1 tbsp mild curry powder
- 2 tbsp vegetable oil

Dough
- 450 g (1 lb) self-raising flour
- 1 tbsp sunflower oil
- Warm water (or liquid from the cooked chickpeas or can) to mix

For the filling
1 Cook the soaked chickpeas in a pan of water until soft, drain and skin or use tinned.
2 Grind coarsely in a food processor.
3 Fry onions and curry in oil until tender.
4 Add the chickpeas to onion mixture and fry, adding more oil if required.
5 Set aside.

For the dough
6 Mix flour, oil and warm water to form a soft dough.
7 Cut the dough into balls and roll them with your hands, then roll out into small circles with a rolling pin.
8 Fill with 1 tbsp of the filling, bring the edges together and close tightly.
9 Heat oil in a frying pan, fry sambusak on both sides until golden brown.
10 Meat option: Can add 225 g (8 oz) cooked chicken, added at number 4 above.

This Sambusak is a Middle Eastern dish. Robin's mum, Angeline Shohet, makes these regularly and they are absolutely delicious. They are similar to samosas. She makes them in delicate bite-sized moon shapes whereas Joan makes them four times as big, similar to small croissants.

SWEET ONION AND POTATO PIE
(Serves 6)

- *4 large potatoes, peeled and sliced*
- *Large knob of butter*
- *1 tbsp olive oil*
- *3 large onions, sliced*
- *2 tsp Demerara sugar*
- *225 g (8 oz) puff pastry, thawed if frozen*
- *1 egg yolk*
- *Salt and black pepper*

1 Preheat oven 200ºC (400ºF/Gas 6).
2 Put potatoes in salted water. Bring to the boil reduce heat and simmer until just cooked, about 10 minutes.
3 Heat butter and olive oil, fry onion until golden brown. Add sugar, and cook until caramelised. Season.
4 Roll out pastry into two circles, one 20 cm (8") and the other 25 cm (9¾") in diameter.
5 Place smaller circle onto a baking tray lined with non-stick paper.
6 Arrange a layer of potatoes on the pastry circle leaving a 2 cm (¾") border.
7 Top with a thin layer of caramelised onions.
8 Continue until all potatoes and onions are used and it is dome shaped.
9 Brush around the edge of the pastry with egg yolk and cover with the other pastry disc.
10 Seal edges and brush pie with egg yolk.
11 Bake for 20 minutes until golden brown.

CARROT AND ORANGE SALAD

- 4 carrots, grated
- A handful of raisins
- 2-3 tbsp orange juice.

1 Put all ingredients in bowl, mix and serve.

DUKE OF CAMBRIDGE TART

- *125 g (4 oz) shortcrust pastry*
- *125 g (4 oz) raisins*
- *50 g (2 oz) glace cherries, chopped*
- *75 g (3 oz) butter or margarine*
- *75 g (3 oz) caster sugar*
- *2 egg yolks (you can use the spare whites to make lemon meringue pie)*
- *2 tbsp of rum or brandy*
- *Fresh cream*

1 Preheat oven 190ºC (375ºF/Gas 5).
2 Line an 18 cm (7") pie dish with pastry.
3 Prick with a fork and blind bake for about 10 minutes.
4 In a pan, cover raisins with cold water and bring to the boil.
5 Allow to stand for 5 minutes and strain.
6 Put raisins and cherries into the lined pie dish.
7 Melt butter or margarine and sugar in a pan and bring to the boil.
8 Remove from heat and add egg yolks and rum or brandy.
9 Pour over the raisins and cherries and bake for about 40 minutes.
10 Serve with fresh cream.

LEMON MERINGUE PIE

- *225 g (8 oz) shortcrust pastry*
- *2 lemons*
- *(35 g (1¼ oz) cornflour*
- *25 g (1 oz) butter or margarine*
- *4 oz caster sugar*
- *2 eggs (separated)*

1 Preheat oven 190ºC (375ºF/Gas 5).
2 Roll out pastry and line an 18 cm (7") round pie dish.
3 Prick the base of the pastry with a fork and bake blind for about 5-10 minutes until pale brown.
4 Grate lemon zest into a pan.
5 Add juice of lemons and water to make up 12 fl oz (1½ cups).
6 Mix cornflour with a little of the lemon liquid to form a slightly runny paste.
7 Put the rest of the lemon liquid on to boil and then pour over paste, stirring continuously. Put mixture back into the pan on a low heat and stir until it thickens.
8 Add the butter or margarine, stirring until melted.
9 Add half the sugar.
10 Add egg yolks to the pan, stir and remove from the heat.
11 Allow to cool for about 2-3 minutes and pour into the pastry case.
12 Whisk egg whites until stiff and fold in rest of sugar and spread the mixture over the lemon base.
13 Bake in slow oven for about 20 minutes or until it is golden brown.

This recipe was donated by Alma Noblett, Joan's mother.

PLAYBACK MENU 3

SPINACH AND POTATO TORTILLA

- *450 g (1 lb) potatoes, scrubbed and sliced*
- *2 tbsp olive oil*
- *2 onions, chopped*
- *1 garlic clove, crushed*
- *225 g (8 oz/1 cup) spinach, cooked and chopped*
- *6 eggs*
- *Salt and black pepper*

1 Put potatoes in a pan of salted water, bring to the boil, reduce heat and simmer for about 10 minutes or until tender.
2 Heat oil in a pan and sauté onions until transparent.
3 Add garlic and potatoes and sauté until just browned.
4 Add spinach and cook for one minute.
5 Whisk eggs with seasoning and pour into the pan with the vegetables and mix together.
6 Cook gently for about 10 minutes until nearly set.
7 Place under a hot grill for about 3 minutes until brown.
8 Let the tortilla stand for about 1-2 minutes, turn out onto a plate and serve.

This recipe was given to us by Sandra Fraser, a fabulous Playgroup leader, cook and lover of all things Italian. (Yes, we do know that this recipe is Spanish!)

AFRICAN CHICKPEA, DATE AND LIME STEW

- *1 tbsp olive oil*
- *1 medium onion, finely chopped*
- *1 large garlic clove, chopped*
- *1 tbsp fresh ginger root, chopped*
- *350 g (12 oz) fresh tomatoes, chopped*
- *2 tsp ground cumin*
- *1 tsp ground coriander*
- *Salt and black pepper*

1 Heat oil in a pan and sauté onion, garlic and ginger for about 5 minutes.
2 Add tomatoes and cook for 5 minutes.
3 Add cumin, coriander, salt, pepper, and cayenne pepper and cook for one minute.
4 Add the chickpeas, water, honey and dates. Cover, bring to boil, reduce heat and simmer for about 15 minutes.
5 Just before serving, stir in lime juice.

BOILED FRUIT CAKE

- *300 ml (½ pint/¼ cups) milk*
- *50 g (2 oz) margarine*
- *175 g (6 oz) Demerara sugar*
- *275 g (10 oz) mixed fruit*
- *2 tsp mixed spice*
- *1 tsp bicarbonate of soda*
- *280 g (10 oz) self-raising flour*
- *1 egg*

1 Preheat oven 180°C (350°F/Gas 4).
2 In a pan, place milk, margarine, sugar, mixed fruit, mixed spice and boil for 5 minutes.
3 Remove from heat, add bicarbonate of soda whilst mixture is still hot.
4 Leave to cool.
5 Add the flour, egg and mix well.
6 Bake for 1½ hours in the oven.

Joan's sister, Joy, gave us this recipe. She makes many exotic cakes. However, this one is made in a saucepan and is very practical.

You have now reached the end of The Boxing Clever Cookbook. We hope it has taught you to box clever with your veggies and you, like us, have had many more happy moments in the kitchen and around the table with family and friends because of it.

If, however, you are still struggling with your box, try this way of making it work, courtesy of the Viennese Vegetable Orchestra.

Forget the Stradivarius and the Yamaha, the Viennese Vegetable Orchestra consists exclusively of vegetable-based instruments. The musicians blow carved-out carrots, tap turnips, clap with eggplant cymbals, twang on rhubarb fibres and rustle parsley and greens. Where necessary, additional kitchen utensils such as knives or mixers are employed.

As if that were not bizarre enough, after the concert the stage is left to the cooks who turn the instruments into a tasty vegetable soup enjoyed at a post-performance party by both the audience and musicians.

CONVERSION TABLES

The tables below give three measurements, metric, imperial and American cups. The equivalents given are approximate only, but are close enough to ensure successful results in the kitchen.

WEIGHT

METRIC	IMPERIAL	AMERICAN
15 g	½ oz	
25 - 30 g	1 oz	
45 g	1½ oz	
50 - 60 g	2 oz	¼ cup
75 g	3 oz	
90 g	3½ oz	
100 - 125 g	4 oz	½ cup
150 g	5 oz	
175 g	6 oz	
225 g	8 oz	1 cup
275 g	10 oz	
325 - 350 g	12 oz	1½ cups
400 g	14 oz	
450 g	1 lb	2 cups
700 g	1½ lb	3 cups
900 g	2 lb	4 cups
1.1 kg	2½ lb	5 cups
1.4 kg	3 lb	6 cups
2 kg	4½ lb	9 cups
2.3 kg	5 lb	10 cups

1 metric cup = 250 ml   1 American cup = 237 ml
1 metric tbsp = 15 ml   1 American tbsp = 15 ml

LIQUID CAPACITY

METRIC	IMPERIAL	AMERICAN
25 ml	1 fl oz	
50 ml	2 fl oz	¼ cup
75 ml	3 fl oz	
100-125 ml	4 fl oz	½ cup
150 ml	5 fl oz/¼ pint	
175 ml	6 fl oz	¾ cup
200 ml	7 fl oz	
225 ml	8 fl oz	1 cup
250 ml	9 fl oz	
275-300 ml	10 fl oz/½ pint	1¼ cups
350 ml	12 fl oz	1½ cups
425 ml	15 fl oz/¾ pint	
450 ml	16 fl oz	2 cups
500 ml	18 fl oz	2¼ cups
575-600 ml	20 fl oz/1 pint	2½ cups
650 ml	24 fl oz	3 cups
725 ml	27 fl oz	
850-900 ml	30 fl oz/1½ pints	3¾ cups
980 ml	35 fl oz/1¾ pints	
1litre	36 fl oz	4½ cups

LENGTH

METRIC	IMPERIAL
(Centimetres)	(Inches)
0.6 cm	¼ in
1.2 cm	½ in
1.9 cm	¾ in
2.5 cm	1 in
3.2 cm	1¼ in
3.8 cm	1½ in
4.5 cm	1¾ in
5 cm	2 in
12.7 cm	5 in
22.8 cm	9 in
25.4 cm	10 in
30.5 cm	12 in

OVEN TEMPERATURES

°C	°F	GAS MARK
130	250	½
140	275	1
150	300	2
160-170	325	3
180	350	4
190	375	5
200	400	6
210-220	425	7
230	450	8
240	475	9

USEFUL RESOURCES AND REFERENCES

J & J Publishing
Ty Crwn, East Grange, Kinloss, Forres, Moray,
Scotland, IV36 2UD
01343 850 123
Website:
www.jjpublishing.co.uk
email: jacquij999@gmail.com

The Soil Association
https://www.soilassociation.org/contact/

Where is my nearest organic vegetable box scheme?

https://www.soilassociation.org/organic-living/buy-organic/find-an-organic-box-scheme/

INDEX OF RECIPES

194

Who doesn't want a world with good food, where we live in harmony with nature and where a safe climate is restored?

At the Soil Association we're on a mission to deliver that world, and we know it is possible. But first we need to dramatically change the way we produce our food. We must take care of our vital soils, we must stop our reliance on pesticides, we must ensure the highest standards of farm animal welfare.

With the support of our members, we're already making a difference: on the land working with farmers to find innovative solutions; on the streets campaigning with our communities; in schools and hospitals improving the food on the menu; and in Parliament lobbying for ambitious changes to farming legislation.

When you join the Soil Association, you're joining the charity digging deeper to transform the way we eat, farm and care for our natural world. **Together we can make a world of difference.**

Visit **www.soilassociation.org/clever** or call **0300 330 0022** to find out more and join today.

Printed in Great Britain
by Amazon